Johann Sebastian Bach's
Chamber Music

Figure 1. Johann Sebastian Bach in his youth. Portrait by Johann Ernst Rentsch, the elder (?).

Hans Vogt

Johann Sebastian Bach's Chamber Music

Background, Analyses, Individual Works

Translated by Kenn Johnson
Reinhard G. Pauly, General Editor

AMADEUS PRESS
Portland, Oregon

Translation © 1988 by Amadeus Press
ISBN 0-931340-04-7
Printed in Singapore

Amadeus Press
9999 S.W. Wilshire
Portland, Oregon 97225

Library of Congress Cataloging-in-Publication Data

Vogt, Hans, 1911–
    [Johann Sebastian Bachs Kammermusik. English]
    Johann Sebastian Bach's chamber music : background, analyses,
 individual works / Hans Vogt ; translated by Kenn Johnson ; Reinhard
 G. Pauly, general editor.
       p.   cm.
    Translation of: Johann Sebastian Bachs Kammermusik.
    Bibliography: p.
    Includes index.
    ISBN 0-931340-04-7
    1. Bach, Johann Sebastian, 1685-1750. Chamber music. 2. Chamber
 music--18th century--History and criticism.   I. Pauly, Reinhard G.
 II. Title.
 ML410.B13V5813 1988
 785.7'0092'4--dc19   88-10427
                                                 CIP
                                                 MN

*To my wife Erni
and to my children, Marianne and Sebastian*

There are some ponderous people who pass judgment on music in the name of classic laws of form. Don't they know that, when it came to form and structure in music, no one spoke up more loudly and boldly in favor of freedom and imagination than did Bach, one of the great law makers in music?

Claude Debussy, *Monsieur Croche*

Contents

Preface

While working on this book I experienced two surprises. First, when I began a systematic search for literature on Bach's chamber music, I learned that despite the abundance of publications on Bach, there had not been a comprehensive work dealing with his chamber music as a whole, at least not during the past hundred years. In the standard works by Philipp Spitta, Albert Schweitzer and others, the chamber music is mentioned only in passing. True, there are some interesting monographs on this or that aspect of the chamber music, as well as several books, for example, Hans Eppstein's 1966 Uppsala dissertation[1], which is important to the topic. But all these works proceed from specialized premises and deal with isolated problems. While detailed studies on the cantatas, the piano and organ music, and the *Brandenburg Concertos* have long been available, there is nothing of the kind on Bach's chamber music.

The second surprise: a late afternoon in Boston, Mass., the Park Street Subway Station during rush hour. A young violinist, in the midst of a crowd of people, playing the finale of the C Major Sonata for Solo Violin—not a first-class performance, to be sure, but a good one, one worth listening to. And even if the problematic notes m. 89 ff. were a bit off, it had as a whole something of that American drive which thoroughly suits the vitality of the composition and brings it to full expression. Success, applause and dollar bills were forthcoming.

To me, these two experiences appear symptomatic of the current state of Bach's chamber music. It is seldom the subject of scholarly research—but it is alive and well. In essence this is the best thing that can happen to an art form, and the question arises whether things should not be left as they are. I, too, had to ask myself this question. My answer: this book is not a piece of scholarly research. It was written by a composer out of the immediacy of his artistic experience. I have been involved with Bach's chamber music ever since I learned to think musically, that is, for more than half a century. And though I have obviously been involved with a great deal of other music, old and new, my own and others', this group of Bach's works always draws me back under its spell. It demands to be worked and thought through, there are new things to discover, it fascinates by its unabated vitality. These pieces never let one down, whether one approaches them purely with the intent of making music or with reflective intelligence.

This book was written both for professional musicians and for amateurs. The latter, in my experience, often become intensely involved with the chamber music, either as players or as listeners, and in the process, questions arise. I am attempting to answer some of them, or better, to suggest answers to them. Even career musicians desire more information on the topic. Here I am particularly addressing those who feel that Bach should be left to the specialists and who consequently keep themselves at an all too respectful distance and, indeed, often avoid him. This kind of thing is unfortunately no rarity. Check concert and radio programs: the A Major Sonata for Violin and Piano by César Franck can be heard at least three times a week; a violin sonata by Bach, on the other hand, very rarely.

A book on Bach's chamber music cannot leave out a description of the milieu. This forms the content of Part I, "The Background." At this point I should like to emphasize that I am not a research scholar, but deal only with the historical facts provided by musicology. Naturally, that encompasses a great deal. I have therefore been compelled to be selective and have frequently had to decide which of the facts available seemed most convincing to me, for scholars are not always in agreement.

In some cases, opposing the positions of musicologists was unavoidable, for example, regarding the authenticity of works. This difficult field, fraught with errors, cannot be left exclusively to scholars; composers must also have their say. A pure concern for precision and "verifiability" occasionally distorts the scholar's view of things which the artist sees differently. Especially where the authenticity of Bach's chamber music is concerned, scholarship must not be the sole criterion. In so saying, I do not wish to reopen the senseless rift between the theory and the practice of art, for the very reason that I am obligated and indebted to musicology in many respects, not only with regard to Bach. Moreover, I am taking a position not only against musicology, but also against a currently widespread historicism in performances, against the mischief—it cannot be called anything else—currently rampant in Bach performances, even on recordings, which style themselves as "faithful to the original" and "historically accurate." One and all, they rest on a fallacy. To put it succinctly; I would like to encourage people to play Bach, even if they do not own a harpsichord.

Part II, the compositional analyses, should help people become better acquainted with Bach and perhaps better understand many aspects of his works. Even though written from the perspective of the composer, the chapters contain no arcane knowledge,—and if at times we go beyond the boundaries of "Johann Sebastian Bach's Chamber Music," this is due to the fact that virtually every existing problem of composition can be demonstrated in Bach's work.

In Part III the works are treated individually. Part III should be used together with Part II, and in general, the book might better be read back and forth rather than from beginning to end.

The music scores are based on the old Complete Edition (BGA) and the New Bach Edition (NBA), along with various others designated as *Urtext* editions, in cases where the respective volumes of the NBA are not yet available. The following terminology should be noted: works in which the clavier merely represents the *basso continuo*, the thorough bass, are indicated as "with b.c." whereas works in which the keyboard instrument has an obbligato part are indicated as ". . . and clavier," regardless of whether a harpsichord, a pianoforte or another keyboard instrument is used. A list of abbreviations can be found in the appendix. Sources are cited only when they directly concern the text. It would be senseless to reproduce here yet another of the many Bach bibliographies.[2]

In the preparation of a work such as this, one is indebted to many assistants. My gratitude extends to the following institutions: The Music Department of the

Bavarian State Library in Munich, the libraries of the Musicological Seminars at the Universities of Heidelberg and Tübingen, the library of the State Music Academy of Mannheim-Heidelberg, The Municipal Music Library of Mannheim, the library of the Musicology Department of the Istituto storico tedesco (Institute of German History) in Rome, and the Bach Archives in Leipzig. Further, I must express my gratitude to many musicians who gave me help and suggestions in various particulars. Since it is impossible to list them all, I shall name the two who were most important: Wolfgang Boettcher and Siegfried Matthus. Finally, I would also like to thank Dr. Mathias Bielitz of the Musicological Seminar of the University of Heidelberg, who assisted me with bibliographic research and Barbara Schaper, who provided the music examples.

Every work on Johann Sebastian Bach remains fragmentary. His stature is too immense; important things remain unsaid. Thus I resort to a quote from Lessing, who wrote in his "Hamburg Dramaturgy" (No. 95, March 29, 1768):

I remind my readers that these pages contain nothing resembling a system. I am therefore not obliged to unravel all the difficulties I create. My thoughts may tend to connect less and less, indeed they often may seem to contradict each other—but they should provide food for further thought. My only desire here is to disseminate *fermenta cognitionis*.

Hans Vogt

Part I

The Background

Chapter 1

The Scope of Bach's Chamber Music

At the outset of a work on Bach's chamber music stands the question of which of his works are to be included in this category. Only at first glance does the answer appear simple; closer inspection turns up uncertainties of all kinds. Even though the term "chamber music" was already employed during Bach's time, it did not denote a clearly defined category. Works like the concertos for solo instruments with orchestral accompaniment, the *Brandenburg Concertos,* occasionally even the four great orchestral suites, were included in the category of chamber music, pieces which today would definitely be classified as orchestral music. In Bach's time the term included all instrumental ensemble music, without any distinction between the various genres. A "chamber" meant any room where music was performed, even a concert hall—in contrast to a "church" or "theater;" for the categorization of musical genres in the 18th century derived from the church, the theater and the chamber, respectively. Johann Mattheson, the music encyclopedist of that epoch, in his *Der vollkommene Capellmeister* of 1739, makes a precise distinction between "church style," "theatrical style" and "instrumental style." The latter he also calls *"the style of writing for the chamber,"* the "chamber style," or, characteristically enough, the "domestic style;" for, as he says, "in a concert hall one can perform a religious piece as well as a dinner concert: hence, it is appropriate to modify the term 'chamber style' with the adjective, 'domestic.'"[1] He includes "sonate da camera, concerti grossi, suites and the like" among the chamber works and even cites typical structural characteristics:

> This style in the chamber also requires far more diligence and perfection than elsewhere, and must have pleasant, clear *interior* parts which, as it were, continually contend for precedence with the upper parts in an agreeable manner. Slurs, syncopations, arpeggios, alternations between tutti and solo, between adagio and allegro, etc., are such essential and characteristic things that one for the most part seeks them in vain in churches and on the stage: because there is more reliance upon the prominence of the human voices, and the instrumental style is only used there to improve and to accompany or strengthen; whereas it clearly asserts superiority in the chamber; indeed, if the melody should occasionally suffer a little thereby, it is still embellished, ornamented and effervescent. That is its distinctness.[2]

Similar views are found in Quantz's work, and this widening of the concept of chamber music had an impact on the "old" Bach Edition (BGA), which appeared in 46 volumes between 1851 and 1899. There, too, all the concertos for solo instruments with string orchestral accompaniment, as well as the six *Brandenburg Concertos,* are collectively designated as chamber music. Today we can no longer adhere to such a categorization, even if it were possible or conceivable to perform some works from this group with a chamber ensemble. For this reason, the new edition of Bach's collected works (NBA), which began appearing in 1952, completely avoids the term 'chamber music' as a category and speaks only of "works for violin," "works for flute," etc. Wolfgang Schmieder, however, in his *Catalogue of Bach's Works,* (BWV) [3] uses the umbrella term "chamber music" for the works BWV 1001 to 1040 (see the listings of the works on p. 15ff). He does not include the *Brandenburg Concertos* or the instrumental concertos in the chamber works; but he also omits the works for lute (BWV 995–1000) and the trio sonata from the *Musical Offering*—the latter forming a separate section along with *The Art of Fugue* (BWV 1079 and 1080).

In the face of such inconsistencies it seems essential to define the characteristics which a work must exhibit in order to belong unquestionably to the category of chamber music. There has been agreement since about the time of Beethoven: a piece in which each instrumental voice is performed by one player is called chamber music. To this may be added, from the late 19th and early 20th centuries: a piece is termed chamber music if it is rehearsed and performed by a team rather than under the direction of a conductor. A conductor/director is not involved, so that during a performance the individual players provide the necessary leads and cues. This holds true from Beethoven's to around Reger's time; it is not yet wholly true for Mozart, for his wind serenades, although scored for soloists, today frequently are conducted. And although works since Hindemith's *Chamber Music #1* (1921) or Schoenberg's *Serenade,* at the latest, are chamber music, they cannot be performed without a conductor, not to mention contemporary music, in which it is not uncommon for a group of only three players to require a conductor. Contemporary works typically diverge from traditional categories. The umbrella term 'chamber ensemble' has thus become commonly accepted in contemporary music.

In Bach's case, such considerations do not offer much help. There is no definitive answer as to which of his works are *not yet* and which ones are *no longer* to be considered chamber music. The solo pieces for violin and for cello, as well as those for lute, are customarily called chamber music. But doesn't that mean that all the music for clavier and even the organ sonatas would also have to be so categorized? We find ourselves on unsure footing and recognize only one fundamental principle: any overly rigid classification is subject to question. Such categorizations only encourage intellectual pigeonholing. Nevertheless, we cannot get along entirely without these concepts. Not only does the abundance of extant music make certain groupings indispensable because they facilitate an overview, but distinctions between genres also work their way into the substance of the music itself. We shall pursue these questions further in Part II. For the purposes of this book we must employ a somewhat flexible standard of judgment; hence, the following:

1. Works for clavier solo are excluded: they form a category by themselves. If we tried to include them here, the aims of the book would be completely altered and its length would be increased many times over. In addition, *The Well-tempered Clavier* and the 2- and 3-Part Inventions or *sinfonie,* works which have little to do with chamber music, would then be admitted into our field of study.

2. Also excluded are all instrumental concertos with orchestral accompaniment, even if the accompaniment in question is only a small string orchestra and the

works were performed along with true chamber music, according to the practices of Bach's time. Instrumental concertos are more closely related to chamber music than clavier music; but they must be regarded as special genre in themselves.

3. Works were also omitted whose status as chamber music is still the subject of serious debate; for example, the 6th *Brandenburg Concerto in B-flat Major* (BWV 1051) for 2 violas, 2 gambas, cello, bass and b.c. The same is true of the 3rd *Brandenburg Concerto in G Major* (BWV 1048), and perhaps also for the *Ouverture* (Suite) *#2 in B Minor* (BWV 1067) for flute and strings. All these works have been successfully arranged soloistically and are often performed without a conductor. It does not, however, seem conscionable to remove individual works from the set (6 *Brandenburg Concertos*, 4 *Ouvertures*) in which Bach placed them. This was done in only one case—that of the Trio Sonata in C Minor for flute, violin and b.c. from the *Musical Offering* (BWV 1079). This piece is furnished with precise directions regarding the instrumentation. None of the other pieces of the *Musical Offering* has such directions. For that reason it can be considered separately.

4. The works for lute. The reason for including them here as chamber music is not only that they approach it more closely than does the clavier music, which can be seen in the fact that several of them are transcriptions from other chamber music pieces. More importantly, a study of them appears to fill an essential need. Today, when the lute is experiencing a revival and its sister instrument, the guitar, is the most popular instrument of the times (so that guitarists, if they play serious music, must necessarily encounter this branch of Bach's work), these compositions, after long having led a shadowy existence, happily have stepped back into view.

This is the group of works we shall be studying. In the following list, works which have been declared doubtful in the Bach literature are marked with an asterisk. The reader will find details in the second chapter.

Chamber Music Works by Johann Sebastian Bach

1. Three Sonatas and Three Partitas for Violin Solo

    Sonata in G Minor BWV 1001, Partita in B Minor BWV 1002,
    Sonata in A Minor BWV 1003, Partita in D Minor BWV 1004,
    Sonata in C Major BWV 1005, Partita in E Major BWV 1006.

    In Schmieder's catalog a second version of the E Major Partita appears as 1006a. This was apparently a transcription of the work for lute which Bach undertook in Leipzig in 1737.

2. Six Suites for Cello Solo

    Suite in G Major BWV 1007, Suite in D Minor, BWV 1008, Suite in C Major BWV 1009, Suite in E-Flat Major 1010, Suite in C Minor BWV 1011, Suite in D Major (for five-stringed cello) BWV 1012.

3. Partita in A Minor for Flute Solo BWV 1013

   Schmieder classifies this work as a *sonata* for reasons that are not altogether clear, although it is unmistakably a partita (suite). The NBA calls it *Partita*. Bach himself, according to the only source we possess, namely a manuscript from the Köthen period, simply entitled it, *Solo pour la flûte traversière*.

4. Six Sonatas for Violin and Clavier

   Sonata in B Minor BWV 1014, Sonata in A Major BWV 1015, Sonata in E Major BWV 1016, Sonata in C Minor BWV 1017, Sonata in F Minor BWV 1018, Sonata in G Major BWV 1019.

   There are two versions of the third movement (Adagio) of the F Minor Sonata and three of the G Major Sonata. More details will be found in the following chapter.

5. Works for Violin and b.c.

   Sonata in G Major BWV 1021, Sonata in E Minor BWV 1023, *Sonata in C Minor BWV 1024, *Suite in A Major BWV 1025, *Fugue in G Minor BWV 1026.

   We should also mention the *Sonata in G Minor for Violin and Clavier BWV 1020, which is also performed as a flute sonata,[4] but does not appear in either the violin or the flute volume of the NBA; and also the Sonata in F Major for Violin and Clavier BWV 1022, which is a reworking of the Trio Sonata in G Major BWV 1038 transposed to F Major.

6. Three Sonatas for Viola da gamba and Clavier

   Sonata in G Major BWV 1027, Sonata in D Major BWV 1028, Sonata in G Minor BWV 1029.

7. Three Sonatas for Flute and Clavier

   Sonata in B Minor BWV 1030, *Sonata in E-Flat Major BWV 1031, Sonata in A Major BWV 1032 (fragment).

8. Three Sonatas for Flute and b.c.

   *Sonata in C Major BWV 1033, Sonata in E Minor BWV 1034, Sonata in E Major BWV 1035.

9. Trio Sonatas for Two Melody Instruments and b.c.

   *Sonata for 2 Violins and b.c. in C Major BWV 1037, *Sonata for Flute, Violin and b.c. in G Major BWV 1038, Sonata for Flute and Violin in C Minor BWV 1079 (*Musical Offering*), Sonata for 2 Flutes and b.c. in G Major BWV 1039.

   Schmieder also lists a *Trio Sonata in D Minor for 2 Violins and b.c. BWV 1036 (it appears elsewhere arranged for oboe, violin and b.c.), though its authenticity is seriously in doubt—as well as a short movement of only 27 measures, a trio in F Major for Oboe, Violin and b.c. BWV 1040. The Trio

Sonata in C Minor from the *Musical Offering* also contains as an "Appendix" the *Canone perpetuo* in C Minor BWV 1079 with the same scoring.

10. Works for Lute

Suite in G Minor BWV 995, *Suite in E Minor BWV 996, Partita in C Minor BWV 997, Prelude, Fugue and Allegro in E-Flat Major BWV 998, Prelude in C Minor BWV 999, Fugue in G Minor BWV 1000, Partita in E Major BWV 1006a.

Of the works mentioned, some are identical, i.e., they were transcribed by Bach from one instrumentation to another. Details of this will be found in the next chapter.

Chapter 2

Dates and Authenticity of the Works

The dates of Bach's chamber works can be precisely determined only in a few cases. Bach was not in the habit of keeping a list of works, as Mozart did in his later years, nor did he use opus numbers.[5] It is very seldom that one finds a dated manuscript, as in the case of the famous autograph of the violin solo works, with the inscription "1720." But that by no means proves that this was the date of composition; 1720 may have been the year in which the clean copy was written. Thus, the only certainty is that the work cannot have been composed any later than 1720.

In order to clarify the dates of composition, we must consider Bach's official position at the time and the duties he was contracted to fulfill. In the 18th century, a Kapellmeister, cantor or organist was also hired as a composer; a large percentage of the music he performed was supposed to be of his own composition. This was inevitable, for there was no repertoire or collection of well-known works in print. Self-sufficiency was the rule. This was still true for Haydn, and likewise for Mozart as long as he was in Salzburg. During his second stay in Weimar (1708–17), Bach was court organist; thus many of his great organ works were written during this period. In 1714 he gained the additional title of "Court Concert Master:" now he was expected to write cantatas as well. In Köthen, his next place of work, (1717–23), he produced no church or organ music. The court belonged to the Protestant-Reformed faith; church services required only the singing of simple chorales. For this reason Bach's tasks did not include church music. As "Court Kapellmeister" he directed a small group of court instrumentalists, with the occasional addition of a female singer. Thus in his six years in Köthen he wrote almost exclusively instrumental works: orchestral, clavier and chamber music. After 1723, when he was appointed cantor at St. Thomas in Leipzig, he again became a church musician and was required to steadily produce church cantatas and other religious vocal music; for he was responsible for providing music for several churches every Sunday. The demands of the Leipzig position on the composer were enormous. Though there may have been pieces of church music by his predecessors, nobody wanted to hear them, for the church cantata was in vogue at the time. It was another fifteen years before the demand for compositions abated somewhat. By that time Bach had produced a repertoire to fall back on and was able to turn to new projects of personal interest for which he had previously had no time. He wrote Book Two of *The Well-Tempered Clavier* and the third and fourth parts of the *Clavier-Übung,* edited his organ works and some of the chamber pieces, readied several collections of earlier works for the engraver and transcribed some previously written violin and wind concertos into clavier concertos for performances at the *Collegium musicum.* Then in the last years of his life came the cyclical magna opera, *Musical Offering* and *The Art of Fugue.*

In Bach's early period, the years before 1708, he was still relatively free in his choice of compositional projects. The demands of his position were not so explicit, and we see more variety in his catalogue of works. He wrote more according to the requirements of the moment. From the Mühlhausen period (1706–08) we have only organ works and a few cantatas, among them the Electoral Cantata, "Gott ist mein König," (God is My King," No. 71), the composition occasioned by Mühlhausen's status as an independent imperial city. There are no works of note from the first brief Weimar period (1703). Among the works written later when he was organist in Arnstadt (1703–06), we find Bach's first cantata, "Denn du wirst meine Seele nicht in der Hölle lassen," (For Thou wilt not leave my soul in hell, No. 15) which is still a rather conventional work. But during this time he also wrote the splendid clavier Capriccio BWV 992, "Sopra la lontananza del suo fratello dilettissimo," (On the Departure of My Dearest Brother). Unfortunately, we do not know whether he had a hand in the composition of an opera with the charming title, "The Wisdom of the City Fathers in Ordaining the Brewing of Beer."[6] The opera was performed in 1705, during Bach's tenure in Arnstadt at the court of Count Anton Günther von Schwarzburg-Rudolstadt; perhaps Bach was there playing the continuo harpsichord or at the concert master's stand.

But as far as Bach's chamber music is concerned, the time he spent in Köthen is of primary interest, since this was the period (1717–23) when he composed most of his chamber works.[7] He wrote these works for concerts at court, of which there were a large number, especially in the years before the marriage of Bach's sovereign, the young Prince Leopold von Anhalt-Köthen, who had a greater than average interest in music. When Bach arrived the prince was only twenty-three years old and assuredly not overworked by governing his small estates. He was therefore able to devote considerable attention to the small but musically competent orchestra. It existed not only for purposes of prestige. He often sat in with the ensemble as violinist or gamba player (see Chapter 3).

But although Köthen had a very busy musical life, its influence was narrow and confined to the small court. This is a further reason for our difficulty in fixing dates, or even verifying the authorship of many of Bach's chamber works: the works were never printed. They existed only in handwritten form, which of course sufficed for the needs of Köthen.

Of all the chamber works of Johann Sebastian Bach, only the Trio Sonata from the *Musical Offering* (1747) was published during his lifetime. And that was not because a publisher happened to express interest in the work—which would have been conceivable, considering the reputation Bach enjoyed at the time—but rather because Bach wanted to dedicate to Frederick the Great a personal copy worthy of a king. So Bach supervised the engraving of the *Musical Offering* himself. Apart from that, however, handwritten copies sufficed for his chamber music. This does not mean that during his lifetime he was neglected as a composer of chamber music (even though others, such as Telemann, were more "famous" than he was) —it was merely the custom of the times. Music publication was still in its infancy and very little music was printed.[8]

Owing to these circumstances, dating and authenticating the manuscripts present substantial problems. The number of Bach's chamber works in autograph manuscript is small (see p. 30). Copies made by his students or colleagues are not always reliable. Copyists were not overly fastidious; often only individual parts were reproduced, not the complete score. Nobody was concerned about precision in the notation of phrasing, details of rhythm and dynamics. Copyists copied from each other, so that errors were perpetuated; many of them probably thought they understood the music better than the composer and introduced arbitrary changes. Bach himself did the same thing and may well have had reason to do so. The composer's name was also treated in a cavalier manner: there was no such thing as copyright. Often the composer's name was entirely omitted. Thus it sometimes happened that the signature of the copyist, which was affixed to the end of the copy according to the practice of the time, was later taken for the signature of the composer. It was also customary to bind copies of works by different composers together in one volume, without any concern that the sheets were of different sizes. True, we gain a vivid picture of the musical repertoire of the time from such collections; but they do not make it any easier to connect the pieces to a particular composer or a date of composition. Handwritten copies were scattered to the four winds: whoever copied a work or commissioned and paid for a copy considered the music his own property. Bach himself was no different. For this reason the existence of a Bach autograph is by no means proof of his authorship.

An additional difficulty arises in Bach's case: his second wife, Anna Magdalena, wrote many of his manuscripts for him. But her musical handwriting came to resemble her husband's so closely that for a long time Anna Magdalena's manuscripts were mistaken for autographs—for example, the most important source for the Six Suites for Cello Solo or the manuscript of the Sonata for Violin and b.c. in G Major BWV 1021, which was not discovered until 1928. Researchers have only been able to straighten these matters out in the last few decades.[9]

Such was the situation facing those who in the mid-19th century began to systematically publish Bach's works in the first complete edition (BGA), the so-called "old" Bach edition. Knowledge relative to the chamber music was especially tenuous; for while the *Well-Tempered Clavier* or the passions and motets all continued to exist in some form during the epoch of Viennese classicism, the chamber music seems to have completely disappeared for a time after Bach's death. The first of these works to be printed, nearly half a century later, was the fugue from the Sonata in C Major for Violin Solo. It appeared in 1798 in Paris in the anthology *L'art du violon*, whose publisher was the French violinist and pupil of Viotti, Jean-Baptiste Cartier. Otherwise, the publishers of the BGA were faced with material that was for the most part unauthenticated, and it was impossible to clarify all the doubtful cases by the time the most important chamber music volumes appeared.[10] But this does not at all diminish the achievement of the editors; on the contrary, despite being built on a shaky foundation, these editions are still indispensable today, scholarly advances notwithstanding.[11]

The appearance of the first complete edition of Bach's works gave new impetus to research. As a consequence, our knowledge of the sources changed and continues to change. In the meantime research methods have been developed that are extremely meticulous, and might even be likened to detective work. Insofar as possible, the history of the manuscript is traced from the time of its composition to the present. The most precise graphological investigations are made, the results of which, among other things, have included the above-mentioned important distinction between Anna Magdalena's and Johann Sebastian Bach's musical handwriting. Paper types and water marks have been examined, enabling scholars to draw some conclusions about the dates of writing; for it was possible to trace which paper mill used which water mark in which year. Finally, all available contemporary documents relating to the first performance of a work were brought together—a process which admittedly did little for the chamber music, as there is almost no mention of it in the contemporary records—which can probably be explained by the fact that chamber music concerts then were not held in public. [12]

Nor can we pass over the added complication that the substantial Bach holdings in what was the Prussian State Library in Berlin were dispersed during World War II in an attempt to save them from destruction. Substantial numbers of the works can be found today in the collection of the *Stiftung Preussischer Kulturbesitz* as well as in the successor to the Berlin Library, the [East] German National Library in East Berlin. Individual works are found elsewhere, and not a few pieces remain missing. [13]

Today, Bach research is concentrated in the Göttingen Johann Sebastian Bach Institute, under the direction of Georg von Dadelson and Alfred Dürr, and the Bach Archives in Leipzig, under the direction of Hans Joachim Schulze, which often assign individual research topics to outside musicologists. On the basis of these studies, work was begun on a new edition of Bach's collected works (NBA) after World War II. But even though this project is still far from complete, some of the volumes published have already had to be revised as a result of new findings. Wolfgang Schmieder's statement still holds true that "in questions of authenticity and of the historical chronology of the works of Bach, there will probably never be the last word." [14] And Alfred Dürr is of the same opinion when he writes, "It is precisely the most conscientious experts who, by reason of their conscientiousness—and especially as their knowledge of Bach's work increases—have refrained from all too categorical repudiations or authentications." [15]

A brief history of one of Bach's most important chamber music manuscripts gives us a vivid picture of the situation. The work in question is Bach's autograph of the Six Sonatas and Partitas for Violin Solo, one of the most beautiful Bach manuscripts in existence and one which has often been reproduced in facsimile (compare Figure 7, p. 168). It was not available to Dörffel for his first edition of the BGA; indeed it did not surface until 1890, when it was surprisingly offered for sale by Rosenthal, a dealer in antiquarian music from Munich, to the Viennese music scholar Eusebius Mandyczewski, along with a Haydn autograph. Mandyczewski was archivist for the *Gesellschaft der Musikfreunde* in Vienna, of which Brahms was a board member. Since at that time the Gesellschaft did not have sufficient funds for the purchase, Mandyczewski passed the offer on to his friend, Brahms. Brahms was a passionate collector of autograph manuscripts, and Mandyczewski was able to offer him the work with a clear conscience, for Brahms had already drawn up a will bequeathing all his treasures to the Society. Mandyczewski wrote to Brahms as follows: "Whether the manuscript is in Bach's own hand, I dare not commit myself. It is written with extraordinary neatness; it is virtually a masterpiece of musical handwriting."[16] Brahms wrote in response, "But, my good man, what about the price? Is one supposed to bid on the treasures? And how much? . . . In the meantime I am trying to find out more about Bach."[17] Apparently Brahms had some doubts as to its authenticity, but the next day he received fresh details from Mandyczewski: "Last night I received news from Munich that the manuscripts, which are only to be sold together, cost 1200 Marks. . . . I have compared the sonatas to the sheet in our museum, and it now seems more probable to me that they were written by the same hand. If that is the case, it may be an incomparable discovery. For the sonatas are beautifully written, a clean copy the like of which is very rare among Bach's works—a real masterpiece. . . . I've looked in Spitta and in the Bach Edition—this piece is unknown."[18] Brahms travelled to Vienna a few days later and looked at the autograph, but he did not decide to buy it—which can hardly have been due to financial considerations. When Spitta, the Bach biographer, did not respond to an enquiry by Mandyczewski (Mandyczewski wrote to Brahms a few weeks later, "Spitta did not answer, and so the piece has fallen into God knows whose hands."),[19] the plan to purchase the work was scrapped. However, the autograph must have come into the possession of Wilhelm Rust, one of the chief editors of the BGA, who naturally had an intense interest in it. After Rust's death in 1892, his widow loaned it to Erich Prieger, a collector and dealer of autograph manuscripts in Bonn. He was probably to have facilitated a sale to the Royal Berlin Library, with which he was in constant contact. It was not until 1917, however, that the Berlin Library decided to purchase it.

Joseph Joachim first saw the autograph manuscript when it was in the possession of Prieger. He was the first violinist who had the courage to perform the works for violin in public concerts. Now, on the basis of his experiences and after examining the autograph manuscript, he prepared a new edition which was completed by Andreas Moser after Joachim's death in 1907 and was printed by the Berlin music publishers Bote and Bock in 1908. This was the first edition which could claim to be based on an authenticated source!

Then, after the autograph was safely ensconced in the Berlin Library, scholars proceeded to reconstruct the stages through which it had passed since it was written in Köthen in 1720. It was learned that it had apparently remained in Bach's possession until his death. When his estate was divided among his children, mainly those from his first marriage, it did not pass into the hands of Carl Philipp Emanuel, like so many of Bach's works. Carl Philipp Emanuel looked after his inheritance carefully, which cannot be said of his older brother, Wilhelm Friedemann, whose property was scattered to the winds. After his death in 1788, Carl Philipp Emanuel's portion of the estate went to the music scholar Georg Pölchau, but only after some of it had passed through the hands of Johann Nikolaus Forkel, who published the first biography of Bach in 1802. Pölchau died in 1836; most of the works in his estate went to the Berlin *Singakademie.* In 1854, this organization, formerly the Zelter Institute, found itself in financial difficulties and sold these works to the Royal Library in Berlin for the ridiculous price of 1400 Thaler. The sale included priceless pieces, such as the autograph parts of the St. Matthew Passion![20] This sale helped to clarify the history of many Bach manuscripts, but the original manuscript of the works for violin solo was not among them; nor could Carl Philipp Emanuel himself have owned it. But on the cover of the autograph volume, which resurfaced in 1890, there was a handwritten entry: "Louisa Bach/Bückeburg/1842." This referred to Christiane Louisa, a granddaughter of the St. Thomas cantor and daughter of Bach's son Johann Christoph Friedrich (1732–95), who had been active in the small principality of Schaumburg-Lippe (he became known as "the Bückeburg Bach"). Louise, his third child, remained unmarried, lived to the age of ninety and died in Bückeburg in 1852. Two nieces inherited the manuscript from her; they were daughters of her brother, Wilhelm Friedrich Ernst Bach (1759–1845), who was harpsichordist at the court of Queen Luise in Berlin. Both nieces likewise remained unmarried and died in 1852 and 1858, respectively. They may have been the last descendants of Johann Sebastian Bach to bear his surname. What happened to the manuscript after that is unclear. It was a stroke of luck that it turned up again in 1890. It had not been available for any of the editions to appear in print before the 1908 Joachim-Moser edition; and that was 11 in all since Simrock had published the first collected edition in Bonn in 1802.

We have thus been able to trace a complex, but still relatively comprehensible history of a Bach autograph.[21] Other cases have been beset with difficulties which have not been worked out up to the present day. To illustrate the point: the Swedish-German musicologist, Hans Eppstein, has researched the source material of the suites for solo cello for more than a decade without yet being in a position to edit the corresponding volume of the NBA.[22]

Given such chance occurrences and incomplete documentation, it is extremely risky to say whether one work is by Bach and another is not. When such judgments have been made, it occasionally smacks of circumstantial evidence. Although much of the Bach research has been laudable and indispensable, it has not always been innocent of the charge that more credence has been given to a paper type or a handwriting characteristic than to the music itself. The results have at times been so erroneous that an experienced practicing musician can only shake his head.[23] Take the Trio Sonata for 2 Violins and b.c. in C Major BWV 1037, for example: was it really written by Johann Gottlieb Goldberg, as is currently maintained? Its merits would not be diminished if that were true, but we are then left with the incomprehensible fact that a man who as a composer produced virtually nothing is supposed to have written such a work of genius. Is it not more likely that a Bach autograph manuscript has travelled a circuitous route and finally been lost, with only a copy remaining? Let us consider as grounds for this argument: the only existing manuscript of the Trio Sonata can be found in a collection which also contains a copy of three movements of the Trio Sonata for 2 Violins and b.c. in F Major, Op. 2, No. 5, by Handel. The works bear the heading "di J. G. Goldberg," in a different hand from that of the copyist. We know Johann Gottlieb Goldberg (also written "Gollberg" or "Golberg") from his association with Bach's *Goldberg Variations* for harpsichord. Born in Danzig in 1727, he was court harpsichordist for Count Keyserlingk, who was the Russian ambassador in Dresden. Later, when Keyserlingk left Dresden, Goldberg remained behind and joined Count Brühl's ensemble. He died in Dresden in 1756, before his thirtieth birthday. Goldberg had been a pupil of Wilhelm Friedemann Bach in Dresden. For many reasons it is difficult to imagine that he was ever a regular student of Johann Sebastian Bach, not the least of which was the distance between Dresden and Leipzig.[24] We know only that he once stayed in Leipzig for a few months in the company of one of Keyserlingk's sons. He surely had some contact there with the elder Bach, and perhaps Bach looked over some of his compositions. But to explain the extraordinary quality of the Trio Sonata as a result of Bach's corrections or of his having supervised its writing is a hypothesis which belies experience. No teacher of composition can conjure up qualities in a pupil that the pupil does not already possess. In this case I feel that speculation has reached the limits of credibility. More trust should be placed in the artistic merit of a piece which far surpasses the level of even the better than average trio sonatas of the time.[25]

There are several cases like this in Bach's chamber music. The Sonata in E-Flat Major for Flute and Clavier BWV 1031 is likewise not considered an authentic Bach work. In analyzing it more closely, it might indeed seem that certain details point to the generation after Bach, perhaps to the circle of Carl Phillip Emanuel Bach. But at least as many facts point to the contrary. How opinions regarding a work like this change is demonstrated in a statement by Werner Danckert, an analyst of style who must be taken seriously. In 1934, when the authenticity of the sonata was not yet in doubt, he wrote about the main theme of the first movement that "It firmly seizes the momentum at the outset. Despite the fluidity of rhythm appropriate to the flute, the line retains a substantiality, a conciseness, that is unmistakably Bach. It does not dally or languish like the flute figures of the Rococo, for the thorough bass, striding firmly and implacably along, does not give it a moment's freedom."[26]

The argument against authenticity, on the other hand, was substantiated in part by the fact that the bass at no time participates in the theme of the E-Flat Major Sonata. But that is also true of the great B Minor Flute Sonata BWV 1030. It was also argued that elsewhere Bach had never allowed the clavier to perform alone as long as he did in the first movement of this sonata. But exactly the same thing occurs in the A Major Sonata for Flute and Clavier BWV 1032, and nobody questions its authenticity; furthermore, the Sonata in G Minor BWV 1020, which has legitimately been claimed by flautists for their instrument, is composed according to the same principles. The parallels between these sonatas will be taken up later (see p. 26). As for the supposedly "unbachian" clavier solos within a piece of chamber music, the Sonata for Violin and Clavier in G Major BWV 1019 contains an entire movement for solo clavier in two of its three versions. Thus the argument against authenticity is based on shaky foundations.

The beautiful middle movement of the E-Flat Major Flute Sonata, "Siciliano," in G Minor with a clear division between "melody" (flute) and sixteenth "accompaniment," which, it is claimed, also diverges from stylistic norms and hence cannot be attributed to Bach, has an exact counterpart in the first movement of the Sonata for Violin and Clavier in C Minor BWV 1017. Moreover, in inspiration and execution it is indisputably superior to the supposedly authentic, but unfortunately rather dry middle movement of the Sonata for Flute and Clavier in A Major BWV 1032— likewise a 6/8 andante. Finally, as to the similarity in style to Carl Phillip Emanuel Bach, this is even more apparent in many details of the Trio Sonata in C Minor from the *Musical Offering*, whose typical "sentimental sighs" in the 3rd movement would go well with a Watteau, Rococo painting. The only certain thing that can be said about the entire complex of BWV 1031 is that it is a very beautiful work which flautists should be eager to play.

Another controversial case: the Trio Sonata for Flute, Violin and b.c. in G Major BWV 1038. After Friedrich Blume's discovery of the parallel version of the work in 1928, the Sonata for Violin and b.c. in G Major BWV 1021, which has only the bass in common with the trio sonata, its reputation has suffered greatly in the eyes of Bach experts, for its authenticity was not absolutely verifiable. A questionable tendency showed itself here: once doubt was cast on the authenticity of a work, critics suddenly began to discover countless weaknesses in the work.[27] In response to this, one must first counter that even Bach was not immune to occasional weaknesses in composition; this in itself is not an argument against authenticity. However, in the case of this trio sonata, a piece which is perhaps not first-rate, but still reaches the level of Handel's or Telemann's trio sonatas, the critics seem to have become blinded to quality. What about the main theme of its 3rd movement (adagio) and the movement "Gute Nacht, o Wesen" from the motet *Jesu, meine Freude* (Example 1)? Is the fact that they are identical of no significance? Is this not an indication of Bach's authorship? Further: none of the publishers of the violin sonata has pointed out that its finale (4th movement) represents only a meager surrogate of a structure originally conceived as a three-part fugue, which is exactly what the trio sonata presents in this movement. There is an additional version of the trio sonata, the Sonata for Violin and Clavier in F Major (BWV 1022). Here, as in the G Major Violin Sonata, the third instrumental part *is* present in the finale. At that, the F Major Violin Sonata contains not only the bass, but also both of the upper parts of the trio sonata, with the right hand of the keyboard taking the flute part. Thus there is complete agreement between BWV 1022 and BWV 1038. The violin sonata has merely been transposed a full step down, and it accordingly calls for a violin tuned a whole tone down (*violino discordato*). There is one exception: the 2nd movement of the violin sonata is expanded considerably over that of the trio sonata. The continuous 2nd movement of the trio sonata, which contains only a modulation to the parallel minor, in BWV 1022 becomes a two-part movement with an additional modulation to the dominant. This in turn introduces a new theme, which appears twice (Example 2).

Example 1. a. Trio Sonata in G Major BWV 1038, 3rd movement, m. 1–3
      b. Motet *Jesu, meine Freude* BWV 227, 9th movement, "Gute Nacht, o Wesen," m. 1–8. In the repetition of m. 1–2 the soprano parts are exchanged. When the passage returns in m. 37–42, the repetition is omitted.

It is precisely from this characteristic variant that I recognize Bach's signature, especially in the new theme, which bears his unmistakable stamp. As a whole it is much more than a mere correction made by a copyist, and Bach himself would hardly have invested so much energy in someone else's work. This Violin Sonata in F Major BWV 1022 has no doubt been underestimated. In my opinion it represents the later, more mature version of the trio sonata, which can be seen especially in the more skillful voice leading, as shown in the following examples. Example 3 (b) shows how the awkwardness of having the two embellishments occur simultaneously in the trio sonata is avoided in the violin sonata.

In his dissertation on Bach's sonatas for melody instruments and clavier,[28] Hans Eppstein proposed and substantiated the thesis that nearly all the great violin/clavier, gamba/clavier and flute/clavier sonatas were originally trio sonatas. In fact, the parallel version of the Viola da gamba Sonata in G Major BWV 1027, is provided by the Trio Sonata for Two Flutes and b.c. BWV 1039. Why, then, should not the Trio Sonata BWV 1038 be an earlier version of the Violin/Clavier Sonata BWV 1022, since both works, as we attempted to show, exhibit a considerable number of Bach characteristics?

Example 2. Sonata for Violin and Clavier in F Major, BWV 1022, 2nd movement, m. 20–27, without violin part

Example 3. a. Trio Sonata in G Major BWV 1038, 3rd Movement, Adagio, m. 17
          b. The same m. 17 in the Sonata for Violin and Clavier in F Major BWV 1022

We cannot, of course, deal with all the questions of authenticity in this study. But we do need to spend at least a little more time on the parallel works BWV 1038, 1021 and 1022. All three have a bass line which is essentially the same but not completely identical. Its authenticity was also in doubt. The critical notes to Volume VI, 1 of the NBA (which contains the works for violin) devote much space to the question of the authenticity of these three works.[29] But the authors repeatedly show considerable insecurity in the evaluation of compositional matters. They claim that the written out repetition of both parts of the first movement (*Largo*) of the trio sonata "shows a surprising rhythmic punctuation of the two upper parts for flute and violin which substantially weakens the compactness of the passage." This thesis does not hold up. The variation of a repetition is a common practice in Baroque music. In this case, Bach was only carrying the principle to an extreme. The varied repetitions, therefore, had to be written down. The bass was simplified for the same reason; the statement that the bass "was forced into a mechanical eighth note pattern so that the original, basic structure is strongly disturbed," shows ignorance of an elementary requirement of composition: when the upper parts are changed to have dotted note passages, the bass must be simplified. Rhythmic combinations like this are not found any earlier than Brahms. Only two pages later, however, the authors present a contrary argument: now the bass in the same passage of the Violin Sonata in F Major BWV 1022, which is strengthened by the addition of thirty-seconds, is "given a more or less capricious structure, which seems to be characteristic of a later period." There is a lack of consensus as to which criteria are to be accepted: whether Bach simplifies or ornaments the bass, both practices are considered as evidence that the work is not authentic. Notwithstanding this, comparable bass variants can be found in a similar constellation of works: the parallels between the Trio Sonata for Two Flutes and b.c. in G Major BWV 1039 and the Sonata for Viola de Gamba and Clavier in G Major BWV 1027; but both these works are authentic beyond any doubt.[30]

It is also unlikely that a work like the Sonata for Flute and b.c. in C Major BWV 1033 could have been written by Bach: it sounds like the work of a student. This is proven by the music alone. He never produced cadences as primitive as those in the 1st movement, and he never wrote run-of-the-mill sequences like those in the allegro which follows. The concluding minuet, in which the clavier part suddenly becomes obbligato, seems to belong to an entirely different work. On the other hand, the Sonata for Violin (or Flute) and Clavier in G Minor BWV 1020 seems to me a truly authentic Bach work and completely worthy of him. It is currently attributed to Carl Philipp Emanuel Bach; but I find fewer similarities between this sonata and his other chamber music than between this and Johann Sebastian's compositional style.

The first thing to be mentioned is its obvious structural affinity to the E-Flat Major Flute Sonata BWV 1031, which we already discussed. Both works have quite lengthy clavier solos in the 1st movement, and in both movements the flute starts with its own theme, which even begins with a rising sixth in both cases. Furthermore, both sonatas, when compared with the sonatas for violin and clavier or for violin solo, for example, display notable compactness in their overall structure, which in both cases consists of three movements; and both feature a free 6/8 siciliano middle movement. Now in the face of such arguments, proponents of the thesis of unauthenticity would certainly object that the E-Flat Major Sonata is also unauthentic, and even if parallels did exist, this would furnish further proof of the unauthenticity of the G Minor Sonata. But there is a third flute and clavier sonata by Bach, the one in A Major BWV 1032, which has the same characteristics: clavier solos, separate clavier and flute themes in the 1st movement, concise diction, Siciliano middle movement,—qualitites which can be seen clearly even in the fragmentary 1st movement of this sonata. There is no doubt about its authenticity! Indeed, there are even similarities to the great B Minor Sonata for Flute and Clavier BWV 1030, which also has a Siciliano-like middle movement. To me this means that at least in the A Major, B Major and G Minor sonatas, Bach was attempting to create a type of flute sonata which had nothing in common with the Sonatas for violin and clavier, but because of the characteristics already cited, together with its three movement structure, diverged from them and from the church sonata scheme in general. Those who join me in viewing the two-part final movement of the great B Minor Sonata as a unit will also place this work in a similar category;—in any case, it has nothing in common with a "sonata da chiesa." The B Minor Sonata is distinguishable from the other three flute and clavier sonatas only by its expanded dimensions.

I also find it hard to believe that similarity between a chamber movement and an aria always means that the vocal work has been adapted—that its text simply has been removed. Musical ideas manifest themselves in the most disparate ways. Moreover, Johann Sebastian Bach is not the only composer who was inspired to write chamber music pieces based on vocal models. There is only one case in which Bach indisputably incorporated an aria into his chamber music: the 3rd movement (cantabile, ma un poco adagio in G Major, 6/8) of the second version (B) of the Sonata for Violin and Clavier in G Major BWV 1019a. Originally it was an aria in the cantata, *Gott, man lobet dich in der Stille,* No. 120 and in *Herr Gott, Beherrscher aller Dinge,* No. 120a.

Such considerations take us far into the realm of stylistic analysis and criticism. They certainly carry more weight than does pure historical paleography in decisions concerning the authenticity and dating of works. Nevertheless, even stylistic analysis has its limitations when it comes to making such decisions. One should never say that a work cannot be by Bach because it contains elements not found in any of his other works. Artistic creation is incalculable. If certain elements appear only once in a composer's work, this alone does not constitute proof that the work is not authentic. Bach always liked to try out new ideas and to experiment with his new insights, especially during the Köthen period.[31] In contrast to Telemann, for instance, he always avoided serial production and repetition according to a tried-and-true scheme; instead he was continually seeking individual solutions. If one has considered the limitations set by the period, and has eliminated all poor workmanship, then it is rarely possible to maintain with absolute confidence that "Bach could never have written this." There are no proofs of this kind in art. If the study of style were based only on analogies, we might indeed wind up with a "standard" Bach, but it would be a sterile and entirely lifeless one. This, however, would be utterly inconsistent with the totality of his artistic nature.

Still another, more fundamental aspect of the "authenticity question" must be mentioned. We indicated above that everybody begins to find weaknesses in a work whose authenticity cannot be proved. The opposite case, when a work which has been established as "authentic" now is praised as a work of genius, is typical of our contemporary need for security. The courage to place one's trust in the substance of the music is lacking; if there is any uncertainty, we seek security in "verifiable," or,

Figure 2. Autograph of the Sonata for Flute and Clavier in A Major BWV 1032 (below) and the Concerto for 2 Claviers and Strings in C Minor BWV 1062

one might say, legally valid facts. That way there is no risk. However, such facts are only secondary in comparison with the unambiguous language of the music itself. Such an approach to music perpetuates a tendency which has long been the bane of the fine arts: obeisance to established authenticity.[32] We shall return to this question in Chapter 6.

It is understandable that the publishers of the NBA omitted works whose authenticity they felt to be unverifiable. But it is regrettable that in so doing they sacrificed several excellent pieces of chamber music. No one should feel compelled by this fact to refrain from playing these works; their quality remains the same now as always. This is the reason that they are being included in our study. Perhaps some day the NBA will publish a supplementary volume including such borderline cases.

What follows is a listing of chamber music autograph manuscripts which are judged to be authentic based on the latest musicological findings. The dates of the manuscripts are included, when known.

1.   Sonatas and Partitas for Violin Solo

   Complete. (1720).

2.   Sonatas for Violin and Clavier
   The only extant autograph is the keyboard part of the 6th Sonata in G Major BWV 1019, version B (see p. 32), and only the 3rd, 4th and 5th movements.

3.   Sonatas for Viola da Gamba and Clavier

   Sonata #1 in G Major BWV 1027 survives intact (1735–45). The autograph of Sonata #3 in G Minor BWV 1029 was available to the editors of the BGA, but is lost today.

4.   Sonatas for Flute and Clavier

   The Sonata in B Minor BWV 1030 survives intact without the flute part (1736–37), as does the fragmentary score of the Sonata in A Major BWV 1032, which Bach wrote down at the bottom of the score of the Concerto for Two Claviers and Strings in C Minor BWV 1062 (see Figure 2). Almost half of the 1st movement is cut off and has been lost. The date of the Clavier Concerto: 1736.

5.   Works for Lute

   The Suite in G Minor BWV 995 (1727–31); Prelude, Fugue and Allegro in E-flat Major BWV 998 (1740–1750); and the Suite in E Major BWV 1006a (1737).

6.   Trio Sonatas

   The entire Trio Sonata in G Major (flute, violin, b.c.) BWV 1038 survives in autograph parts. The Trio Sonata in C Minor from the *Musical Offering* BWV 1079 is preserved not as an autograph manuscript, but in the first edition printed in 1747, which Bach supervised. The short trio sonata movement in F Major BWV 1040 (Ob., Vl., b.c.) was written by Bach on half of the last page of the score of Cantata #208 (*Was mir behagt, ist nur die muntre Jagd*). The cantata was written in Weimar in 1716. Three parts for the Trio Sonata in G Major BWV

1039 (2 Flutes and b.c.) bear the additional inscription by Zelter, "in his own hand."[33]

There are two interesting things about this list: first, only a few works survive in autograph manuscript. The majority exist only as copies. We can assume that Bach edited Anna Magdalena's manuscripts, and this can also be assumed to a certain extent for the copies made by his pupils, Altnikol and Kirnberger. Secondly, most of the autographs originated in Leipzig, although we know for certain that the chamber music was mostly written in Köthen. This would mean that they were also used and played in Leipzig. The dates of the manuscripts that are not autographs would confirm this. At the very least, Bach was still involved with his chamber music when he was in Leipzig and made a "critical revision" of it, as he did with much of his organ music. There would have been no lack of opportunity to perform the pieces at home or in the *collegium musicum.*

With the exception of some of the lute pieces (see p. 31), only the Trio Sonata from the *Musical Offering* was definitely rewritten in Leipzig; this was done in 1747. I would add to the list of compositions reworked in Leipzig the Sonata for Flute and b.c. in E Major BWV 1035, not only on the basis of the existing documentation,[34] but chiefly because in format and execution it bears all the signs of a mature work. Though it may on the surface appear to be a conventional work, this may have been due to the person to whom it was dedicated, a man named Fredersdorf, who was the chamberlain of Frederick II. For the king himself Bach wrote more difficult, that is, more challenging works, as exemplified by the trio sonata. But in the E Major Sonata Bach elevated the tradition of the through bass sonata to an incomparably higher spiritual plane. In effect, it was a sublimation in this genre of the work of several generations of composers. It is indisputable that there is a link between the sonata and one of Bach's two journeys to Berlin in 1741 and 1747.

Some parts of the lute music also belong to the Leipzig period, and perhaps the B minor version of the great Flute and Clavier Sonata BWV 1030 was also a Leipzig creation. In any case its famous, calligraphically masterful autograph was not written until 1736–37, whereas the G minor copy of the same work was done in Köthen. The transcription of the Trio Sonata for 2 Flutes and b.c. in G Major BWV 1039 into the Gamba Sonata 1027 also may have been made in Leipzig.

Nevertheless, Köthen remains the place where the majority and the most significant of Bach's chamber music pieces were composed. This puts them between the years 1717 and 1723. According to Eppstein's studies,[35] the three groups of sonatas written for melody instruments and obbligato clavier during these six years appeared in the following sequence: Flute Sonatas BWV 1030 (G Minor version), 1031 and 1032, Viola da Gamba Sonatas BWV 1027, 1028 and 1029, Violin Sonatas BWV 1014, 1015, 1016, 1017, 1018 and 1019 (1019a). The BWV numbers bear no relation to the sequence of composition within the individual groups. Accordingly, the violin sonatas would have been the last in the series. This is a plausible conclusion because the compositional principles of this genre were certainly carried out with maximum sovereignty in these works.

The period from 1717 to 1720 would seem to be appropriate for the works for violin solo, according to the surviving autograph title page. The contention that the Suites for Cello Solo were written *after* them was undisputed until Eppstein declared the contrary to be true; according to him, the comparatively conventional cello suites came first, and then the sonatas and partitas for violin solo, which display a great deal more virtuosity—from the standpoint of composition, not performance technique.[36] Scholarship also places the b.c. sonatas in the Köthen period; we have already shown why we make an exception of the E Major Flute Sonata. The Trio Sonatas in C Major for 2 Violins and b.c. BWV 1037 and in G Major for Flute, Violin and b.c. BWV 1038 have yet to be placed in the sequence. Schmieder dates them (as he does nearly all the chamber works) simply, "Köthen, circa 1720." The Trio Sonata for Flute is surely the earlier of the two; we might be inclined to place it in the Weimar period, if we did not know that before Köthen Bach never used the transverse flute—the *traversa* or *flûte allemande*. The Trio Sonata for 2 Flutes and b.c. in G Major BWV 1039, the prototype for the first gamba sonata, clearly belongs to the Köthen years.

The current literature views the Sonata for Violin and b.c. in E Minor BWV 1023 as a work of the last Weimar years. This assumption is supported by the rather tentative structure of the piece, which contains two sonata and two suite movements, the beginning of which seems to have been intended more for the organ.

The works for lute pose several riddles. The BGA nearly always casts doubts on their original composition as lute works and leaves open the possibility that they might just as well have been keyboard works. It was not until quite recently that the painstaking research of Thomas Kohlhase has clarified this matter.[37] According to Kohlhase the following works are primarily intended for the lute: Suite in G Minor BWV 995, Partita in C Minor BWV 997, Prelude in C Minor BWV 999 and Fugue in G Minor BWV 1000. All of these are authentic Bach works. Since, however, the last-named work, a transcription of the fugue from the Sonata for Violin Solo in G Minor BWV 1001, survives only as a tablature copy made by a contemporary of Bach named Weyrauch, it is possible that Weyrauch himself was responsible for the lute version. However, this thesis is contradicted by the rather significant altering of the lute version compared to the violin version. BWV 995 is a transcription of the Cello Solo Suite in C Minor BWV 1011. The transcription, however, survives as an autograph manuscript and contains, moreover, obvious extensions of the polyphony of the primary work in the 6/8 allegro passage of the prelude, leaving no doubt as to Bach's authorship of the lute version. As a transcription it is clearly superior to that of the Violin Solo Partita in E Major BWV 1006 for the lute (BWV 1006a), which does survive as a Bach autograph, but is rather superficial and careless. There still remain BWV 996, the Suite in E Minor, and BWV 998, the Prelude, Fugue and Allegro in E-flat Major. The former work is one of the few compositions from before the Köthen period,—probably between 1707 and 1717. Certain instances of awkwardness relative to lute technique have given rise to doubts as to its authenticity, although its inventiveness and measured proportion strongly suggest Johann Sebastian Bach. The piece originally may well have been written in D Minor; this would correspond to the normal tuning of the lute at that time and would make it more suitable for the technique of the instrument. BWV 998, the work in E-flat Major, was written in the last decade of Bach's life. In the meantime, doubts have been eliminated as to its authenticity; and we no longer believe that it is an unfinished work.[38] It should be noted that of all the lute works, only the short C Minor Prelude BWV 999 was composed in Köthen. The original versions of BWV 995, 1000 and 1006a are obviously not included in this observation. But in BWV 996, 997 and 998, original works for lute, we have three highly interesting pieces which provide insight into the development of Bach's instrumental style outside Köthen (see Part III, pp. 229 ff.). A vivid example of this is the very unconventional fugue theme of the C minor Partita (Example 4).

Example 4. Partita in C Minor for Lute BWV 997, 2nd movement,
Fugue, m. 1–3

Nevertheless, in some instances there remain uncertainties regarding the lute works. We should not let this situation annoy us, as the quality of the works remains quite untouched. And since the literature for Baroque lute is rather sparse, such substantial compositions are in any case a welcome addition to the repertoire. Whether and to what extent the lute works may also be performed on the guitar will be examined in Chapter 6.

We have repeatedly encountered several versions of the same work. It is a matter of speculation why Bach transcribed many of his works. There are many possible explanations: for one, the pressure of time so often imposed on him, especially in Leipzig, where constant demands for church music did not allow for work on new chamber music pieces. The transcription of the sonatas for melody instruments and clavier from what had previously been trio sonatas (which is admittedly hypothetical, with the exception of BWV 1039 to BWV 1027) is often accounted for by Bach's intense involvement with the clavier. A certain delight in experimentation may also have been a factor. But a more weighty consideration seems to have been Bach's desire to have his chamber works remembered, for which reason he gave some of his works a "new relevance" by rewriting them.

It is another matter though when a work is not merely re-scored (which always includes minor structural changes, revisions of the bass, cuts and additions, and so forth), but when Bach kept polishing the very substance of the work because it had not yet reached its final, definitive form. A prime example of this is the Violin and Clavier Sonata in G Major BWV 1029, of which there are three versions. We shall list them now in the sequence of composition suggested by Eppstein: [39]

Sonata for Violin and Clavier in G major BWV 1019/1019a

Version A: 1. Vivace 4/4 G major (identical to B1 and C1)
               2. Largo 3/4 E minor (identical to B2 and C2)
               3. Unspecified 3/8 E minor (clavier solo)
               4. Adagio 4/4 B minor (identical to B4)
               5. Violino solo e Basso l'accompagnato 2/2 in G minor
               6. Repetition of 1.

Version B: 1. Presto 4/4 in G major (identical to A1 and C1)
               2. Largo 3/4 in E minor (identical to A2 and C2)
               3. Cantabile, ma un poco adagio, 6/8 in G major
               4. Adagio 4/4 in B minor (identical to A4)
               5. Repetition of 1

Version C: 1. Allegro 4/4 in G major (identical to A1 and B1)
2. Largo 3/4 in E minor (identical to A2 and B2)
3. Unspecified 4/4 in E minor (clavier solo)
4. Adagio 4/4 in B minor
5. Allegro 6/8 in G major

It is extremely interesting to see how Bach struggles with the five-movement structure of this concept, which does not appear quite like this in any of his other instrumental works. First, in A and B, he attempts to tie the movements together by means of the da capo of the beginning movement. He drops the idea in the end and writes a new final movement for version C. Another idea present from the start is the clavier solo movement. It vanishes in B but returns in C, albeit with completely different material. The rhythm and key of the adagio of the fourth movement seems to have been firmly established from the beginning. As beautiful as A4 and B4 are, within the sonata we must give preference to the C4 movement, built as it is around a new expansive theme. All in all, version C, which is printed in all the Bach editions, is without doubt the best solution.

The 5th movement of version A seems to have been incorporated into the sonata by chance. It does appear in the autograph manuscript, but only the bass part. The violin part is unknown. It seems to have little in common with the movements of any of the other versions. It would be quite unusual for Bach to employ the identical minor key in a sonata (in contrast to a suite) movement. Furthermore, what do we make of a thorough bass movement in a sonata grouping which otherwise features only obbligato clavier? At any rate, Bach did not scrap movements 3 and 5 of the A version; he later incorporated them into the E Minor Clavier Partita BWV 830 as *Courante* and *Tempo di Gavotta.*

It has already been mentioned that the cantabile movement which appears in version B is a literal transcription of an aria from two Leipzig cantatas BWV 120 and 120a. In both versions of the aria the voice is accompanied by a concertante solo violin. The latter remains unchanged in the sonata as a violin part, while the vocal part is transferred to the right hand of the keyboard. Bach did find himself compelled to add ornamentation; the tone of the harpsichord was apparently too thin for him (in other transpositions he did not show such scruples). The types of embellishing techniques used in Bach's time are revealed by comparing the vocal and the harpsichord versions. Despite the great musical beauty of this movement, which is much more effective in the vocal version, Bach removed it from version C of the sonata and replaced it with the comfortably dancelike harpsichord movement; in so doing he followed his original idea.[40]

Later, Bach also revised the 3rd movement (adagio) of the Violin and Clavier Sonata in F Major BWV 1018. His first draft, which features simple sixteenth arpeggios in place of the thirty-seconds of the clavier part, was apparently too colorless for him.[41]

The following is a list of all the works or parts of works which exist in more than one version:

1. a) Trio Sonata for 2 Flutes and b.c. in G Major BWV 1039
    b) Sonata for Viola da Gamba and Clavier in G Major BWV 1027
    c) 1st, 2nd and 4th movements for Organ or Pedal Clavier
        (Schmieder lists the 4th movement as BWV 1027a)

2. a) Trio Sonata for Flute, Violin and b.c. in G Major BWV 1038
    b) Sonata for Violin and Clavier in F Major BWV 1022
    c) Sonata for Violin and b.c. in G Major BWV 1021
        (2c has only the bass in common with 2a and 2b, with the exception of the final movement, which takes over the fugue theme)

3. a) Sonata for Flute and Clavier in B Minor BWV 1030
    b) Sonata for Flute and Clavier in G Minor (not in the BWV)
        (3b is identical to 3a except for minor differences, but only the clavier part of 3b is extant. 3b is also performed on the oboe, but there is no record of this.

4. a) Suite for Violoncello Solo in C Minor BWV 1011
    b) Suite for Lute in G Minor BWV 995

5. a) Sonata for Violin and Clavier in G Major BWV 1019 (version A)
    b) Sonata for Violin and Clavier in G Major BWV 1019 (version B)
    c) Sonata for Violin and Clavier in G Major BWV 1019 (version C)
    d) Movements A3 and A5 as Courante and Tempo di Gavotta in Partita #6 for Clavier solo in E Minor BWV 830 (here also the upper part for A5)
    e) Movement B3 as a soprano aria in the Cantatas BWV 120 and BWV 120a

6. a) Sonata for Violin and Clavier in F Minor (BWV 1018), 3rd movement (sixteenth-note version) BWV 1018a
    b) Sonata for Violin and Clavier in F Minor BWV 1018, 3rd movement, (thirty-second-note version)

7. a) Sonata for Flute and Clavier in A Major BWV 1032, 2nd movement, Largo e dolce
    b) Trio movement for Violin, Cello and b.c. Largo (not in the BWV; reproduced in NBA VI, 3, Critical Notes, p. 55)

8. a) Partita for Violin Solo in E Major BWV 1006
    b) Suite for Lute in E Major BWV 1006a

9. a) Sonata for Violin Solo in G Minor BWV 1001, 2nd movement (fugue)
    b) Fugue for Lute in G Minor BWV 1000
    c) Fugue for Organ in D Minor BWV 539, 2nd movement

Even if an examination and comparison of these multiple versions may help to clarify some questions of dates of composition, we are still left with guesswork. But such a comparison gives us some interesting angles on their composition. In which passages did Bach make his revisions? What was corrected? What was retained in all versions?

There are other works of chamber music whose authenticity remains doubtful. Since some of them are listed in the BWV or contained in the BGA; they will now be listed and briefly described:

1. Sonata for Violin and b.c. in C Minor BWV 1024
    The first three movements might be attributed to a composer at the turn of the 18th century who was active shortly before Bach. The 4th (final) movement is obviously from a later period, probably from the time of the older sons of Bach,

and was probably not originally part of the sonata. Most valuable is the 1st movement, which recalls Heinrich Ignaz Franz Biber with its extravagant Baroque violin patterns.

2. Suite for Violin and Clavier in A Major BWV 1025
    A mediocre, utilitarian composition, which shows Italian rather than German influence.

3. Fugue for Violin and b.c. in G Minor BWV 1026
    In respect to polyphony, the piece has long passages where there are more than just two parts. They always occur in the violin part; the clavier part remains a simple b.c. As is the case of the fugues in the sonatas for violin solo, there are non-thematic episodes with virtuoso passage work. Although not very satisfying to perform, the piece is a good composition. Its great length (181 measures) does not lack substance.

4. Sonata for Violin and Clavier in D Minor BWV 1036
    In the BWV the work appears as a "Trio," but this trio version goes back to an arrangement by Max Seiffert, who published it in 1930.[42] Seiffert considers this work to be authentic, but this has since been refuted. The sonata belongs to the circle of Carl Phillip Emanuel Bach; it seldom rises above mediocrity.

5. Sonata for Flute and b.c. (in Minuet I, Flute and Clavier) in C Major BWV 1033. It has already been discussed on p. 26.

6. 4 Inventions for Violin and b.c. BWV App., 173–176
    These inventions, which comprise four individual movements and are by no means uninteresting, are by Francesco Antonio Bonporti (1672–1749). They were considered authentic for a time, since Bach had made copies of them.

Other chamber music pieces which occasionally have been attributed to Johann Sebastian Bach need not be considered here. On the other hand, I would like to emphasize that in my opinion the following works are authentic and should for this reason be included in our study:

1. Trio Sonata for Flute, Violin and b.c. in G Major BWV 1038
2. Trio Sonata for 2 Violins and b.c. in C Major BWV 1037
3. Sonata for Flute and Clavier in E-Flat Major BWV 1031
4. Sonata for Violin (or Flute) and Clavier in G Minor BWV 1020
5. Sonata for Violin and Clavier in F Major BWV 1022 (adapted from the Trio Sonata BWV 1038)
6. Suite for Lute in E Minor BWV 996

Chapter 3

Historical and Social Background

In Bach's time it was unthinkable for a composer to have written "for his desk drawer." Music was only composed when it was sure to be used, i.e. performed, and accepted by its public. Practically all of Bach's works were produced in this way: the *Art of Fugue* was perhaps the only work he wrote for himself, although we do it no injustice to imagine that Bach intended it for a "learned" group such as the "Mizler Society." We have already noted that Bach's works were intimately connected with the position he held at the time he wrote them. Thus the question: "for what audience was it intended?" also applies to the chamber music. The question has two components: the first has to do with the specific situation in Köthen, which is indisputably of primary importance for the chamber music; the second is more general: who were the people who played chamber music in the second half of the 18th century, and on what occasions did they play it?[43]

The second question is the broader of the two, so we shall deal with it first. In the first half of the 18th century there was no concert life that could be compared with what we know today, or even with that of the 19th century. Public performances of instrumental music, for which one paid admission, were seldom offered. Examples of such exceptions were the performances organized by Telemann beginning in 1721 in the "Drill House" in Hamburg; the *Society of Music* founded by Young, a member of the Royal British Chapel, in 1724; or Philidor's *Concert sp;ituel,* which began in 1725. But Bach had no connection with these enterprises, and it is uncertain how much or how little chamber music they offered.

When Bach embarked on his musical career at the turn of the 18th century, the church and the aristocracy were virtually the only patrons of music. The few "free lance" musicians who were active—town pipers and fiddlers—belonged to an inferior class and were beneath his consideration. In the realm of instrumental music, it was the aim of the various greater and lesser "serenissimi" to maintain a theatre for opera and ballet, or, when that exceeded their means, as was the case in Köthen, at least to have their own group of musicians, a small orchestra. This cultivation of music was largely a matter of social status. If a prince entertained guests, they were regaled with music, and if he travelled, the number of musicians accompanying him was a measure of his prestige. This does not mean that musicians had the status of menial servants, which was how Mozart thought of himself in Salzburg. Their existence—modest as it was—was secure, and their artistic freedom for the most part uncircumscribed; in any case, they enjoyed more freedom than during the period of the Viennese censorship in the 19th century or in totalitarian states today. And their music often held the genuine interest of their patrons.

Church music followed much the same course; to a large extent it, too, served the demands of prestige, especially when associated with the court of a prince. And even more so at the See of a bishop: the reputation of a prince of the church was mirrored in the splendor and variety of his sacred music. Consider Orazio Benevoli's polychoral mass for the dedication of the Salzburg Cathedral.[44] But the parish community was also a supporter of church music, especially in Protestant lands. The imperial and Hanseatic cities, be it Mühlhausen or Hamburg, Leipzig or

Lübeck, all regarded the cultivation of music as an important responsibility. Hamburg was the first city which dared to open and maintain an opera house independent of an aristocratic court; the building on the Gänsemarkt would be called a municipal opera house today. At any rate, the institution remained in existence for 60 years; Keiser, Telemann, Mattheson, and the young Handel were active there. It was no accident that the free cities took the first steps toward independent patronage of music, as this reflected a rising "culturally conscious" bourgeoisie. In Lübeck one even dared to perform church music apart from a church service in the evening concerts of religious music (Geistliche Abendmusik).

Yet amidst all this activity we search in vain for chamber music. Chamber music does not lend itself to upholding status—ostentation is contrary to its nature—and this may be one of the reasons why it is so rarely mentioned during this period. But it had played a significant role since Corelli's time: it was composed, played and in demand. How otherwise to explain Telemann's vast output of chamber music if there was "no market for it"? But where was this market?

Throughout early 18th-century Europe there existed, along with opera and church music, private groups of active musical devotees. They went by various names: "Collegium musicum," "Musikalische Gesellschaft," "Musik-Societät" ("Akademie"), and in France and England, "salon," "club," "consort." Music lovers and in some cases professional musicians congregated in pursuit of their common aim. They took turns meeting in private homes, as often as four times a week. The host provided beer and bread and arranged the lighting. Gatherings of this kind lasted for hours, and the amount of music played was enormous.

In 1712, a Frankfurt resident and music lover, Johann Friedrich von Uffenbach, reported from Strassburg that he had encountered several societies of this kind there.[45] One of these was composed of the following members: four vocalists, clavier, gamba, two violins, and two transverse flutes. So they also performed vocal music, surely pieces from operas and cantatas. Male and female singers are included in nearly all illustrations of such "Collegia musica." In Chodowiecki's well-known engraving, "Das Konzert," we see a male singer along with two violins, viola, gamba and clavier; and the depiction of a "Collegium musicum" from Thun, Switzerland, shows 12 people, including four vocalists, being conducted by one of them in the foreground.[46]

The repertoires of these societies consisted largely of original works— Telemann, Vivaldi and Pepusch were mentioned. With such small ensembles, drawing a clear distinction between chamber and orchestral music is impossible. All the trio and duet sonatas which the period so richly featured were surely played in these circles.

The instrumentation fluctuated, consisting of whatever players happened to be present. Thus it was probably necessary to have a stock of duet or trio sonatas on hand. As late as 1800, a music society in Königsberg reported that its members agreed to play "vollstimmige Sachen" (works for larger ensembles) from 5 to 8 o'clock, and then "quartets, etc.," from 9:30 to 10 o'clock. "Vollstimmige Sachen" were probably sinfonies, divertimenti and the like, whereas in Bach's time we must think rather of suites or overtures, of which Telemann alone supposedly wrote over 1,000.

In many places, a "learned" tone was set, as in the Mizler Society in Leipzig, to which Bach belonged after 1747. Anyone wishing to join such a society had to write a "trial piece". For this purpose Bach wrote his Canon in Six Voices BWV 1076,

Figure 3. *The Rémy Family in Coblence.* Painting by Januarius Zick (1776).

which he is holding in his hand in the well-known portrait by Hausmann. This circle preferred to be called an "academy," and cultivated challenging music which was probably discussed even more than it was played. The word "academy," meaning "concert," was still in use in Beethoven's time, and is derived from these societies.[48]

We now understand why Mattheson spoke of the "domestic style."

At first, audiences were not really wanted at gatherings of this kind. Many contemporary graphic representations, however, depict other people along with the musicians. In Januarius Zick's painting, "the Rémy Family in Coblenz" (1776), we can see, besides the six musicians—three violins, a cello, a clavichord, and a female singer—people drinking tea, playing billiards, and two men apparently engaged in lively conversation. Allowing for the artist's license in creating a well-proportioned painting, we can assume that most of the non-musicians were enjoying an "intermission" (see Figure 3).

Such groups wanted to be left to themselves, at least in the early part of the century. It was personalities like Telemann—who was indefatigable not only as a composer, but also as an organizer—who went public and attempted to attract an audience. He founded "Collegia musica" in Leipzig, Frankfurt am Main and Hamburg. We know that Bach, who from 1729 to 1738 directed the "Collegium musicum" founded by Telemann in Leipzig, happened on just such a transitional phase, in which musical performances were no longer confined to a domestic circle (they met at the Zimmermann Cafe), but could not yet be considered true public concerts.[49] In the university town of Leipzig, a substantial portion of the musicians were music-loving students. As we know, they were also an important component of Bach's church music, and thus they were able to "practice" with the "Collegium musicum," and even now and again earn extra money at birthday serenades and the like, until they were in a more favorable position to apply for stipends, having been volunteer musicians in the churches. Leipzig had several such "Collegia musica." Along with the *Grosses Konzert,* which was founded in 1743 by Bach's pupil and later cantor at St. Thomas, Johann Doles, and which consisted of 16 persons of both the aristocratic and the burgher classes, they formed the core of the *Gewandhaus* concerts, which came into being as public concerts in 1781, and which, incidentally, have continued to offer a chamber music series up to the present day.

Naturally, there were also professional musicians in these circles, who performed on instruments which otherwise could not have been included. This tendency to select a professional musician as "guiding spirit" also existed elsewhere. Bach and Telemann served in just such a capacity. It must, however, be emphasized that the amateurs were in the majority. The nobility and burghers, officers and students, but above all, men and women, played together as equals, without class distinctions. The music provided a democratic common ground.

Besides the "collegia," however, music also was being played by family members in private homes. The same players for whom the *Inventions, Suites* and *The Well-Tempered Clavier* were intended had most certainly played some of the persons. works for solo strings or duet sonatas in their own homes. We note, however, that Bach never furnished his chamber music pieces with dedications like "For the delectation of music lovers," which were so widespread at the time, although he occasionally did so elsewhere.[50] The sonatas and partitas for violin solo and the suites for cello and flute solo were in any case clearly study pieces and no thought was given to their "performance."

Court orchestras, especially if they were not too large, also needed chamber music. When not performing as a full orchestra, they were usually obliged to "come up with" chamber music. Even in capitals with opera houses (Vienna, Paris, Berlin), the leading players were required to play chamber music, which they usually did gladly. The smaller courts which had no operas also had smaller music groups, and apart from the fact that playing music was their "job" and thus they rehearsed somewhat more conscientiously, their repertoire probably differed little from that of the collegia musica. In Bach's case we can draw some conclusions based on the small size of the court orchestra in Celle (as well as his Köthen experience, which will be discussed later), which he frequently listened to, and in which he may even have served as an assistant during his Lüneburg period (1700–1703). Celle was an important stopover for him; there, for the first time, he encountered independent instrumental music of a high quality. The orchestra at Celle consisted of the following:[51]

Two violists who play both regular and French style
One gamba player
One organist
One trombonist or bassoonist who can also sing a part and play violin in regular and French style
One cornetto player who plays violin in French style
Two choir boys
One Calcante (orchestra assistant and probably copyist)

In addition, there were "A Director Musices, an alto" (probably a castrato), and "a tenor who could also play violin in the French style," so that in total there were 13 persons. It is interesting that there were only two full-time violinists; the other four "violists" were primarily singers or wind players. With the exception of the trombonists, they were employed as violinists only in "French" music, from which we can conclude that this was the strictly instrumental music. They probably served as ripieno or tutti players. Leaving aside the "choir boys," i.e. apprentices, and the "calcante," there were 10 active players; for the "Director Musices" also had to serve as violinist or harpsichordist. Under these circumstances, the distinction between orchestral and chamber music had to remain fluid, even if one assumes that apart from this ten-man formation there were two or three trumpet players and timpanists (who were always listed separately in the court records of the period). So in terms of members, the orchestra at Celle did not differ greatly from a collegium musicum. Their respective "audiences" were another matter; in the former case, only members of the nobility were present, and if any of the illustrious company felt the urge, he (or she) would pick up an instrument and play along.[52]

All this gives us a certain picture of the atmosphere in which the chamber music of Bach and his contemporaries was first heard. For the sake of completeness, we mention two other types of chamber music instrumentation. In Venice, Vivaldi introduced *concerti soli*, by which we mean both concertos and sonatas, during the intermissions of opera performances. This practice also became accepted north of the Alps. And finally, instrumental solos were occasionally performed during communion in church services.

We now turn specifically to the situation in Köthen.[53] On the surface, things did not seem to be any different there than in countless other small German principalities. But Bach's sovereign, Prince Leopold von Anhalt-Köthen (1694–1728), was an exceptional patron of music. He had a veritable passion for this art and was reputedly quite a good musician in his own right. In 1707, when he was still the crown prince, he prevailed upon his mother, the Princess-widow Gisela Agnes, who administered the regency for him, to appoint three court musicians, as he wanted to have competent partners for chamber music. Later he was sent to study at the "Ritterakademie" in Berlin; there he became acquainted with the members of the court orchestra of Frederick I of Prussia. He became an accomplished violinist, gamba, and harpsichord player, and by all accounts also had a good bass singing voice. This exposure to the music of Berlin later proved to be significant for Köthen and for Bach. In 1710, after his studies in Berlin, Leopold embarked on the customary educational tour for young aristocrats. He visited Holland, England and Italy. Everywhere he went he was intensely interested in the music—where music was being performed, what was being played, and in what form. In Rome he cultivated a friendship with the German composer and Kapellmeister, Johann David Heinichen, who probably also gave him instruction. After returning to Köthen in 1713, he assumed the reigns of government at the age of nineteen. One of his first acts was to appoint Augustin Reinhard Stricker as Kapellmeister. Stricker attracted other musicians from Berlin to Köthen. Frederick William I, who had recently come to power as King of Prussia, had drastically reduced the luxurious conditions at his father's (Frederick I) court, and had begun by dismissing the entire court orchestra. These musicians were glad to have new positions, and Köthen likewise benefited from the influx of qualified artists.[54] The Prince was more pleased than anybody. Now he not only had good musicians, but he had known them previously as musical colleagues.

This was the situation when Bach assumed the position of "Ducal Kapellmeister of Anhalt-Köthen" and "Director of Court Chamber Music" in 1717. Leopold had made his acquaintance in Weissenfels at another prince's birthday celebration, to which Bach, at that time still in Weimar, had contributed the cantata *Was mir behagt, ist nur die muntre Jagd* (No. 208). When Stricker left Köthen, Johann Sebastian Bach was appointed immediately. Bach tried hard to leave Weimar, where he rightly felt discriminated against; it is well known that he pursued his dismissal so vigorously that his sovereign in Weimar put him in jail for a month before releasing him to go to Köthen.

In the meantime, the orchestra at the court of Köthen had grown to 18 musicians. Significantly, the orchestra was now known as "collegium musicum." From salary records of 1717 we know the names of its members and their instruments. First listed are the "Ducal Chamber Players" (the first three and the sixth and seventh on the list were from Berlin):

Joseph Spiess, "Premier Cammer-Musicus"—violin
Martin Friedrich Marcus—violin
Johann Ludwig Rose—oboe
Johann Heinrich Freytag (I)—flute
Johann Gottlieb Würdig—flute
Johann Christoph Torlee (Torlén)—bassoon
C. Bernhard Linike—cello
Christian Ferdinand Abel[55]—gamba

Additional musicians included Johann Freytag, the elder (II), Wilhelm Harbordt, Adam Weber (whose instruments are not named), the trumpet players Johann

Ludwig Schreiber and Johann Christoph Krahl, the timpanist, Anton Unger and another Freytag (III), whose function, however, remains unclear. Last on the list are the copyists Johann Kreyser (also written 'Keyser') and Johann Bernhard Göbel. Counting Kapellmeister Bach, who also played, following the practices of the time (he is said to have preferred to lead the ensemble from the violist's chair and there is no violist mentioned among the musicians), the total comes to 18.[56]

The list of names and salaries is interesting for many reasons. The Kapellmeister, Bach, appropriately received the highest salary, approximately 400 Thaler annually. If we add to that the salary of his second wife, Anna Magdalena, who had performed as a soprano at the court since 1721, we find that the Bachs were more than amply remunerated in Köthen, for Anna Magdalena was paid about 200 Thaler, as much as the Konzertmeister, Spiess, who was the highest paid player. Striking differences are found in the salaries of the other musicians. For Freytag III we even find the notation, "Should receive 5 Thaler quarterly, but has not been paid." The discrepancies can probably be explained by the fact that some of the Köthen town musicians had to be incorporated into the court orchestra. We know that this caused bad blood, because they were not considered when the first three court musicians were hired.

The trumpeters and timpanist were not normally used during daily music making. They were employed only on certain occasions. The timpanist, Unger, even had permission to moonlight as an innkeeper. The copyists did not play either. But the orchestra's great demand for music can be seen in the employment of two copyists. Copyists, by the way, were by no means uneducated and, at the very least, had to be able to read a music score. Kreyser later even attained the position of court organist. It is also conceivable that now and then servants took part in performances to reinforce the "tutti." At any rate, after Bach's departure a certain Mattstedt appears in the records as a servant in charge of the "silver service," who received 85 Thaler annually and a bonus of 16 groschen plus livery, as well as 35 Thaler as a musician.[57]

This, then, was Johann Sebastian Bach's ensemble. The first eight on the list, the "Kammermusici," were the first ones to rehearse new chamber music works. Quite often the prince joined them as a player. He also saw to it that good instruments were available, or had Bach do so. A 1773 inventory of the court's music room lists among other things several instruments made by Stainer, string instruments by the Leipzig violin maker J. C. Hoffmann, three wing-shaped harpsichords, a spinet and a small portable harpsichord. Listed as curiosities were "2 boxes containing horns, a couple of violins and Dis trumpets, a tromp. Mariae." The latter is a bowdlerized version of "tromba marina," a one-stringed instrument. The inventory also includes a catalogue of music, but it has little significance for us, since most of the works are from the period following Bach's departure from Köthen.

Especially significant for Bach was the acquisition of a new "clavecyn," a harpsichord that had been ordered from Berlin. It was delivered in 1719 at a cost of 130 thalers, with additional charges for shipping.[58] The new instrument undoubtedly inspired Bach to write the great new clavier works which originated in Köthen, especially the sonatas for melody instruments and obbligato clavier, with which he created an entirely new genre.

It is significant that Bach was able to score all the Brandenburg Concertos for the Köthen orchestra with the exception of the first, for which two horns were lacking. However, Terry[59] found in the Köthen payroll accounts of June 6, 1722, the entry, "To the two French horn players who have been performing here, 15 thalers." From this we can infer that the 1st Brandenburg Concerto was also performed in Köthen. The harpsichord soloist in the 5th Concerto was, of course, Bach himself.

How are we to picture Bach as a practicing musician? Carl Philipp Emanuel Bach has left us the following vivid portrayal:

> He was able to hear the slightest wrong note in the heaviest instrumentation. Possessing the greatest knowledge and judgment of harmony, he preferred to play the viola with suitable dynamics. From his youth until he was quite old he played the violin clearly and penetratingly and thereby kept the orchestra in better order than he would have been able to do from the clavier. He perfectly understood the potential of all the string instruments. This is demonstrated by his solos for the violin and for the cello without bass. One of our greatest violinists once said to me that he knew of no better way to become a good violinist and could recommend no other study for the ambitious student than the above-mentioned violin solos without bass. Owing to his mastery of harmony, more than once he accompanied trios, and, being congenial and knowing that the composer of these trios would not take it amiss, he improvised a perfect fourth part from a miserably figured continuo part which had been placed before him, so that the composer of the trios was astounded. When listening to a heavily instrumented fugue in many parts, he knew as soon as the theme appeared what contrapuntal artifices could possibly be brought into play, and how the composer by rights ought to apply them. Whenever I was standing next to him, he would nudge me when he was pleased that his expectations had been met. He had a good, resonant voice with great range, and used it well.[60]

The six years in Köthen have been unanimously characterized as a particularly happy period by all Bach biographers. In fact, his relationship with the young prince, at least until the latter's marriage, seems to have been unstrained, if not warm. There is no record of any friction, such as Bach had experienced in Weimar and Arnstadt and which he was later to have in Leipzig. He was able to work in peace and compose exactly what he wanted, secure in the knowledge that his music was appreciated. He thus enjoyed an atmosphere which encouraged an incredibly rich and inspired production and which, in contrast to that of many of his contemporaries, shows no signs of a "routine." Bach composed fully conscious of his mastery. To the present day, the works of the Köthen years have lost none of their freshness. Unhindered by church and organist duties,[61] he was able to further develop the ideas he had gained in Celle and Weimar. He was able to experiment[62] without the pressure of a deadline. He had interested, willing, and competent colleagues. Considering the stature of the Köthen years in the context of Bach's work, it is difficult to understand why, of all the instrumental ensemble music written during that time, only the Brandenburg Concertos have achieved real popularity. All the rest, in contrast, has remained more or less music for the connoisseur. Surely it cannot be said that Bach's chamber music is especially "difficult," or, compared with *The Well-Tempered Clavier*, especially "learned." On the contrary, much of it bears the stamp of truly popular music, and was anything but "pedantic."

There is no indication that Bach gradually became oppressed by the narrowness of life in Köthen. It can be assumed that the performance of music there was more or less a family affair, and not only because the rehearsals were usually held in Bach's home.[63] The audience attending these concerts several times a week—the court society—was always the same, so that one knew in advance how each person would react and what he thought he was expected to say about the music. Bach always enjoyed travelling; he did this in Köthen, too, and Leopold did not stand in his way. Indeed, only two weeks after his arrival in Köthen, in December, 1717, he travelled to Leipzig to inspect and approve a new organ, and later to Halle on a similar mission. He had hoped to meet Handel there, but was unsuccessful. In 1718 and again in 1720, Leopold took Bach and 6 other musicians (the "Kammermusici" already mentioned) with him to Karlsbad for several weeks. After the second trip to Karlsbad Bach returned to find that his wife, Maria Barbara, was no longer among the living; no one had sent him the news of her death. Should we assume that his application, a few months later, for the position of organist at St. Jacob's Church in Hamburg was connected with the loss of his wife, that it pained him to remain in Köthen? Other factors were probably also involved. Hamburg was by all accounts one of the more prestigious places for a musician at that time. As comfortable as Bach may have felt in Köthen, he apparently did not view his position there as a permanent one.

In 1721, Bach was married for a second time, to Anna Magdalena Wülckeln,[64] the daughter of a court trumpet player in Weissenfels, and a trained soprano. It was she who made the numerous music copies which were long considered Bach autographs. Only two weeks later, the young prince was also married, to his cousin, Friedericia Henriette von Anhalt-Bernburg, of whom Bach later wrote in unflattering terms that "she seemed to be unmusical."[65] From that time on Leopold's interest in music seems to have waned. He accompanied the orchestra less frequently, and the number of performances dropped. The princess was probably not solely responsible for this; the prince's brother, August Ludwig, who was constantly in financial difficulties, also considered court music to be a superfluous luxury. When he took over the government after Leopold's untimely death in 1728, he allowed the orchestra to deteriorate rapidly. But even before that, when Bach left Köthen in 1723, no effort was made to find a qualified successor. Still, as long as he was employed in Köthen, he gave no indication of disenchantment with his work. Perhaps he had more time for composing when he had less to do as Kapellmeister. That he finally did leave Köthen, a decision which, despite everything, does not seem to have been an easy one for him,[66] can probably be attributed to his understandable desire to have a position with greater influence; and Leipzig was indeed such a place in comparison with Köthen. Bach parted on completely friendly terms, and he remained the "honorary" Köthen Kapellmeister; that is, he still provided services on special occasions.[67] He performed this function twice; once on the birthday of Leopold's second wife in 1725 (the "unmusical" princess had died in 1723), and again in 1729, when, with musicians from St. Thomas in Leipzig, he performed a requiem for double choir, a large work, in memory of the prince who had died the previous year. This work seems for the most part to have consisted of music from the *St. Matthew Passion* for which new texts had been supplied.

With that, Bach's activity in Köthen came to an end. Leopold had only lived to the age of thirty-four, but his love of music and his good fortune in engaging the services of Bach enabled the small residency to achieve a unique brilliance. Yet walking through Köthen today, one finds few traces of Bach's presence there. Only a few groups of old houses in the heart of the town furnish an idea of how it must have looked in Bach's time. We do not know where he lived; it is assumed that he changed lodgings several times. In one place, the noise of a nearby water wheel bothered him when he was trying to work; but that does not help in locating the house as there were many water mills in Köthen at the time. The cemetery where his first wife, Maria Barbara, was buried in Bach's absence, still exists, but the location of the grave is not known. However, the splendid sarcophagi of Leopold, his mother, Gisela Agnes, and the "unmusical" Friedricia Henriette can still be viewed in the crypt of St. Jacob's Church. This, the largest church in Köthen (its two towers were erected in the 19th century), was avoided by Bach during his years there, for Bach was a devout Lutheran. As the court church, St. Jacob's was of course reformed. Bach attended services at the small Baroque Lutheran Church, St. Agnes, where his name appears repeatedly on the communion register.[68] St. Agnes was also the church where he played the organ when he felt so moved. We recall that the great Organ Fantasia and Fugue in G Minor BWV 542 was written in Köthen. And it is virtually certain that he first played the work on the organ at St. Agnes (which, however, was replaced in the 19th century). Bach directed music at St. Jacob only once, during the memorial service for Leopold in 1729.

Of greatest interest is the site where Bach held his court concerts. The castle in Köthen has two concert halls, a small Baroque hall on the ground floor and a larger, splendidly decorated "hall of mirrors" from the classicistic period on the 3rd floor. The two halls have vied for the honor of having been the stage for Johann Sebastian Bach's music. But most likely this honor must be given to the small Baroque hall. The classicistic extension (it was not a remodeling) of the castle was documented in 1823. The small auditorium, now called the "Bach-Saal," can hold up to 100 people. The place for the musicians was on the narrow side opposite where the podium stands today. A small continuo organ is said to have stood there earlier. Recently the hall was simply and tastefully restored. The floor, which had been built up after Bach's time, has the right height again. Only the podium is not in its original place, for practical reasons. One cannot help but be moved when entering the room in which so many great works of Western music were heard for the first time.[69]

Chapter 4

The Instruments

We want to interpret Bach's music in a manner that does justice to his style, and this we view as an artistic necessity. Bach's music should sound the same way today that it did in his own time; more precisely, the way Bach wanted it to sound; or, even more precisely: the way we *assume* Bach intended it. The reader will note the distinctions made here; we shall say more about this later. The first thing we must do is determine how the musical practices of Bach's time differ from those of the present. In so doing we shall restrict ourselves to the chamber music and consider the total scope of Bach performance practice (which covers a very broad field indeed and has been intensively studied by musicians and scholars alike[70]), only insofar as it sheds light on the chamber music.

The difference between the way instruments were made in Bach's time and our own relates to changed concepts of an ideal sound. From around the beginning of the 19th century there has been a distinct tendency (alien to the 18th century) to increase the *volume*. Above all, music had to be loud; the halls now were larger, the orchestras had more players, the tonal range of the instruments expanded. This tendency can be seen everywhere, in keyboard instruments as well as wind and string instruments. Thus, in Mozart's music, for example, the trombone provides a characteristic color; in Wagner (*Tannhäuser Overture*) it only has to be powerful. Most dramatically affected by this development was organ building. By the end of the 19th century, the organ had become simply a "noise-maker"; nearly all the tonal differentiations had been sacrificed to a tremendous increase in volume. But the predictable reaction that set in at the end of this period occurred precisely in the area of organ building. The so-called "organ movement"[71] which began after World War I suddenly made people realize the great advantages of the Baroque ideal of sound. This Baroque ideal was totally different from that of the period 1820–1920. Its intention was to develop individual, characteristic timbres. Music was not meant to be voluminous, but rather transparent, so that its polyphonic structure could be heard—musicians, in a word, played softer. All the differences between instruments then and now can be explained by this phenomenon; once we understand this the details will fall in place.

The instruments Bach employs in his chamber music are the violin, cello, viola da gamba, transverse flute, clavier (i.e. harpsichord, sometimes clavichord), and lute—not many, considering the large number of instruments available to him. It is surprising, for example, that the oboe is not used in his chamber works. After all, it was the oboe which inspired some of his most beautiful ideas in the cantatas and passions, and in Köthen he had a great oboist at his disposal in Johann Ludwig Rose from Berlin. There may simply have been no occasion to write a substantial chamber work for oboe.[72]

Violin. Compared with the modern violin, the instrument of Bach's time had a shorter neck and, consequently, a shorter fingerboard. The latter was about 5–6.5 cm shorter, quite sufficient for the required upper notes. The highest note Bach wrote for the violin was g^3.[73] Furthermore, the bridge of the instrument was lower, thicker and less arched, which matched the flatter fingerboard.

Even though the classic Stradivarius model (characterized by a flatter curvature of the back and belly than the older Amati model) already existed in Bach's time, the musicians Bach worked with probably played instruments with a pronounced curvature, after the old tradition of German and Austrian violin-making. From the side, one could see through both F-holes. The neck was not placed at an oblique angle to the sound box, but extended straight out from it. The required angle of the fingerboard was set by inserting a wedge.

The instruments were all strung with gut; only occasionally G strings were wound with metal wire. In general, the strings were thinner than they are today and consequently had less tension.

The greatest difference between violins of that time and the models used today was in the violin *bow*. It was shorter, curved outward (convex), and had a so-called "pike-tip." Not until the second half of the 18th century did the axe-shaped point become prevalent, when bows became more concave, leaving a greater distance between the stick and the hair (see Figure 4). The frog screw, however, had become

N° 1. —Mersenne, 1620.

N° 2. —Kircher, 1640.

N° 3. —Castrovillari, 1660.

N° 4. — Bassani, 1680.

N° 5. — Corelli, 1700.

N° 6. — Tartini, 1740.

N° 7. — Cramer, 1770.

N° 8. — Viotti, 1790.

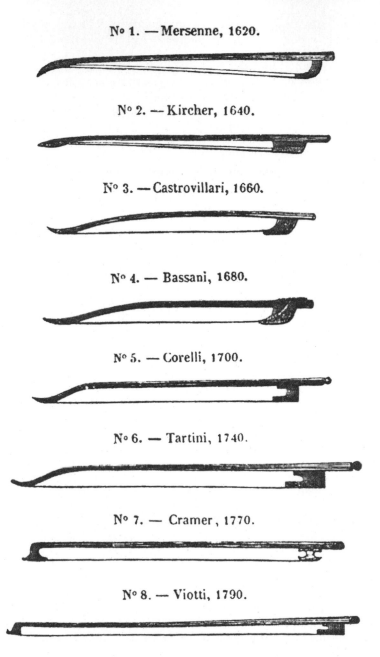

Figure 4. Development of the Violin Bow from Mersenne (1620) to Viotti (1790)

widely used after 1720 to regulate the tension of the bow hair. Only the short bows of simple dance fiddles were still tightened in the primitive manner, with wedges or a loop at the frog.

But it is precisely in regard to the violin bow of Bach's time that there are contradictions, ambiguities and even legends. The convex curvature of the bow stick is depicted in most of the contemporary illustrations, but this is not seen on the Corelli bow of 1700 nor the Tartini bow of 1740 (see Figure 4). It seems not to have been prevalent everywhere in Europe and perhaps was predominant only in Germany. According to David D. Boyden, it was "not adequate for sustaining three-note or even four-note chords, as is often claimed."[74] The length of the bows also appears to have varied greatly. In France shorter bows were preferred (Bach surely encountered such bows in Celle), but in Italy and Germany, after 1720 at the very latest, the "sonata bow" became popular. At 70–71 cm. its hair length was even greater than that of today's bows (hair length 64–65 cm). Figure 4 shows such an elongated bow.

Much confusion was unleashed in the early 20th century when Arnold Schering thought he had rediscovered the "authentic Bach bow," a bow with a stick curved outward like a whip. The distance between the stick and the hair was said to have been as much as 12 cm. There was a mechanical lever on the frog to regulate the tension of the hair, but it could only be crudely adjusted. Any fine adjustments had to be made with the fingers of the right hand while playing.[75] Albert Schweitzer was emphatic about the authenticity of this bow.[76] Since then, however, we have confirmed through painstaking scholarly research that this "Bach bow" never existed. It is an invention of our century, as was the "Bach trumpet."

The **cello** was similar in construction to the violin, but its proportions appear to have varied significantly. We find both larger and smaller models than today's. They were all bulkier and had a considerably shorter neck. This made it difficult to play in the upper positions and was probably why the cello played such a minor role before Johann Sebastian Bach.[77] The solo string instrument in the tenor range at that time and up through the period of Viennese classicism was the **viola da gamba.** Cellos were used primarily to support the thorough bass. Wolfgang Boettcher writes, "We know that Bach complained about the clumsiness of the cello. The lexicographer Gerber tells us, 'In view of the lively bass lines in Bach's works, the stiff manner in which the cello was played in his time compelled him to invent what he called the viola pomposa . . .' Thus one can assume that the level of cello technique in Bach's time was not very high. It is all the more astonishing that Bach makes such great demands on the cello in his suites."[78]

Cellos were strung in various ways: three, four or five strings were used, as needed. One of the oldest extant models was made by Andrea Amati in Cremona in 1572. In 1618 Michael Praetorius wrote that the cello was called the "bass viol da braccio" and had five strings: F_1, C, G, d, a.[79] But the tuning seems to have varied, for in the same paragraph Praetorius writes, "Take heed, now, / it is of no great import / how this or that person tunes his violin or viola / if only he can perform on it / accurately, clearly and in tune." The form of the cello as we know it today became established around 1700. The instrument made by Stradivarius in 1720 (thus, during Bach's Köthen period) may have served as a model; it was played during the 19th century by the well-known Italian cellist Alfredo Piatti (1822–1901), incidentally, still without an end pin, just as in Bach's time. The cello was held between the knees and the lower leg. This brought about a more direct physical contact between player and instrument, but it detracted from the resonance; also, the freedom of the left hand must have been restricted. This was solved by the invention of the end pin in the 19th century by the Belgian, Adrien François Servais (1846–1901), a son of Liszt and the Princess of Sayn-Wittgenstein.[80]

An important difference in technique between then and now: Bach was not acquainted with the thumb position. Consequently, he goes no higher than the fourth position, and the highest note he demands from the cello is g^1 (in the 5th Suite, it is an f^1 with a down-tuned A-string). The 6th Suite is the only exception. It calls for a 5-stringed instrument to which a high e^1 string was added. Nevertheless, the range he requires in the higher registers in this suite is unusual: up to g^2. Consistent with his customary practice of not requiring any notes beyond the fourth position, it should actually only have been d^2. This fact has given rise to speculation that the 6th suite was written for the legendary viola pomposa, a hypothesis, however, which does not bear scrutiny. At that time there were many five-stringed cellos, the highest string of which was usually tuned to d^1, according to the French practice. Perhaps this D major suite was the piece (since five-stringed cellos were rare) which, owing to its higher registers, accelerated the use of the thumb position, which was already used in Italy and France in Bach's time. It is thought to have been invented by the cellist Franciscello Geminiani (not to be confused with the more famous violinist of the same name, Francesco Saverio Geminiani, c. 1680–1762), about whom little more is known than that he probably died in 1750, the same year as Bach. Geminiani's thumb position was adopted by the German, Jean-Baptiste Stück (also known as Batistin) who was born in Florence in 1680, later went to France and played in the orchestra of Louis XIV. Thus the thumb position came to France, where it received theoretical support in Michel Corrette's 1741 treatise, *Méthode théorétique et pratique pour apprendre en peu de temps le violoncelle* (Theoretical and Practical Method of Learning the Cello in a Short Time). The thumb position fundamentally revolutionized the playing technique of the left hand. The cello was now able to reach higher registers than previously thought possible. As Haydn's work demonstrates, the new technique gained rapid acceptance.

There were also differences in bowing technique. The traditional underhand bow-grip probably was still used; that is, the bow was gripped from behind, as with the gamba (and still is today, primarily, with the contrabass). Even if the player held it from above, the position was probably looser and not calculated for displays of power.

We have already mentioned that the **viola da gamba** was preferred over the cello. This is confirmed not only by Hubert LeBlanc's curious work, *Défense de la basse viole contra les entreprises du violon et les prétensions du violoncel,* (A Defense of the Bass Viol Against the Enterprises of the Double Bass and the Pretensions of the Cello),[81] in which the cello is downgraded for "deficiencies in the vibrations of the strings, which are veritable ship-hawsers." But there was also Leopold Mozart, who wrote in his *Violinschule* of 1756, "Finally, the viola da gamba differs from the cello in many ways. It has six, or even seven strings, while the Bassel (cello) has only four. It also has a completely different tuning, a more pleasing tone, and is usually used for a higher part."[82] Opinions like this were still being voiced at a time when the cello had long since become the more important instrument. Apart from Carl Friedrich Abel (1723–1787), the son of Bach's orchestra member in Köthen, Christian Ferdinand Abel, there were hardly any other gambists in the late 18th century. Still, it is understandable that Bach chose the gamba, and not the cello, as he began composing his sonatas for a tenor string instrument and clavier. The cello was untested in such works—he was only following the customs of the time.

The pedigree of the viola da gamba differs from that of both the violin and the cello. It belongs to the viol family, external characteristics of which are the flat back, set at an angle where it joins the neck, and "sloping shoulder," that is, the body tapers away from the neck rather than being connected at right angles like the violin, viola and cello. Gambas are somewhat smaller than cellos and, because of their six strings (in Bach's Sonata in D Major a low seventh string is even required), have a broader fingerboard. The latter had only a slight arch, similar to the violins and cellos of the time, and the bridge was correspondingly flatter. A construction of this kind was conducive to playing chords, which was particularly popular with the gamba (as shown by the gambia aria, "Komm, süsses Kreuz," (Come, sweet cross), from the *St. Matthew Passion.* However, it was difficult to play one of the middle strings of the gamba without touching one of the neighboring strings, especially in a forte. The fingerboard of a gamba usually has 7 frets. They were intended to make playing easier but were perceived as a hindrance even before Bach's time, since they made the change of position and pure double-stops difficult. The seven-stringed viol da gamba of Joachim Tielke, Hamburg, 1699, pictured in the supplement to the *Archiv* recording no longer has any frets.

The customary tuning of a six-stringed viola da gamba was and is D, G, c, e, a, d[1]; seven-stringed instruments had an additional lower string, A_1. In his gamba method published in Venice in 1542–1543, Sylvestro Ganassi gave the six strings of the gamba the following names: 1) Bass (D), 2) Bordun (G), 3) Tenor (c), 4) Mezzana (e), 5) Sotana (a), 6) Cantus (d[1]).[83] It should be noted that the highest string, the "cantus," was considered the most important melody string, and hence the sixth string of the lute was called the "chanterelle." When this highest string of the gamba was played, the musician had to hold the right (bow) hand very high. This explains why the terms 'up-bow' and 'down-bow' meant the opposite of what they do today: in playing the cantus string the bow was, in fact, pushed *down* and pulled *up.*[84] Also, musically speaking, what we call upbowing served the function on the viola da gamba of the stressed stroke, falling on accented beats.[85] Leopold Mozart also speaks of "down" and "up" bowing with that meaning.

The gamba was normally played without an end pin, and usually still is today. However, illustrations from the 17th and 18th centuries often picture gambists propping their instruments on a low stool or footrest.

The bow of the gamba is also convex, i.e. curved outward, and is always played with the underhand bow grip. These two factors give rise to the delicate, silvery tone which is critical to the main bow stroke of the Baroque period, the loose *détaché.* This is done so easily, so naturally, on the gamba, that from it we can gather how the violin and the cello were played in Bach's works. We shall let the experts speak: in the foreword to his edition of the suites for cello solo August Wenziger writes, "Bach's articulation makes quite specific demands on bowing technique. When performing Romantic and Post-Romantic music, the modern cellist is almost exclusively trained to play legato and to amplify the tone. But for the string player of the 17th and 18th centuries, the non-legato, the broad *détaché* stroke, was the norm. He was used to producing a continuous musical line with the *détaché* stroke. To tie notes together served to set off a group of notes from the normal flow of the music."[86] And again, Wolfgang Boettcher: "The broad *détaché,* the primary bow stroke of the 17th and 18th centuries, is often not clear enough on the thick low strings of the cello. It can be produced most easily with a "Baroque bow," which in contrast to the bows of today was convexly curved, lighter and more narrowly strung. In practice sessions I like to use a reproduction of a Baroque bow in order to clarify for myself the possibilities of Baroque bowing. Since, however, this bow cannot make the cello vibrate to its full capacity, in concerts I use the modern, concavely curved bow and strive to find articulations which are just as eloquent as those evoked by the old bow."[87]

Other string instruments for which Bach composed are omitted here, since they do not appear in the chamber music. These are the **violino piccolo,** which has one of the concertante parts in the 1st Brandenburg Concerto; the **violoncello piccolo,** which we encounter as an obbligato instrument in the cantata, *Bleib bei uns, denn es will Abend werden,* ("Abide with us, for Evening is Nigh"), of which the Köthen Hofkapelle had two models, the already mentioned **viola pomposa,** and the **viola d'amore,** which is employed in the *St. John Passion.*

The difference in sound between a **flute** of Bach's time and its modern parallel is less than that between the string or keyboard instruments of the two epochs. Bach did not use the flute, also called **traversière, flûte allemande** and **traversa,** before the Köthen period. In the form it had at that time, it was a relatively new instrument, and its rapid ascendance to the status of a fashionable instrument must be attributed to its greater volume, range, and expressive potential which was clearly superior to that of the recorder. Bach used and developed these assets. One can say without exaggeration that his chamber music for flute presents the instrument in a state of perfection that has scarcely been achieved since.

The Bach transverse flute has a range from d^1 to g^3 and, in the Solo Partita in A Minor BWV 1013, as high as a^3. It was almost always fashioned out of wood, and often had ivory decoration; expensive flutes were made entirely of ivory. The metal flutes common today were not yet in use. The instrument had three detachable joints: head, middle and foot. This construction had been invented in France between 1660 and 1670. Likewise familiar was the alternation of conical and cylindrical sections in the overall bore of the flute, although the measurements have somewhat changed since then. The blow hole was generally circular, not oval, as it was after the end of the 18th century, or rectangular with rounded corners and an embouchure plate, as it is today. The flute had six fingerholes and only a single key, the D-sharp key, which allowed for the half-tone above the lowest note. The other intermediate chromatic tones could be produced by cross-fingering; this could also be done by turning the blow-hole. The half-covers for the fingerholes which had been in use before Bach's time and had survived in other instruments, especially the recorder, were rarely employed on the flute—they were too undependable. By modern standards, however, the cross-fingering of the first half of the 18th century must have also been unsatisfactory. It led to impure intonation, and notes produced in this way had a timbre that was clearly different from notes produced in the normal manner. Notes not belonging to a particular key could be recognized by their different timbre. This cannot have been without ramifications on the general perception of music; just as the natural horns and natural trumpets of that time strongly emphasized the key, every modulation on the flute must have been discernable by the change of tone color. Acoustically exceptional tones of this kind often had a special piquancy.

The Berlin Collection of Musical Instruments[88] has in its possession (#2670) a Hotteterre flute made in 1700, which was made in the way described[89]. Its bore is slightly conical in all three parts, though to different degrees. Its tone is described as robust and full especially in the lower middle register; the high notes (over d^3) which Bach demanded, appear to have been quite difficult to reach. Its tuning is surprisingly low. Whereas we usually assume that in Bach's time the tuning was based a half tone below what had been the previous norm of d^1 (435 hertz), this flute is almost a whole step below current orchestral tunings of 442 to 443 hertz. It is interesting that in some places flutes of this type had an interchangeable middle joint, with which the lowest note could be changed from d^1 to e-flat^1, thus expanding the flexibility of the instrument. The d^1 foot made sharp keys possible: hence the many works for flute written in B Minor! The e-flat foot, on the other hand, made the flat keys more accessible, for instance, the Sonata in E-flat Major BWV 1031 and the Trio Sonata in C Minor from the *Musical Offering.* We do not know whether late in life Bach took into account the Quantz flute, which he may have encountered at the latest on his visit to Berlin in 1747. It had seven finger holes and two adjoining keys for d-sharp and e-flat in enharmonic change. It also consisted of five detachable joints. Perhaps this instrument inspired Bach to write the Flute Sonata with b.c. in E Major, BWV 1035.

Special attention is due the keyboard instruments in Bach's chamber music. With the exception of the solo works, the works "senza basso," the clavier is required everywhere, either as a thorough bass instrument or as an obbligato partner, which in addition to the bass is assigned its own upper part in duet with the melody instrument.

Bach was familiar with two kinds of keyboard instruments: the **harpsichord,** on which the strings are plucked, and the **clavichord,** on which the strings are struck with small metal tangents. He also often characterized his works for organ as pieces "for 2 claviers and pedal," but we do not need to concern ourselves with that here. It is unlikely that the clavichord could have played a role in Bach's chamber music. Its delicacy and its intimate mode of expression was hardly conducive to an equal partnership with the flute, the violin or the viol da gamba. Even though we know that these instruments were played more softly than they are today, the clavichord would still not be able to compete with them, even as a b.c. instrument. At the most, a clavichord could have accompanied a recorder, but Bach did not write chamber music for recorder, as Handel, Telemann and others had done. In his works we must therefore think of the clavichord as a solo instrument, as an instrument for music in private, for such works as the *Inventions,* the *French Suites* and many pieces from *The Well-Tempered Clavier.*

The **spinet** would be a much more likely candidate for chamber music. It was a small, one-manual harpsichord with strings set at an oblique angle to the keys. Though lacking the full tone of a wing-shaped harpsichord, it was more powerful than a clavichord and was not subject to the limitation of fretting.

The primary instrument for chamber music is indisputably the wing-shaped harpsichord, the "cembalo." We know for a fact that Bach had several of these instruments in Leipzig. Unfortunately, we have no record of what instruments he personally owned in Köthen, but the Hofkapelle in Köthen apparently had three harpsichords.

The traditional harpsichord of Bach's time had two manuals, even though one-manual instruments were common enough. The two-manual instrument had an 8-foot and a 4-foot register on the lower manual, which was the primary manual in most cases, and another 8-foot register on the upper manual. There was usually also a 'lute' stop, a felt-covered bar, which served as a damper and either extended across all three registers or was attached to the 8-foot register of the upper manual. The registers were not activated by pedals, as they are on modern harpsichords, but by handstops which were located over the manuals. There does not seem to have been a significant difference in volume between the two 8-foot registers, but there was a difference in timbre, since the point where the upper 8-foot strings were plucked was nearer the bridge, which produced an effect similar to the 'près de la table' of the harp. Italian harpsichords from the workshop of Cristofori often had only three 8-foot registers.

The coupling of the upper to the lower manual (sometimes, when the upper manual is constructed as the primary manual, the lower is also coupled to the upper), was achieved in a primitive manner: one of the two keyboards is pushed in or pulled out. The player therefore had to have his hands free for the processes of changing registration and coupling. How this affected musical interpretation is not difficult to imagine.

The Bach harpsichord had no 16-foot register; this was not developed until the second half of the 18th century, when some changes were considered necessary to meet the growing competition of the Hammerklavier—the fortepiano. At that time the two instruments were more similar than they are today. Carl Philipp Emanuel Bach even wrote a concerto for harpsichord, Hammerklavier and orchestra. In the Deutsches Museum in Munich there is even a "combination grand piano" built by Joseph Merlin in London in 1780, which had both quill and hammer action. Until mid-century the 16-foot register was avoided because it presented difficulties in construction: either one had to use covered strings, which did not respond well to quill jacks, or the instruments had to be built to a length of 3 meters or more to accommodate simple metal strings of the requisite low pitch. Incidentally, the lack of a 16-foot register does not mean that these harpsichords lacked a rich sound; tests on historical or reconstructed instruments with the 8-foot—8-foot—4-foot configuration bear this out.

The compass of the instruments Bach had in Köthen and Leipzig is said by Friedrich Ernst to have been G_1–d^3.[90] And in fact, this range is not exceeded in the chamber works. The violin and flute sonatas with clavier are even restricted to B–d^3; Bach requires a range down to G_1 only in the gamba sonatas. Since, however, G-sharp (A-flat) does not occur anywhere, it can be concluded that the instruments had the so-called "short G_1 octave" (Example 5).

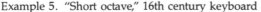

Example 5. "Short octave," 16th century keyboard   "Short octave" of the Bach clavier

Ernst is also of the opinion that Bach had only one-manual harpsichords in Köthen. This is difficult to believe, in view of the obvious provisions he made for so many *forte* and *piano* effects in his chamber music; for example, in the first movement of the gamba-clavier sonata in G minor or the third movement of the violin-clavier sonata in C minor.

There is more precise documentation on one of the instruments. It was ordered during Bach's employment in Köthen from Michael Mietke who built it. Bach took an active interest in its acquisition and made suggestions as to its disposition. It is even speculated that he made a trip to Berlin especially on that account.[91] Considering the high price of 130 Thaler, it can be safely assumed that the instrument had two manuals. After all, it was in Köthen that Bach wrote such great harpsichord works as the *English Suites* and the *5th Brandenburg Concerto.* Of course, musicians were not exactly helpless on a one-manual harpsichord, especially when playing the b.c., as shown by Quantz's directions in his flute method: "On a harpsichord with one clavier, a *piano* can be achieved by using a moderate touch and reducing the voices; the *mezzoforte,* by doubling the octaves in the bass; the *forte,* in the same way, plus having the left hand play some of the consonances belonging to the chord; the *fortissimo,* however, by a rapid upward breaking of the chords; again, by doubling the octaves and consonances in the left hand, and by a more energetic, forceful stroke."[92] It is noteworthy that Quantz indicates the possibility of influencing the volume of the harpsichord by the force of the stroke, which is contrary to everything we know.

The first two-manual harpsichord Bach owned was said to be a wing-shaped harpsichord of the Flemish Rucker type, built in Germany, which he acquired in Leipzig between 1725 and 1730. Ernst also gives its specifications as 8-foot and 4-foot in the lower manual and another 8-foot in the upper manual. The range is again said to have been G_1-d^3, which is surprising, since Bach required a range of up to f^3 in Leipzig, e.g., in the *Triple Concerto* in A Minor BWV 1044. We assume that this was the wing-shaped harpsichord which appears in the estate inventory of 1750 as "1 veneer clavecin for 80 thalers." There were also three other harpsichords, among which was a "smaller one" and, further, two "lute harpsichords" and a "small spinet." Strangely enough, there was no clavichord.

The harpsichord designated as "Bach-Flügel," No. 319 in the instrument collection in Berlin before World War II, has two manuals; on the upper manual an 8-foot and a 4-foot, along with the lute-stop, an 8-foot and a 16-foot on the lower manual. It also has a coupler. However, it has been definitely proven that the instrument was extensively rebuilt in the 19th century, and not entirely successfully. What it looked like before that and whether it really is a harpsichord from Bach's estate cannot be determined.

The harpsichord did not vanish from the musical scene for as long as is usually believed. The last harpsichords were made around 1800. Then, at the 1889 Paris World's Fair, an instrument made by Erard-Pleyel was displayed. With this instrument began the harpsichord revival led by Wanda Landowska of Poland.

In his treatise in defense of the viola da gamba, which we have already mentioned, Hubert LeBlanc writes about the **lute,** the last instrument we shall consider: ". . . the sound of the lute is so beautiful that not even the gamba can compare with it. . . . The difference between the divine sweetness of the gut-strings stretched over a deep arch (lute) and the clangor and tinkling of strings made of iron and brass (harpsichord) is like taking a drink of bitter absinthe. All of Gallus' cries of pain scarcely suffice to describe the brittle spareness of the striking of a raven's quill."[93] LeBlanc was not the only person of his time who had no affection for the harpsichord, but then he was a reactionary romantic. He was unable to halt the decline of the gamba, and he praised the lute at a time when its golden age had long since passed. Even Bach's lute works are latecomers. The instrument which only a century and a half earlier had been the favorite of the musical world (think of the Elizabethan lutenists) was almost forgotten by the end of the Baroque. And the guitar was virtually unknown in Germany at that time; it did not appear from across the Spanish border until the beginning of the Romantic period (Weber, Schubert, Paganini, Berlioz).

Bach's compositions for lute, BWV numbers 995–1000 and 1006a, were thus occasional pieces, written for specific players at specific events,[94] and they were often revised by their recipients. Bach probably did not have a special interest in the lute, which is not to say that these works were of inferior quality. This certainly would not apply to all the adaptations of the solo works for strings, but the original works for lute also hold their own against all his other compositions.

There were numerous types of lutes during the Renaissance and the early Baroque, but by Bach's time only a few models still existed. The so-called Baroque "D minor lute" was considered the norm. Its tuning was also called "neo-French." The instrument had 13 courses of strings, of which the top two were single, and the rest, double. Its appearance differed little from lutes played today: it had a flat belly with a sound rose and a curved, shell shaped body, which was made of glued-together thin wood pieces. The neck and fingerboard were very wide, owing to the great number of strings; the peg-box was turned back and featured a special protruding bout for the lowest strings.[95] Animal gut was used for the strings. From the fifth course down, the strings were usually covered, so that the necessary low pitch could be achieved; for the lute is a tenor instrument.[96] On the fingerboard there were frets, the number of which varied; 12 seems to have been the maximum (Fig. 5). Since there were so many frets, the last ones were located on the belly rather than the fingerboard.

The top 6 courses were used as playing (fingering) courses; the lower ones, the bass or Bordun courses, served primarily as open strings, although occasionally they were also played. This, however, sometimes caused difficulties because of the extraordinary width of the fingerboard; on the 12th and 13th courses, which were no longer on the fingerboard, it may well have been impossible. The strings or courses were tuned as follows, from top to bottom: f^2 - d^2 - a^1 - f^1 - d^1 - a - g - f - e - d - c - B - A. Our music example shows that the two top courses were single strings, the rest, double; it should also be noted that courses 6–10 were tuned in octaves (Example 6).

Example 6. Tuning of the Baroque (D minor) lute. The sound was an octave lower.

The lute had 13 courses and 24 strings. It sounded an octave lower than it was written for, and thus had considerable volume in the bass. To be sure, not all of Bach's works can be played on the 13-course lute. BWV 995, the transcription of the 5th Suite for Cello Solo (C minor for cello, G minor for lute), requires low G (note G_1), which is not present on the lute just described. Hence it is assumed that this piece was written for a 14-course lute with an additional bass G string.[97] There are, in fact, a few authenticated examples of 14-course lutes. Other lutenists are of the opinion that instead of the D minor lute described here, Bach composed for a lute that was tuned one degree lower, thus a "C minor lute" with 13 courses, on which all the compositions for lute, even the works in E minor (BWV 996) and E major (BWV

LAUTENISTIN.

Wann keine Muſic wär auf gantzer Welt zu hören
als eine Laute nur; ſo wär es ſchon genug .
dann wer Sie künſtlich ſpielt zeigt, was in Engels Chören
man faſt erfordern kan : und wie der ſchöne Zug
in unſer Hertz und Ohr, was edeles beginnet
daß man gantz auſſer Sich. und wie nicht recht beſinnet.

Figure 5. Lutenist from the *Musikalisches Theatrum* by Johann Christoph
Weigel. Engraving, (c. 1720)

1006a) could be played.[98] Still other solutions were worked out by Konrad Ragossnig and by Narciso Yepes, the prominent interpreter of Bach's lute music on the phonograph recordings of Archiv Productions.[99] Yepes plays a 14-course lute which was built in Holland in 1972 after old models. He changes the tuning for almost every piece, which corresponds entirely to Baroque practice. Musicians had no fear of scordatura, not even on a lute with 26 pegs!

Kohlhase mentions that Bach was also familiar with lutes that had fewer than 13 courses. "Bach's lute works reflect the multiplicity of types: BWV 999 presupposes 10 courses, BWV 996, eleven (or twelve, depending on the tuning); ... BWV 997, 998, 1000 and 1006a, thirteen (or fourteen, depending on the tuning); finally, BWV 995, fourteen."[100] The chronology of the works leads us to believe that he did not become familiar with the 13-course lute until he was in Köthen. Incidentally, he himself owned a lute, which is listed in the estate inventory. But we do not know what kind of instrument it was or whether he himself played it.

Other questions pertaining to Bach's lute music, among them the problem of notation, will be treated in Part III. Here, we recall yet another instrument frequently mentioned in connection with Bach's works for lute: the lute-harpsichord or "Lautenwerk." It was, roughly speaking, a harpsichord with a set of gut strings whose sound is said to have resembled that of the lute. In the estate inventory already mentioned two such instruments are listed; thus Bach must have played them. We know that he sometimes was interested in the construction of a lute-harpsichord, and according to other sources the initiative for the project came directly from him.[101] Of the various makers of lute-harpsichords, Zacharias Hildebrand of Leipzig, whose workshop produced both of the "Lautenwerke" in Bach's estate in about 1740, must have been on close terms with Bach. Bach must also have known about the work of his cousin, Johann Nikolaus Bach (1669–1753), an organist in Jena, who experimented with instrument-making and created not only lute-harpsichords, but even a gamba that could be played with keys. J. N. Bach used gut strings exclusively and made lute-harpsichords with as many as three manuals.[102] Bach's two instruments, in contrast, had only two gut-string registers and a brass-stringed "little octave," i.e., a 4-foot register.

Since not a single lute-harpsichord has survived we must rely on the scanty descriptions provided by Jacob Adlung in his book, *Musica mechanica organoedi*, published in Berlin in 1768; the author, in turn, relies on Bach's pupil, Johann Friedrich Agricola, whom he quotes literally.[103] A modern reconstruction attempted in 1932 sparked no interest. The entire matter would have solely historical significance if a contemporary copy of the Suite in E minor BWV 996 did not include the subtitle "Aufs Lautenwerk," and if the final movement (gigue and double) of the C minor Suite BWV 997 were not essentially unplayable on the lute owing to its unusual range ($C-f^2$). Finally, there seem to have been lute-harpsichords in use before 1720 and outside of Bach's sphere of influence.[104]

An important fact must still be considered which pertains to all the string instruments: the lower pitch in Bach's time. The result was that the strings were not stretched as tightly as they are today, which means that the bodies of the instruments were not subjected to so much tension, especially since the strings were also thinner. People do not always realize how significantly the pressure on the body of an instrument increases when the tuning is raised by even a few hertz. And the difference between today's tuning and Bach's is more than a half step! For this reason, Hanns Neupert, the well-known maker of modern harpsichords, considered the use of iron frames so that the harpsichord will withstand the tension of today's higher tuning. [105] Obviously musical instruments are so sensitive that any excessive tension of the strings is bound to have an impact on the quality of sound.

Chapter 5

Performance Practices in Bach's Time

The musician of the 20th century has a different relationship to the written or printed music than did the musician of the early 18th century. We have been trained to practice interpretation to the letter, to be "faithful to the original". We demand that a composer be as precise as possible in writing down his intentions. 250 years ago, things were different. The written or printed text of a composition was treated casually; even in the widespread practice of hand-copying, no special effort was made to be accurate. The actual notes largely served as a basis for ornamentation, for improvisation. Certain principles of composition were such common knowledge that it was unnecessary for the composer to write them down.

Today, if we want to interpret a work by Bach, we thus have to supply certain things which the music as written, even if it is an autograph, does not specify at all or only insufficiently. It is necessary to consult other sources, to make comparisons, and so on. The entire matter then becomes fathomable and the real ambiguities are reduced to a minimum.

Abbreviations

We shall begin with the easiest examples. Now and again Bach uses short-hand procedures (as Mozart also did occasionally in his piano concertos). A significant example can be found at the end of the prelude of the D Minor Suite for Cello BWV 1008. Measures 59–63 are notated as simple triads, but except for the last measure, they obviously must be played as sixteenth-note arpeggios (Example 7). In such cases one does not have to limit oneself to simple arpeggios, but can—to a degree—continue patterns set up in the preceding measures. In Example 7 an attempt is made to give some suggestions; another can be seen in Example 158. [106] Similarly arranged is the long episode m. 88–119 in the Chaconne from the D Minor Partita for Violin Solo BWV 1004, in which Bach indicates in the first quarter how the passage is to be executed, and expressly adds the direction "arpeggio." Also in the Sonata for Violin and Clavier in A Major BWV 1015 there is a passage in the violin part (m. 74–91) that should be arpeggiated, but it is evident that measures 81, 83, etc., are not affected. Personally, I do not think m. 92 should be played as an arpeggio either, but rather as a quarter-note double-stop. This preserves the caesura before the entry of the reprise.

Example 7. Suite for Cello Solo in D Minor BWV 1008; 1st movement, Prélude, m. 51–63.

Phrasing

A very extensive area, and certainly where strings are concerned, the most important, is that of *phrasing*.[107] It was customary in Bach's time to write very few legato ties and staccato dots; players were expected to have enough experience and taste to fill these things in according to their own judgment, which may have worked out for some players and not for others. But in any case, phrasing was used; this was particularly true of continuous passage work which, though unmarked for long stretches, never was played without any articulation, even considering the détaché typical of the time (see p. 50). Of course, one should not be content with a mindless ♫♫ ♫♫ , the way many orchestras drill ad nauseam. Bach obviously had his own ideas about phrasing, which diverged from the run of the mill. He also made his intentions explicit in many cases; his directions have only to be precisely read and carried to their logical conclusions. Some examples may clarify this. In the first movement of the G Minor Sonata for Violin Solo BWV 1001, m. 17, first quarter, we find the original notation in Example 8(a): m. 21, first quarter, of the same work contains the original notation 8(b). It is therefore obvious that m. 1, third quarter, must also have a tie (Example 8(c)). In Bach's time, the mere fact that all

Example 8. Sonata for Violin solo in G Minor BWV 1001, 1st movement, Adagio, m. 17, 21, 1

three passages contained an appoggiatura made a tie automatic for the violin. In the A Minor Solo Sonata for Violin BWV 1003, 2nd movement, there is a two-part passage without legato ties (m. 177–178), in which the need for the ties follows from the two-part arrangement itself, since otherwise the long values would be spoiled (Example 9). The same situation prevails in the C Minor Suite for Cello solo BWV

Example 9. Sonata for Violin solo in A Minor BWV 1003, 2nd movement, Fuga, m. 177–178

1011, m. 42. In this example the sixteenths coinciding with the lower part have to be tied, since otherwise the two-part arrangement cannot be represented (Example 10). But by logically extending the tie, in this case unavoidable, the next measures, unphrased by Bach, must in turn be phrased; at least the last four sixteenths of each measure should be played on one bow, as Wenzinger suggests (Example 10, m. 43–45, ties made with solid lines), or the first two sixteenths can also be tied, as is unavoidable in m. 42 (Example 10, ties made with dotted lines). Wenzinger goes a

Example 10. Suite for Cello solo in C Minor BWV 1011, 1st movement, Prélude, m. 42–45

step further in the Allemande of the E-flat Major Suite for Cello solo BWV 1010, when from the original tying in m. 1, first quarter, and m. 17, 1st and 2nd quarters, he proceeds to tie four sixteenths together throughout the movement, taking into consideration Bach's phrasing of m. 7 (Example 11), with the exception, of course,

Example 11. Suite for Cello solo in E-flat Major BWV 1010, 2nd
movement, Allemande
(a) M.1: Only the tie over the 1st quarter is original
(b) M.17: Only the ties over the 1st and 2nd quarters are
original
(c) M. 7: All the ties are original

of those figures which Bach himself phrased differently. If this seems to be a believable projection of Bach's phrasing, then it is incomprehensible why Flesch, in his otherwise so carefully considered edition of the works for violin solo, arbitrarily changed some of the original phrasings, for example in the Sonata in G Minor for Violin solo BWV 1001, 2nd movement, m. 69 ff. (Example 12).

Even if Flesch's solution were more felicitous with respect to today's string technique (it probably is not), Bach's direction should have been investigated rather than simply negated. Numerous editors of "practical editions" have been guilty of such things even up to the beginning of this century, Max Reger not excluded. At the very least, the original phrasing should be included (as, indeed, Flesch does).

How precisely Bach wrote his phrasings, and how unconventional his ideas were in these matters, can be clearly seen in the autograph of the works for violin solo, into which he apparently put special effort. We also find some surprising phrasings elsewhere in his chamber works, more so than in the orchestral music, where he must have had less hope that unconventional ideas would be accepted. We cite as an example m. 47–51 of the Sonata for Violin and Clavier in C Minor BWV 1017, 2nd movement (Example 13). Here the last measure contains an arti-

Original

Flesch

etc.

Example 12. Sonata for violin solo in G Minor BWV 1001, 2nd movement, Fuga, m. 69–72

Example 13. Sonata for Violin and Clavier in C Minor BWV 1017, 2nd movement, Allegro, m. 47–51, violin (dotted ties added)

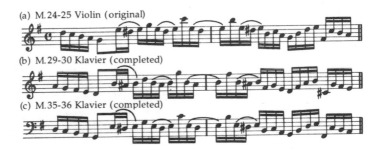

(a) M.24-25 Violin (original)

(b) M.29-30 Klavier (completed)

(c) M.35-36 Klavier (completed)

Example 14. Sonata for Violin and Clavier in G Major BWV 1019, 1st movement, Allegro, m. 24–25, 29–30, 35–36

culation which is characteristic, even typical, of Bach in the figure ♪♫ ♫♪ . In the works with clavier it stands to reason that phrasings of the melody part also have to be taken over by the clavier, as shown in Example 14, from the Sonata in G Major for Violin and Clavier BWV 1019, 1st movement. The violin measures 24–25 (a) are phrased by Bach; however, the clavier measures 29–30 (b) and 35–36 (c) are not. Example 15, which shows measure 8 from the 4th movement of the same sonata, goes one step further. Here the violin part is phrased in the original, but the clavier part is not. We have furnished the necessary additions with dotted lines.

Violin

Clavier

Example 15. Sonata for Violin and Clavier in G Major BWV 1019, 4th movement, Adagio, m. 8

In the theme of the 1st movement of the Sonata in G Major for Gamba and Clavier BWV 1027, in measures 1 and 2, there are staccato dots on the eighth-notes which are extremely important.[108] Not only must they be applied to the corresponding passages if they are missing; they also reveal the charmingly tender quality of the movement desired by the composer (Example 16).

Example 16. Sonata for Gamba and Clavier in G Major BWV 1027, 1st movement, Adagio, m. 1–2, gamba part

Interestingly enough, these dots are not found in the parallel version of the work as a Trio sonata for two flutes and b.c. BWV 1039. In contrast, such a characteristic phrasing as that in measures 29–32 of the 2nd movement of the same sonata, gamba part, also appears in the trio sonata, flute II;[109] nevertheless, when performing one version one should also take a good look at the phrasing of the other.

Further examples could be easily cited. To complete this phase of our inquiry, we shall point to a few more interesting cases, both positive and negative. In the 2nd movement of the D major Sonata for Gamba and Clavier BWV 1028, the articulation of the main theme of the gamba is precisely indicated; it is characterized by the alternation of two détaché and two legato sixteenths (Example 17). Measure 3 is also characteristically phrased. It is incomprehensible that these ties in the original

Example 17. Sonata for Gamba and Clavier in D Major BWV 1028, 2nd movement, Allegro, m. 1–4, gamba

score are simply ignored in the clavier part of the Rolf van Leyden edition in favor of reducing everything to a legato. In the last movement of the same sonata we do not find a single tie in the gamba part; here the typical Baroque *détaché*, of which Wenzinger and Boettcher speak, is definitely appropriate. The same seems to be true of the concluding movement of the Sonata in E-flat Major for Flute and Clavier BWV 1031, where there are no ties at all. But a flute cannot be played *détaché*, so if the movement is played with a light staccato throughout, the flutist may not only tire, but will not be able to take a breath. For this reason, some legato marks could be placed over two sixteenths. Even when passages appear to be similar, due caution should be exercised. The great opening movement of the Sonata for Flute and Clavier in A Minor BWV 1030, measures 9 and 13 for the flute, would surely be phrased identically if Bach had not given two completely different articulations (Example 18). Similar variants can be found in the Sonata in E Major for Flute and b.c. BWV 1035. In the second movement, compare measures 1–4 of the flute part with 33–36. Which version should we accept? The staccato dots of the Siciliano theme (3rd movement) surely demand an additional dot on the first syncopated eighth of the following measure (Example 19).

Example 18. Sonata for Flute and Clavier in B Minor BWV 1030, 1st movement, Andante, m. 9 and 13, flute

Example 19. Sonata for Flute and b.c. in E Major BWV 1035, 3rd movement, Siciliano, m. 1–3. Staccato dots are added where there is a *. Notation of appoggiaturas follows the NBA

But in the following Allegro assai one is reluctant to make additions which appear to be analogous: the theme in measure 1 is articulated differently than in measure 2 and this has to be clearly distinguished in performance (Example 20).

Example 20. Sonata for Flute and b.c. in E Major BWV 1035, 4th movement, Allegro assai, m. 1–2, flute

Note also the articulation of the flute part in m. 32–38 of the same movement. It seems necessary to point out that many of the phrasings suggested by Albert Schweitzer should be viewed with scepticism. Schweitzer was not a string player and in these questions still showed the strong influence of Hugo Riemann. As a last example of converting a Bach direction into modern violin technique, we cite m. 220–223 of the Chaconne, which we show both in the original version and in Carl Flesch's version (Example 21).

Example 21. Partita for Violin solo in D Minor BWV 1004, 5th movement, Chaconne, m. 220–223

We have devoted so much space to the question of appropriate phrasing because we consider it to be the most important part of interpretation, more important than dynamics or tempo. Well-thought-out and convincing articulation is the fundament of any good Bach performance.

Dynamics

Directions concerning the volume of the music, i.e. *forte, piano,* etc., are given by Bach even more seldom than articulation. However, the few directions we do have provide a whole series of reference points that can be pursued further. When, for example, there is a *p* in m. 2 of the Prélude, 6th Suite for Cello solo in D Major BWV 1012, it is clear that the first measure, which has identical notes, must be played *f*. And, in fact, the following third measure again is *f*, the fourth, *p*, the fifth, *f*—which achieves the desired echo effect. In the finale of the E Minor Sonata for Flute and b.c. BWV 1034 we find the same situation: in m. 2 Bach writes *p*. Such evidence indicates that in Bach's time an allegro movement began and ended, as a rule, in *forte*; gradations in between were customary. On the other hand, a slow movement was usually played 'piano'. In this case, however, the evidence is not as clear, since dynamic indications for andante and adagio movements are rarely found. But the flute sonata movement already mentioned is relatively well marked. In two places (m. 37 and 83) there is even an original *pp*; from this we can gather that Bach had in mind three distinct dynamic gradations. Simple echo effects are indicated in the A Major Sonata for Violin and Clavier BWV 1015, 2nd movement, m. 58–69, for example; here too the directions are characteristically found in the clavier part, which means that a two-manual harpsichord was available. Echo effects in the 2nd movement, m 17–18 and 27–28, of the E-flat Major Sonata for Flute and Clavier BWV 1031 can also be safely assumed, although they were not explicitly noted. The 3rd movement of the same sonata leads to the same conclusion; for example, in m ½–¾, 6–7, et al. Even Albert Schweitzer pointed out that such brief echo effects were typical of Bach. Echo effects are part of the stock inventory of Baroque musical devices; hence, Bach knew that the musicians would recognize them in the music without any explicit directions.

But the dynamics of that time are not exhausted by echo effects; then, as now, the contrast between *f* and *p* was used to set off contrasting themes, in the structuring of movements—in short, to clarify the form. If, for example, in the 2nd movement of the Sonata in B Minor for Violin and Clavier BWV 1014 the first section, m. 1–40, was played at a basic *forte* level, the following middle section, m. 41 ff, surely began *p*. This *p* was by no means sustained throughout, but it must have surfaced again starting with m. 95, toward the end of the B section. Even though the concluding cadence, m. 100–101, is again marked *f*, the tripartite form of the movement is dynamically clarified. Almost all of Bach's tripartite sonata movements are similar to this; consider, for example, the violin/clavier sonatas in A major, E major, C minor and G major. In the finale of the Sonata in G major for Gamba and Clavier BWV 1027, it is the divertimentos or episodes (for example, m. 44–59) which have to be set off dynamically, and in the finale of the following Gamba Sonata in D major BWV 1028 there is even a *pp* in the "whispering" episode, m. 84–96. I think, however, it is a mistake to consider dynamic contrasts like this which relate to ongoing passages exclusively in terms of "tutti" and "solo", as in the concerto grosso. The concerto grosso and the instrumental concerto may have been especially well-defined models of this kind of dynamic differentiation, as was the tyical da capo aria, but the procedure also occurred in works whose instrumentation did not offer the prerequisites for such dynamic differentiation: namely, the chamber music. Schematization is alien to the spirit of living music, hence the notion of "terrace dynamics," a notion which was rigidly interpreted well into our own century, is finally due for revision. "Terrace dynamics" mainly involve the organ and the harpsichord and are not necessarily applicable to other instruments.

We have long known that "crescendo" and "decrescendo" were known and practiced even before Bach's time. The Mannheim composers did not invent the effect but only brought it to its greatest level of perfection. Precise 'cresc.' and 'dim.' signs are found, for example, in the *Sonate accademiche* for violin and b.c., op. 2, by Francesco Maria Veracini, which appeared in 1744,[110] where they have the following appearance:

◢ =*dim.*   ◤ =*cresc.*   ◣ = ＜＞ =*messa di voce*

But even when there are no explicit directions, the music clearly reveals where a "crescendo" and a "decrescendo" would be appropriate. On this point Gustav Scheck, well versed in Baroque performance practice, writes, "Undoubtedly, there were also dynamic build-ups and releases of tension between *forte* and *piano*, and vice versa."[111] Thus it follows that m. 37–39 of the Prelude of the 1st Suite for Cello solo in G Major BWV 1007 contain a crescendo; likewise in the Preludio of the Partita in E Major for Violin solo BWV 1006, m. 29–31 are to be played "crescendo," m. 32 dim. and m. 33–36 cresc., as are all the corresponding passages. In addition, we cite two more passages from the *Brandenburg Concertos:* the 1st movement of the Third Concerto (m. 114–119) and the 1st movement of the Fifth Concerto (m. 95–101). Any attempt to suppress a crescendo in these passages would be tantamount to hounding an academic principle to death.

Rhythm

Precision in rhythmic notation was also liberally interpreted by musicians. They knew that ♩ 𝄽 was to be played ♩ 𝄽 and that ♩ 𝄽 when referring to triplets meant ♩, ♪. The various values of dots also had to be standardized in practice, so that the shortest value always serves as a guide (Example 22).

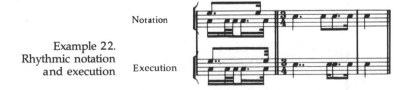

Example 22.
Rhythmic notation
and execution

Notation

Execution

But we must be wary of wholesale simplifications. In their instructional works, Quantz, Leopold Mozart and Carl Philip Emanuel Bach (who, after all, belonged to the same tradition as his father) advocated a careful distinction between eighth triplets and dotted eighth plus sixteenth. In general, it was even recommended that the dotted values be lengthened—thus ♩. ♪ . Johann Friedrich Agricola, Bach's pupil, gave a very clear answer to this question: "It is taught that in dotted notes against triplets, the note after the dot should be played with the third note of the triplet. This is true only at a very fast tempo. Other than that, the note after the dot must be struck not along with, but *after* the last note of the triplet. Otherwise, the distinction between even rhythms, in which such notes appear, and 3/8, 6/8, 9/8 and 12/8 time would be lost. J. S. Bach taught this to all his pupils..."[112] If more proof is needed, we refer to the Recitative #30 from The *St. John Passion (und geisselte ihn;* and flogged him) in Example 23. It shows conclusively that Bach recognized and provided for the distinction; it would be unthinkable that the bass rhythm would change after the introduction of the sixteenth-triplets in the vocal part.

Example 23.
St. John Passion,
Recitative #30

The matter becomes even more dubious when, as has happened, it is proposed that passages like m. 35 ff., 51 ff. and others from the 4th movement of the E Major Sonata for Violin and Clavier BWV 1016 be played so that the lower part conforms to the upper part. Example 24 shows the original notation and the proposed solution.

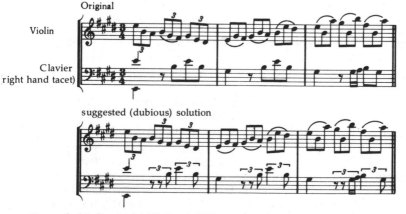

Example 24. Sonata for Violin and Clavier in E Major BWV 1016, 4th movement, Allegro, m. 35–37

Such proposals are not convincing; if this had been the desired solution, then why was the lower part not written with dotted notes, as it was in other cases (Example 25)? In my opinion it was definitely intended the way it was written; that

Example 25.
Sonata for Violin and Clavier
in E Major BWV 1016,
4th movement, Allegro,
m. 35–36

Violin

Clavier

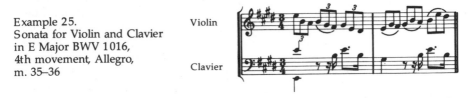

is, Bach chose this notational form because he wanted to clearly distinguish between a 3/4 rhythm divided into 3 × 4 sixteenths, on the one hand, and 3 × 3 eighth triplets, on the other,—a contrast which, as a matter of fact, is the *principium agens* of this movement.[113]

Now is the time to speak of the so-called *notes inégales*. By this we mean a playing convention in which short note values which are written equally are played unequally—a technique which seems to have been fairly common in the Baroque period. The justification for such a change was thought to derive from the distinction between light and heavy metric values, stressed and unstressed notes. It was promulgated as an agogic presentation of "thesis" and "arsis," stressed and unstressed notes.[114] In practice it had the following appearance (Example 26):

Example 26. Notes inégales: (a) notation, (b) execution

In this case, too, I am skeptical. It would contradict our understanding of style if, for example, the Andante from the Sonata for Violin solo in A Minor BWV 1003 were played as follows (Example 27):

Example 27. Sonata for Violin solo in A Minor BWV 1003, 3rd movement, Andante, m. 1–4

There are even crasser examples. However, if this had been Bach's intention he would have written it that way. We have enough examples to confirm this, for instance, the written out repeats in the 1st movement of the Trio Sonata in G Major for Flute, Violin and b.c. BWV 1038. In any case, Bach was more precise in his notation than many of his contemporaries, so we should be extremely careful with "historically accurate" interpretations of his texts. Granted that his contemporaries (especially in his absence) occasionally interpreted his works freely and introduced variations à la mode; but the extent to which this expressed his intentions is at the very least questionable, and I consider it out of the question that he would have expected this. If so, he would have clarified it through notation. Consulting 18th

Century (and current) literature, one encounters many restrictions on the practice of "notes inégales": it was valid only in certain phrasings; was not to be used with the directions "allegro e staccato" or "andante e staccato," nor in movements with continuous rapid motion, such as the Presto of the Violin Solo Sonata in G Minor BWV 1001. Also, "notes inégales" were supposed to have been common only in France, not in Italy, while in Germany no clear principle was followed. Quantz's position is clear: "Every note must be expressed in its true value and its correct tempo. If this were always correctly observed, the notes would then sound the way the composer intended them; for he must never compose without rules. Not all practitioners abide by this principle. Whether out of ignorance or corrupted taste, they often give the following note some of the time that belongs to the preceding one."[115] The whole matter was thus little more than a fad, and we do not have to go far afield to find similar musical fads in our own time. Between about 1920 and 1935 it was impossible to hear running sixteenth-note passages without substantially sustaining the first notes. This can even be heard on old recordings of the cello solo suites by Casals.[116]

Tempo

Questions about the correct tempo of Bach's chamber works cannot be answered definitively, say, by assigning compulsory metronome values. Many factors influence the choice of tempo, each of which is subject to specific variables. A tempo that worked one day in one hall, with certain musicians and a certain audience, can come across completely wrong the next day in a different hall, with different musicians and a different audience, identical metronome values notwithstanding. The problem will be treated in detail in Chapter 6. Here we shall merely try to gain an idea of which tempi Bach might have desired and chosen, i.e. which ones were prevalent and considered correct in his time.

In suite movements Bach gives no tempo directions. He assumed that everybody had a clear idea of the tempo of an Allemande, a Gigue or a Bourrée. Nevertheless, an Allemande is not simply an Allemande, a Gigue not merely a Gigue, etc. An Allemande featuring a great deal of intricate motion in thirty-second notes, as in the Suite in D Major for Cello solo BWV 1012, must be played slower than an Allemande with evenly flowing sixteenths, as in the Suite in G Major for Cello solo BWV 1007. This is generally true, is constantly mentioned in the literature of the time and really is quite obvious. The situation is not so clear when it comes to sonata movements. Even if there are any tempo indications there is much leeway. If a work exists in two versions, the tempo notations may not even be the same for the same music. Thus the first movement of the Trio Sonata in G Major for Flute, Violin and b.c. BWV 1038 is marked Largo, and the analogous movement of the Sonata in G Major for Violin and b.c. BWV 1021, Adagio, while the same passage in BWV 1022, the transcription of the trio sonata into a Sonata for violin and clavier in F major, has no tempo specified at all. The same passages in the 2nd movement of the work are marked "vivace" in the trio sonata and the violin/b.c. sonatas; in the F major sonata, "allegro e presto." In the former case, "largo/adagio," one might suspect that 'largo" was not quite so slow as "adagio;" for the adagio features many thirty-second notes, and the largo does not. This is again contradicted by the notations in the 3rd movement of the same works: how the violin/b.c. sonata is 'largo," although it has many thirty-seconds, while the trio sonata, moving almost exclusively in sixteenths, is "adagio." Hence, our suspicion turns out to be incorrect. For the sake of comparison, we shall consider other works in two versions: the Gamba Sonata in G Major BWV 1027 and the Trio Sonata for Two Flutes and b.c. in G Major BWV 1039. The 3rd movement of the gamba sonata is marked "andante," the 3rd movement of the trio, "adagio e piano." The Suite for Cello solo in C Minor BWV 1011 has a French overture as the first movement. There is no tempo indication at the beginning of the 3/8-section, although a decisive change in tempo from slow to fast takes place. The lute version of the same piece, Suite in G Minor BWV 995, is marked 'très viste" in the same passage. But how fast is "très viste?" Is the movement faster for the cello, or for the lute, or equally fast for both instruments? On records the former is heard more often.

These are all open-ended questions which cannot be answered absolutely. Nevertheless, there is always only *one* correct tempo which must be observed for each piece under specific conditions of time, space, performers and other circumstances.

On the other hand, Bach's tempo directions in his chamber music are by no means always vague, and they should be studied closely. Thus, the notation "allegro ma non tanto" for the 2nd movement of the Sonata in G Major for Gamba and Clavier BWV 1027, is very appropriate for the substance of this movement, which should not be rushed. The "vivace" for the first movement of the G Minor Gamba Sonata BWV 1029 must, of course, be applied to the eighth-notes in the movement, which contains numerous important thirty-second notes. Bach uses the term "presto" for a movement that should be played with great force and speed, as in the finale of the G Minor Sonata for Violin solo BWV 1001. "Grave" applies only to the opening movement of the Violin solo Sonata in A Minor BWV 1003, which in fact does have a somewhat heavy quality. The introductory movements of the two other violin solo sonatas, on the other hand, are appropriately marked "adagio," since they do not have that quality. This makes it evident that the Italian terms for tempo indicate not only speed, but also the character of the music. The two fugues of the violin solo sonatas in A minor and C major have no indications at all. It was probably understood which "tempo giusto" was intended. The simple "dolce" for the 1st movement of the A major sonata for violin and clavier BWV 1015 is very enlightening, as is the "andante un poco" over the 3rd movement of the same sonata. The addition of "ma non tanto" to the "adagio" over the 3rd movement of the E Major Sonata for Violin and Clavier BWV 1016 is also significant. Other directions are not as clear, as when the same notation, "adagio," is employed for movements of completely different character and tempo, i.e. the very slow, meditative 4th movement of the Sonata for Violin and Clavier in G Major BWV 1019, 3rd version, and the gracefully playful 1st movement of the G Major Sonata for Gamba and Clavier BWV 1027. The great introductory movement of the B Minor Sonata for Flute and Clavier BWV 1030, on the other hand, is appropriately marked "andante," particularly since tradition would have led one to expect an allegro here. The examples are chosen arbitrarily and could easily be multiplied.

What do Bach's contemporaries have to say about the problem of tempo? A 'universalist" like Johann Mattheson, who scarcely leaves out a topic worth considering from his *Vollkommene Kapellmeister*, is strangely laconic on this point. Quantz is much more precise. He attempted to find an objective unit of measurement in the human pulse (since in the 18th century there were no metronomes), and he expressed his notions about tempo accordingly. Since these postulates of Quantz became very famous, they will be quoted verbatim here:

Johann Joachim Quantz

Essay of a Method for Playing the Transverse Flute, accompanied by several Remarks of service for the Improvement of Good Taste in Practical Music, and illustrated with examples.*

Chapter VII, Section VII

§ 47

The means that I consider most useful as a guide for tempo is the more convenient because of the ease with which it is obtained, since everyone always has it upon himself. It is *the pulse beat at the hand of a healthy person.* [Emphasis by Quantz] I will attempt to give instructions as to how each of the various distinguishable tempos can be determined without great difficulty by regulating yourself with it. . . .

§ 48

I do not pretend that a whole piece should be measured off in accordance with the pulse beat; this would be absurd and impossible. My aim is simply to show how in at least two, four, six, or eight pulse beats, any tempo you wish can be established, and how you can achieve a knowledge of the various categories of tempo by yourself that will lead you to further inquiry. . . .

§ 49

Before I go further I must first examine these various categories of tempo a little more closely. . . . I will divide these tempos, as they occur in concerto, trio, and solo, into four classes, and will use these classes as the basis [for determining the others]. They are based on common or four-four time, and are as follows: (1) the *Allegro assai*, (2) the *Allegretto*, (3) the *Adagio cantabile*, (4) the *Adagio assai* [Emphasis by Quantz] . . . .

§ 50

The *Allegro assai* is thus the fastest of these four main categories of tempo.** The *Allegretto* is twice as slow. The *Adagio cantabile* is twice as slow as the Allegretto, and the *Adagio assai* twice as slow as the Adagio cantabile. In the Allegro assai the passage-work consists of semiquavers [sixteenth-notes] or quaver [eighth-note] triplets, and in the Allegretto, of demisemiquavers [thirty-second notes] or

---

*Reprinted with permission of Schirmer Books, A Division of Macmillan, Inc. from Johann Joachin Quantz, *On Playing the Flute,* Translated by Edward R. Reilly. Copyright © 1966, 1976, 1985 by Faber & Faber, Ltd.

**What in former times was considered to be quite fast would have been played almost twice as slow as in the present day. . . . The large number of quick notes in the instrumental pieces of the earlier German composers thus looked much more difficult and hazardous than they sounded. . . .

semiquaver [sixteenth-note] triplets. . . . In alla breve time, which the Italians call *tempo maggiore,* and which, whether the tempo is slow or fast, is always indicated with a large C with a line through it, the situation is the same, except that all the notes in it are taken twice as fast as in common time. . . . Just as the Allegro in duple time has two principal categories of tempo, namely a fast and a moderate one, the same is also true of triple metres, such as three-four, three-eight, six-eight, twelve-eight, &c. For example, if in three-four time only quavers [eighth-notes] occur, in three-eight only semiquavers [sixteenth-notes], or in six-eight or twelve-eight only quavers [eighth-notes], the piece is in the fastest tempo. If, however, there are semiquavers [sixteenth-notes] or quaver [eighth-note] triplets in three-four time, demi-semiquavers [32nd notes] or semiquaver [sixteenth-note] triplets in three-eight time, or semiquavers [sixteenth-notes] in six-eight and twelve-eight time, they are in the more moderate tempo, which must be played twice as slow as the former. If the degrees of slowness indicated at the beginning of this paragraph are observed, and attention is paid to whether common time or alla breve is indicated, no further difficulty will be encountered in connexion with the Adagio.

§ 51

To get to the main point, namely how each of the types of metre cited can be put into its proper tempo by using the pulse beat, it must be noted that it is most important to consider both the word indicating the tempo at the beginning of the piece and the fastest notes used in the passage-work. Since no more than eight very fast notes can be executed in the time of a pulse beat, either with double-tonguing or with bowing, it follows that there is

In common time:

In an Allegro assai, the time of a pulse beat for each minim; [half-note]
In an Allegretto, a pulse beat for each crotchet; [quarter-note]
In an Adagio cantabile, a pulse beat for each quaver; [eighth-note]
And in an Adagio assai, two pulse beats for each quaver.

In alla breve time there is:

In an Allegro, a pulse beat for each semibreve;
In an Allegretto, a pulse beat for each minim;
In an Adagio cantabile, a pulse beat for each crotchet;
And in an Adagio assai, two pulse beats for each crotchet;

In two-four time or quick six-eight time a pulse beat occurs on each bar in an Allegro.

In an Allegro in twelve-eight time, two pulse beats fall in each bar, if no semiquavers occur.

In three-four time, if the piece is Allegro and the passage-work in it consists of semiquavers or quaver triplets, a definite tempo cannot be established in a single bar. Taking two bars together, however, it is possible to do so. Then a pulse beat falls on the first and third crotchets of the first bar, and on the second crotchet of the following bar; thus there are three pulse beats for six crotchets. The same is the case in nine-eight time.

In the following paragraphs Quantz presents his method in detail. Of this, only a part of Section 58 will be of interest to the reader:

> The *entrée,* the *loure,* and the *courante* are played majestically, and the bow is detached at each crotchet, whether it is dotted or not. There is a pulse beat on each crotchet.
>
> A *sarabande* has the same movement, but is played with a somewhat more agreeable execution.
>
> A *chaconne* is also played majestically. In it a pulse beat takes the time of two crotchets.
>
> A *passecaille* is like the preceding type, but is played just a little faster. . . .
>
> A *bourrée* and a *rigaudon* are executed gaily, and with a short and light bow-stroke. A pulse beat falls on each bar.
>
> A *gavotte* is almost like a rigaudon, but is a little more moderate in tempo.
>
> A *rondeau* is played rather tranquilly, and a pulse beat occurs approximately every two crotchets, whether in alla breve or in three-four time.
>
> The *gigue* and the *canarie* have the same tempo. If they are in six-eight time, there is a pulse beat on each bar. The gigue is played with a short and light bow-stroke, and the canarie, which is always in dotted notes, with a short and sharp one.
>
> A *menuet* is played springily,[1] the crotchets being marked with a rather heavy, but still short, bow-stroke, with a pulse beat on two crotchets. . . .
>
> A *march* is played seriously. If it is in alla breve or bourrée time, there are two pulse beats on each bar, &c.

Thus Quantz. Fortunately, he had enough experience to view his proposed values only as guidelines, not as dogma. Nevertheless, if put into practice, the results are confusing. Today the average human pulse rate is between 70 and 75 beats per minute. But medical science is certain that people in earlier centuries all had lower blood pressure and a correspondingly slower heartbeat. According to the experts, one might settle on an average rate of 60 beats per minute for people of Bach's time. But even this slow a rate results in tempos which mostly are unrealizable. "No more than 8 notes for each heartbeat,"—in an allegro with simple sixteenth-notes, that amounts to a tempo of $\downarrow = 120$, and this is always too fast. Try to imagine the 2nd movement of the Violin/Clavier Sonata in C Minor BWV 1017 at such a tempo: the result would be a grotesque scramble. Even in the case of extremely fast movements, for example the 4th movement of the violin/clavier sonata in E Major BWV 1016, or the gigue of the suite for cello solo in E-flat Major BWV 1010—in which an eighth-note triplet would have to be assigned a value of 160—we would approach the realm of the unplayable. And the Chaconne with a tempo $\downarrow = 120$, as proposed by Quantz: no one would even consider playing it that fast. The footnote to Section 50 of Quantz' book takes one aback. What did Quantz mean by "earlier times?" His book was published in 1752, shortly after Bach's death. Does "earlier times" perhaps mean the generation of Bach, with whom Quantz had been personally acquainted and whose music he had heard? On the other hand, Marin Mersenne (1588–1648), in his *Harmonie universelle,* published in Paris in 1636, goes even further: he speaks of "no more than 16 notes a second," which in 4/4 would result in a value of quarter note = 240, if the sixteenth is taken as the smallest unit. In the face of such standards, the musician of today is totally lost.

[1]*Hebend.* Literally, this means in a lifting or rising manner.

There is only a single document on Bach's own approach to tempo, the "Nekrolog" published in 1754 by Carl Philipp Emanuel and Bach's pupil, Agricola: "As regards tempo: he usually set a very lively pace and was extremely confident."[118] If one adds to that the other documentation concerning Bach's performances (they come from Carl Philipp Emanuel's letters to Forkel[119] and are extremely vivid), one comes away with the impression that Bach was a very practical musician. As such, he surely was aware of the time-honored principle that "allegro" or "lively" has a relative, not an absolute value in music, and that a moderate tempo in which all polyphonic writing is perceptible, makes the allegro seem faster than a tempo that is more rapid when measured with a metronome, but in which nothing can be distinguished. Questions of tempo are never objective, i.e. can never be resolved mathematically. Measured by metronome, the beats of a slow movement can be faster than those of a rapid one. For example, in the Sonata for Gamba in G Major BWV 1027, the eighth-notes of the 1st movement (Adagio, 12/8) are faster than the quarter notes of the 2nd movement (Allegro, 3/4).

The "Manieren" (Ornaments)

In the 18th century, melody parts, even in duets, were rarely played as simply as they were written. As soon as a note was a bit longer, it was enriched by ornaments, especially at a slow tempo. The procedure was called *diminuieren*, i.e. to reduce in size, to divide up the main value ("diminuieren" does not mean that the music becomes softer, as one might think today). These ornaments were called "Manieren" in Germany, "agréments" in France and "embellishments" in England. Musicians were judged according to their ability to invent and execute such ornaments tastefully, interestingly and effectively.

It must be noted that this did not entail opening the floodgates of unbridled fantasy. There was a veritable repertory of flourishes, formulas and idioms which were continually changing; a young musician had to learn them himself or absorb them by listening to his elders. In written form, several of them were indicated by symbols, but in practice, musicians went even further than this. The symbols were interpreted very freely, and ornaments were brought into play even when there were no signs. The number of ways in which the same symbol can be interpreted is shown in Philipp Emanuel Bach's *Essay on the True Method of Playing the Clavier*, where he gives an example in Table VI, Fig. XCIII (Example 28).[120]

Example 28. Carl Philipp Emanuel Bach, *Essay on the True Method of Playing the Clavier*, Table VI, Fig. XCIII

Leopold Mozart also provides instructive examples for expanding and changing written ornaments in his *Violinschule*, 9th Section, § 22ff. Mattheson likewise treats the topic very thoroughly in his *Der Vollkommene Capellmeister*; he gives us a list of names for the various types of ornaments: Accent, Trillo, Tremblement, Pincé, Groppo, Tirata, Tenuta, Ribattuta, Halbcirckel, etc., and illustrates them with examples, of which at least the *Tenuta* resolved into a *Ribattuta* is cited here (Example 29).

Example 29. Johann Mattheson, *Der vollkommene Capellmeister,* Part 2, Chapter 3, § 48

It is impossible to give here a complete course in ornamentation. But anyone who wishes to interpret Bach's music in the right style needs to study this area intensively. Extensive literature on the subject is available. The most important author is, of course, Johann Sebastian Bach himself, who provides a compilation of the chief ornaments in the *Klavierbüchlein* (Little Clavier Book), which he wrote for his son Wilhelm Friedemann, during the Köthen period.

Having gained a comprehensive view of this subject—which can only be called huge—and learned a few of its fundamental rules (see p. 75), the player will be able to approach such questions with authority. This is necessary if one is to do justice to the subject. To begin with we must recognize that there are no absolute answers about how ornaments are to be played—not even in one single case. It is the nature of ornaments to be improvised, and therefore to be changeable; this is precisely why they were not written as specific notes. It would be a mistake to insist that any individual solution was "the right one," that it must be played thus and not otherwise.

A super-systematic approach like this also runs contrary to the casual way in which ornaments were or were not notated in the 18th century. In textually identical passages, such as passages with the same theme, the first may be marked ∾, the next one *tr* the next one ⌁, the next one, nothing at all. In corresponding places the directions may vary: see the following example from the G Major Sonata for Gamba and Clavier BWV 1027, 1st movement (Example 30): the trill is written in three or four different ways. And so it goes: the confusion is endless. The practice of the Italians was the most rational; in places where they wanted ornaments they simply wrote a "+" over the note and left the rest to the player.

Example 30. Sonata for Viola da Gamba and Clavier in G Major, BWV 1027, 1st movement, Adagio, m. 27–28

The visual aspect of the signs may help a little.[121] The signs ∾, ⌁, ⌁, ⌁, ⌁ represent the progression of the ornament to a certain extent. It is already more complicated with signs like the following: ⌣⌐.⌐⌐.⌐⌐.≈⊤ . They can be found on p. 115 of BGA XVII in the edition of the Clavier Concerto in A Major BWV 1055. It is not without reason that they have been transcribed into small notes in modern editions.[122] Still, the unfixed character of each ornament must not be disregarded. Nor can it be ruled out that a "Manier" be altered in repetitions or parallel passages. The number of possibilities at the disposal of the musician was indeed inexhaustible. One must accept the risk of independently deciding such questions according to one's artistic conscience. The notation provides little solid footing: indeed, it could often be characterized as chaotic. Better clues can be found where we have documentation concerning Bach's own use of ornaments. An important example is the 3rd movement of the 2nd version of the G major Sonata for Violin and Clavier BWV 1019. It is identical with both the aria, "Heil und Segen," from the cantata BWV 120, *Gott, man lobet dich in der Stille* (Leipzig Town Council Election Cantata), and the aria "Leit, o Gott, durch deine Liebe," from cantata BWV 120a, *Herr Gott, Beherrscher aller Dinge* (Wedding Cantata). The right hand of the keyboard part in the violin sonata contains the ornamented vocal part in the arias cited.

Below we present a list, reduced to a bare minimum, of the most important ornaments:

1. *tr, ᴧᴧ, ᴧ* =trill
2. *ᴧᴧ* =upper mordent (from 'mordere,' to bite)
3. *✦* =downward, "inverted" mordent, also trill with after-beat
4. *ᴗᴧ* =mordent with descending turn
5. *ᴧᴧ* =lower mordent with turn from below; can also be a trill beginning with an ascending turn and ending with an after-beat
6. *∞* =turn, starting with upper note turn (in the Baroque era there is no turn from below) [123]
7. *ᴧᴦ* =mordent with ascending slide

Trills virtually always begin with the upper auxiliary note. If they appear on a dotted note, there is a "point d'arrêt" (Example 31 #8).

Example 31

The appoggiaturas, which signify that suspensions are not fully written out, are also important. Another term for them is "long" appoggiaturas. The following principles apply:

1. The suspended note has half the value of the following note. Shorter values may occur, but cannot be inferred from the manner in which the suspension is written—quarter, eighth, sixteenth.

2. In triple time the suspension receives two-thirds of the following note (in this case, too, there are exceptions).

3. The suspension usually falls on the strong part of the beat. It is always tied to the following note. But there are exceptions in which the suspension occurs *before*

Example 32. Sonata for Flute and b.c. in E Major BWV 1035, 1st movement, Adagio ma non tanto, m. 1

the strong beat (Example 32, taken from the E Major Sonata for Flute and b.c. BWV 1035, 1st movement).

The "short" appoggiatura is likewise impossible to recognize from the notation. It occurs rarely in Bach's work. When he did use it, however, he did not write it with a crossed stem or flag, as has been customary since the Classic period. In the 1st movement of the E major flute sonata, Gustav Scheck plays all the appoggiaturas before the sixteenth-note triplets short, i.e., as "grace notes" which is convincing, although they are no differently marked than the long appoggiaturas of the same movement (Example 33). I must say that current editing practices in this regard still

Notation (Short grace notes)

Example 33. Sonata for Flute and b.c. in E Major BWV 1035, 1st movement, Adagio ma non tanto, m. 15

are unsatisfactory. The 3rd movement, Siciliano, of the same sonata has different appoggiaturas in the NBA, VI, 3, than does an edition put out by another publisher, which is likewise called an *Urtext*. In this instance, three (in the NBA, two) different notations are used for the same musical situation. Where there are two different versions of the same work, as in the C Minor Suite for Cello solo BWV 1011 and the Lute Suite in G Minor BWV 995, comparisons can be instructive.

We shall conclude this nearly inexhaustible subject with an example which may seem insignificant, but which nevertheless clearly illustrates the extent of the problem. The passage in question is the main theme, or, more correctly, one of the two main thematic lines, of the 4th movement of the Sonata in D Major for Gamba and Clavier BWV 1028 (Example 34). It first appears in the gamba part without ornament, as in Example 34; but when it is repeated in the clavier part, m. 5–6, it has the following ornament (Example 35): (Here again, the turn is facing the wrong

Example 34. Sonata for Gamba and Clavier in D Major, BWV 1028, 4th movement, Allegro, m. 1–2

Example 35. Sonata for Gamba and Clavier in D Major, BWV 1028, 4th movement, Allegro, m. 5–6

way.) Then, in m. 17, with the motif in A major, there is no ornament, and the same in m. 21, with the motif in B minor, m. 51–52, first a 𝄗 , then a ∿ m. 97, again ∿ ; the motif occurs only once here. Then, in m. 111–112, G major, both times 𝄗 ; m. 115–116, both times ∿. Without going into all the details at this point, there should certainly be some ornament on the third eighth note. Which one? A trill or a turn would be likely candidates. Following Baroque practice, a trill would always begin with the upper note; that would result in Example 36 (a). The turn would be executed either as in 36 (b) or 36 (c). Version (a) is unlikely. The lines d-e-f# and, in the following measure, e-f#-g (in the original key) which ascend by degrees, are lost because a skip of a third follows after the d or e; this, by the way, also detracts from the culminating point f# /g. Even in the Baroque period such cases were

Example 36. Sonata for Gamba and Clavier in D Major, BWV 1028, 4th movement, Allegro, different possibilities

regarded as troublesome. In order to find a solution, an ascending slide was added to the note before the ornament, as shown in Fig. 36 (d). But considering the rapid tempo of this movement (eighth-notes about 184, dotted quarter-notes about 62), this solution is impossible here. Solution (a) is also too ponderous for the required tempo. So a choice has to be made between (b) and (c); and then it must be decided whether the motif will be played with an ornament each time it appears, or only in certain places, which places, and for what reason. One other possibility remains—that of alternating between (b) and (c). Problems aplenty for such a simple case! In the same movement the question of the trill termination remains to be analyzed. In m. 12 the gamba has a simple sixteenth anticipation after the trill (the B obviously has to have a trill; see m. 16, clavier). In m. 16 the passage is arranged identically, but the clavier now has an after-beat, whereas the gamba, running in parallel sixths, only has an anticipation (Example 37). Such discrepancies are especially common in cadential ornaments. Harmonic clashes such as Example 38, which result from the mixture of anticipation and suspension, were apparently not taken too seriously; this kind of dissonance was not felt to be irritating. There was more emphasis on horizontal than on vertical listening.

Example 37. Sonata for Gamba and Clavier in D Major, BWV 1028, 4th movement, Allegro, m. 15

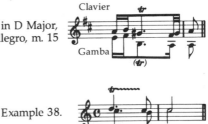

Example 38.

Interestingly enough, the gamba sonatas are especially rich in ornaments. It may be that someone other than Bach added them; generally, we have the impression that Johann Sebastian Bach was not fond of excessive ornamentation. His own directions, especially in the chamber music, are relatively sparse, compared, for example, with François Couperin. Bach probably wanted the musicians to play only what he had written; in this respect he anticipated what later became Beethoven's *conditio sine qua non.*

Basso Continuo

Historically, the age of the basso continuo (b.c.), also called "figured bass" or "thorough bass," begins with the transition from Renaissance polyphony to early Baroque monody. This process sets in around the turn of the 17th century, and for us it is chiefly associated with the names Monteverdi and Schütz. After the death of Johann Sebastian Bach in the mid-18th century, the reign of the b.c. is essentially over. However, during those 150 years there was virtually no music that was not accompanied by a chordal instrument which sustained (and in many cases, it would be more correct to say, "led") the bass and the harmonic structure. When Bach expressly noted on the title page of his 6 Partitas and Sonatas for Violin Solo, "senza basso," he was describing the situation perfectly: works without the thorough-bass were the exception.

Instruments carrying the b.c. were the harpsichord, organ, clavichord or lute; in the early stages four viols were also used. Another instrument was usually added to reinforce the thorough bass: a cello or a small contrabass. Illustrations from the 17th and 18th centuries often show a harpsichordist and, next to him, at the center of the ensemble, the cellist; they formed the core of the group.

In Bach's chamber music the b.c. is played almost exclusively by the harpsichord. If only *one* melody instrument was used in a piece (for Bach this meant either a violin, gamba or flute), the cello reinforcement was usually omitted, but in trio sonatas and quartets it was always present. Whenever the harpsichord had no obbligato melody line, its function is clear: the left hand plays the bass, which was written by the composer, and the right hand plays accompanying chords which are derived from the figuration of the bass. At times, however, this figuration is lacking; then the continuo player must derive his chords from the context of the melody part(s) and the bass. In Bach's works we occasionally encounter such gaps in the figuration, probably because he himself played b.c. and knew what was expected.

The demands made on the interpreter of the thorough bass should not be underestimated. He was expected to be able to improvise chords according to the figuration and in so doing to avoid major blunders in the voice leading. Today this ability has mostly been lost. Modern editions of Baroque music therefore have the thorough-bass "realized" for the player: the music to be played by the right hand is written out in individual notes by an editor. Thus, the keyboard player now has a "part", like everyone else. Still, b.c. players should remember that the right hand part is variable; the chords can be filled in or reduced according to spatial or other exigencies. This flexibility of the b.c. is of special significance in orchestral and vocal music: by using a heavy or a light, transparent texture the player can adapt to whatever instrumentation is available, can support the ensemble rhythmically, strengthen weak middle parts and should always be in the center of the group. There is less occasion for this in chamber music, with its comparative lack of fluctuation in the instrumentation. But then the chord progressions in the right hand must be worked out more carefully. If we take the original thorough bass (harpsichord) part from the Trio Sonata in C minor from the *Musical Offering*, for example (see Figure 6), and consider the accomplishment of the musician who had only this part (there was no score!), our respect for the ability of the musicians of that time grows.

There is one extant example of a continuo part done under Bach's supervision: this is a realization of the thorough bass of the trio sonata from the *Musical Offering* done by Bach's pupil, Johann Philipp Kirnberger.[124] The work was carried out meticulously; the voice leading of the harmonic parts (three lines, most of the time) is flawless. But this is an ideal situation. Baroque musicians, if not Bach himself, could only have produced such an immaculate and precise continuo part after thorough preparation. We know that Bach assigned tasks like this to his pupils to

Figure 6. Continuo part of the Trio Sonata in C Minor, BWV 1079 from the original edition of the *Musical Offering*, Leipzig, 1747. A score was not published.

give them practice in correct voice leading and connection of chords. In contrast to modern practice, there were at that time no "harmony text books;" composers went immediately to work on practical tasks.[125]

A special problem is posed by the b.c. in all the sonatas for melody instruments and obbligato clavier. In these works the parts for both hands of the keyboard player are written out and thereby fixed, and the right hand, which carries the melody, is usually so intensely occupied that there can be no thought of also fleshing out the chords. For this reason Bach entirely omits figuration of the bass in these sonatas. Nevertheless, even in these pieces thorough bass chords are necessary now and then, especially during a rest in one of the upper parts. The keyboard player of that time would probably have played them routinely. Three examples will serve to elucidate. In Example 39 the violin and the left hand parts are original; the right hand chords are by Hans Eppstein.[126] After m. 5, the right hand has its own melody part; further chords are dispensed with.

Example 39. Sonata for Violin and Clavier in B Minor BWV 1014, 2nd movement, Allegro, m. 1–5

Example 40 shows the same situation in a slow movement. Here the right hand part is by Rolf van Leyden;[127] Although only in two-part writing it is almost too elaborate. With the last note of m. 2, C-sharp², the b.c. filler ends and the original duet part begins.

Finally, Example 41 shows what the result could be if the melody instrument has a rest and only the clavier is playing (realization by the author).

But as a rule one should be cautious about making such additions. The special case of the Sonata for Violin and Clavier in E Major BWV 1016 will be discussed in depth in Part III, p. 190.

A few decades ago an attempt was made to resolve the problem of the thorough bass in the sonatas with obbligato clavier in the following manner: two harpsichords were included, one of which played the original part, the second (supported by a cello) playing a simplified bass and, in the right hand, its harmonic implications. Thus, along with the melody instruments, four players take part in the performance of the sonata. It is difficult to imagine that Bach could have made use of such an apparatus. Musically, nothing is gained by the arrangement; on the contrary, the polyphony becomes muddled. But in the works for three parts, Bach's counterpoint is so admirable, the harmonic structure so completely realized in the lines, that they require no complementary chords. Even the occasional two-part passages are possible without b.c. support, if necessary. It would be worth trying to play the pure trio sonatas with only the two melodic instruments and with a cello for

Gamba

(Realization)

Clavier

(Bach)

Example 40. Sonata for Viola da Gamba and Clavier in D Major, BWV 1028, 3rd movement, Andante, m. 1–2

(Bach)

Clavier

(Lower voice: Bach
Middle voices: realization)

Example 41. Sonata for Viola da Gamba and Clavier in G Minor, BWV 1029, 4th movement, Allegro, m. 1–2

the bass line. People will be surprised at how much transparency the polyphony gains and will probably repeat the experiment.

Chapter 6

Aspects of Modern Performance Practice

In Chapters 4 and 5 the instruments and playing techniques of Bach's time were described, insofar as they were used in chamber music and based on our current knowledge. This chapter will deal with modern performance, which to now we have only mentioned in passing.

The musicians of today seldom feel as confident interpreting a violin sonata by

Bach as they do a sonata by Brahms or César Franck. Ever since we developed, early in the 20th century, an awareness of historical styles, it has been thought that Bach's music was to be played differently than the works of the Classic and Romantic periods. Since that time the question of how to recreate the performance techniques of the Bach epoch has not been laid to rest. How could Bach's music be performed in a manner that did justice to his style and was faithful to the original—to use terms still common today? After World War II there were a number of thorough, but often merely well-meaning, publications which brought this question to the attention of the general musical public, who were now offered numerous performances and recordings, often of extremely dubious quality, claiming to be "the original Bach." It began with the harpsichord revival. Bach on a modern piano? Sacrilege! It developed into a veritable holy war, in which logical argumentation was lost sight of. In the process it was studiously overlooked that the harpsichords built in the 20th century differed significantly from Bach's harpsichord. We quote a specialist in the matter, Raymond Russell:

It is unfortunate that the type of harpsichord which has usually attracted modern instrument makers, and from which they have developed their plans, is the instrument which—already decadent—was condemned by the composers and overwhelmed by the pianoforte of the late eighteenth century. The swell, the machine stop, and various other devices planned to vary tone color were a last attempt to display powers of romantic expression comparable with those of the pianoforte. It is interesting to see this same phenomenon displayed by many harpsichord makers today, whose preoccupation with contrasted tone color and with expressive powers inherent in the pianoforte but foreign to the harpsichord betrays both a lack of appreciation of the sterling musical quality of the classical instrument and also doubts concerning its popular acceptance.

Modern harpsichords are fitted with pedals instead of hand stops, and a 16-foot register is almost always included. Leather is more often used for plectra than quill, and is far more reliable, though formerly quill was almost invariably used. Covered strings are usually found in the bass, because convenience of transport and modern living conditions demand an instrument as short as possible. The tone of covered strings is, however, very inferior to that of uncovered. The casework and frame are much heavier than the old harpsichords. This is due partly to the influence of pianoforte-making, and partly to the fact that many makers use a much heavier stringing than was formerly thought necessary, which requires a stronger frame to bear the extra tension. The result of this, inevitably, is that most modern harpsichords are far less resonant and possess far less carrying power than their predecessors. Electrical amplification is therefore sometimes resorted to in concert performance—quite unnecessary when old instruments in good condition are used.

Individual features in modern harpsichords are good, but one undeniable fact must be faced: all the greatest masters of harpsichord-writing and playing—Byrd, Bull, Gibbons, Frescobaldi, Chambonnières, Louis Couperin, Purcell, François Couperin, Scarlatti, Rameau, Handel, and Bach—were content with small or moderate-sized instruments with one or two manuals, a maximum of two 8-foot and one 4-foot, and without means of changing the stops while playing. . . . There is no evidence that any of these great composers and players had access to harpsichords with a 16-foot or with pedals for working the stops. [128]

All this is confirmed when we hear an unrestored instrument from Bach's time which is still playable: the difference is surprising. Add to this the awkwardness in the change of registers, which was pointed out in Chapter 4. The register knobs and couplers could only be used during rests since both hands were required to manipulate them. Today, the pedal mechanism makes it easier to play and expedites rapid changes of register, but "original" it is not. On the other hand, today's higher pitch and the resulting increase in tension adversely affects an instrument's resonance.

An incontrovertible advantage of the harpsichord revival is the contribution of a new and very attractive tone color, a welcome addition to the family of plucked instruments, which are somewhat underrepresented in our modern inventory. But still unresolved is the difference in volume between the harpsichord and other instruments—the crass disproportion which occurs, for instance, when a modern violin or flute teams up with a harpsichord in a performance of one of the sonatas with obbligato clavier. As soon as the violin or flute begins to play, the upper part of the harpsichord is absolutely impossible to hear, and only a vague rumbling can be heard from the bass region. It is incomprehensible that serious musicians can be insensitive to the gross distortion of Bach's sound that ensues in this situation, i.e. by the loss of the second melody part. The sound is not as disproportionate in the gamba sonatas, since the gamba is somewhat more delicate and moves in the lower middle range, so that the upper part of the clavier is not covered up. But even here the result cannot be very satisfying. We shall only mention in passing the total distortion which occurs in a harpsichord concerto accompanied by a string orchestra (which cannot be eliminated even in a recording), and likewise the distressing fact that a harpsichord in a large orchestra is useful only in *pianissimo*, since it cannot assert itself in any other way. Whether amplification techniques can ever bring about a change, perhaps by means of a contact microphone or some device similar to that used in the electric guitar, remains to be seen. Up to now the situation has been completely unsatisfactory. Enlisting the harpsichord with the aim of recreating Baroque sound is only meaningful when a lower tuning is used and a gut-stringed, short-necked violin with a convex bow or an 18th-century flute are added to the ensemble. In this case, the relationship is still not completely smooth, but it is at least workable, as long as the room in which they are playing is not too large.

It has already been established (p. 52) that the clavichord is unsuitable as a chamber music partner. But it is a keyboard instrument which is capable of satisfactory articulation, particularly legato and staccato. This may be the reason why Bach preferred it to the harpsichord, especially in legato. In contrast to string and wind instruments, instruments with "quick-attack" sound-production (plucked and percussion instruments) can only produce a good legato indirectly. In the latter instruments each note is essentially a "sforzato"—stronger or weaker, according to the basic volume, with an ensuing diminuendo, graphically depicted $sf \Longrightarrow$. A legato line is thus a $sf \Longrightarrow sf \Longrightarrow sf \Longrightarrow sf \Longrightarrow$, exactly the opposite of what a legato should be. Hence, only the illusion of a legato can be created on these instruments, namely by playing the individual sforzati with precisely the same force. On the clavichord, harp, guitar, lute, and of course the modern piano, it is the player who has direct control, since the attack is transmitted to the instrument directly with the hand. But on the harpsichord an inanimate mechanism intercedes between the hand and the production of the sound. The player sets it in motion, but other than that, he has no immediate control. Thus, every legato remains lifeless. One has to take a certain pleasure in perverted sounds not to admit this; for instance, the hopeless inadequacy of harpsichord cantilenas like that of the 2nd movement of the Clavier Concerto in D Minor BWV 1052, or, in chamber music, the weakness of the main theme in the clavier part in the 1st movement of the Violin/Clavier Sonata in F Minor BWV 1018 (Example 42). Here, in a line that is very expressive, the harpsichord fails to do real justice to the music. It is best employed in rousing arpeggios and brilliant passage work. The instrument is also deprived of its potential for differentiation if it is constantly forced to employ a heavy registration in concert with modern instruments. This rigidity of tone was the point of departure for Manuel de Falla's harpsichord concerto, which in my opinion owes its convincing quality to de Falla's keen recognition of the specific potential of the instrument as well as its limitations.

Example 42. Sonata for Violin and Clavier in F Minor BWV 1018, 1st movement, largo, m. 1–2

Those opposed to Bach's music being performed on a modern piano like to point out that Johann Sebastian himself did not have a high opinion of the Hammerklavier or fortepiano.[129] It is, in fact, documented that although otherwise open to all innovations in instrument-making, he greeted the first fortepianos to which he was introduced by Gottfried Silbermann in Freiberg "coolly, indeed quite negatively."[130] The only written evidence on the subject, Johann Friedrich Agricola's article in Adlung's *Musica mechanica organoedi,*[131] notes that Bach only expressed a partial rejection. It is also unknown whether Bach at a later time listened to the fortepiano that Silbermann improved after Bach's critique. In an case, there are two things to keep in mind: 1) The first fortepianos did indeed have a very thin upper range, even inferior to that of the harpsichord; and 2) Bach was acquainted only with fortepianos from Saxony. He never heard the southern German instruments which go back to Johann Andreas Stein and were much better. Yet these were the very instruments which gave real competition to the harpsichord shortly after Bach's death. In an case, Bach also made negative comments about the harpsichord.[132] The harpsichord did not escape controversy even in the 18th century; Voltaire called it "an instrument for coppersmiths," and LeBlanc wrote that it was "suitable for having fun and making noise, nothing more; it can do nothing but chirp, . . . cannot bring out a theme."[133]

We have given a great deal of space to these critical views of the harpsichord, with one intent: no one should feel intimidated about playing Bach's chamber music on a modern piano. The demands made by the clavier part in Bach's chamber music can certainly be better met by a pianoforte than by a harpsichord. Our modern piano has a very broad range of expression and does not have to be played in a "Romantic blur" or with "thunderous pedal effects," or whatever other criticisms are made. Such qualities are only required by Busoni's organ-like adaptations for the modern piano, which only strive for effect. It is apparent from Bach's score that one does not need to use a Brahms sound: he demands a clear, lucid playing style, uncluttered articulation and transparent dynamics within a limited range. All this can be achieved on a modern piano which, moreover, allows for a better legato and a resonant high range. Why, then, pursue a phantom of historicism, when contemporary harpsichords do not sound like those of Bach's time anyway? Granted, a harpsichord can be used for thorough bass, but even at that it needs support from a cello. Consciously and intelligently played, the fortepiano can achieve the same results.

The situation with string instruments is similar, though not quite as precarious. An instrument by an Italian master or even a newer model, whether it be a violin or a cello, cannot be brought to full resonance with gut strings, low tuning and a convex bow. More than half of its potential is lost. Naturally, the players have to be knowledgeable about the techniques of playing Baroque music and must have a notion of what was desired musically. However, they must try to achieve all this with *our* instrumental means. This has been shown to be possible more than once, and the charge of ignoring history or doing violence to the work is not cogent; if it were, every performance of a Mozart or Beethoven sonata would ignore history.[134]

Occasionally one also encounters the argument that string instruments and a modern grand piano or a flute and a modern grand piano "do not sound good together."[135] Apart from the fact that this is a question of individual taste—obviously a matter that one can argue about—it must be said that "sounding good together"cannot be equated with having the same means of sound production. A string quartet is a group of instruments with homogeneous sound; the sonata for flute, viola and harp by Claude Debussy uses a group of instruments with heterogeneous sound. Both, however, are optimal combinations. The charm of a combination of instruments can lie precisely in the different timbres: wind, bowed, percussion, plucked instruments. In Bach's cantatas there are examples of acoustic subtlety which derive specifically from the differences between the instruments. Moreover, the demand for blending sounds is a typically late Romantic ideal; in Bach's time tone colors were juxtaposed honestly and sharply.

The combination of gamba and harpsichord is less problematic. This is due to the fact that modern gambas bear a stronger resemblance to older models than do violins or cellos. But the problem of the higher modern pitch and the prevalent use of covered strings still remains. Gambists are expected to avoid applying techniques of sound production associated with the cello. Not only must they avoid any kind of *spiccato*—that was also true for Baroque violinists and cellists, since the old convex bows could not bounce—but they must also avoid putting excessive pressure on the strings. Even the chords which are so characteristic for the gamba should always be played arpeggio and never produced by power or pressure.

The flutes of Bach's time can hardly be played satisfactorily today. Intonation of the half-steps on a flute with only one key creates considerable difficulties for our wind players who are no longer trained in this technique. Since, however, the differences in sound between a Baroque flute and a modern silver Böhm-Schwedler flute are not substantial, satisfactory Bach interpretations can be rendered on the latter. Indeed, after his Köthen period, Bach favored the flute, precisely because of its expressive qualities which are approximated by the modern flute.

As yet there is no satisfactory answer to the question of whether and to what extent Bach's lute works can or should be played on the modern guitar. The guitar is the most popular instrument of our time, and since its literature is limited, contemporary guitarists are forced to resort to the old lute repertory, and there they encounter Bach. A work composed for a 13 or 14-course lute, however, cannot simply be transposed for a six-string guitar with today's e^2-b^1-g^1-d^1-a-e- tuning; it requires extensive changes, and many of the works have to be transposed. Of course we can take the stand that it is better to play Bach's works for lute on the guitar than not at all; after all, Bach himself transcribed works for other instruments, and in any case a good half of his works for lute are themselves transcriptions. It must, however, be viewed as at least questionable when the works BWV 995 (Suite in G Minor), BWV 996 (Suite in E Minor) and BWV 997 (Partita in C Minor) in a Bach recital for guitar (at which I was present) were all played in A Minor.

A larger consideration is the difference in plucking technique between the lute and the guitar and the resulting acoustic contrast. This is compounded by the difference in the construction of the instruments and by the double-course stringing of the lute versus the single courses of the guitar. In this matter, which has seldom been aired publicly, we again defer to an expert, the lutenist and guitarist Siegfried Behrend: ". . . I generally believe that Bach's works for the lute certainly can be played on the guitar. A transcription is needed, because playing technique as well as the tuning of the lute prohibit one simply playing from the same music. Unfortunately, there are no good transcriptions. . . . Diligent work is needed to transcribe these lute pieces for the guitar so that they do justice to the work. The result—if well done—will of course not be a Bach work for the lute, but rather a Bach work made playable on the guitar by so-and-so."[136]

But the crux of all the questions relating to modern performance is not the instruments. They are important, of course, since it is the instruments which first enter the consciousness of the listener, but there are other, more decisive factors. Playing a piece "correctly" is not solely a matter of having the right instrument, but equally, if not more so, a matter of correct tempo, correct phrasing and dynamics. All of these can be accomplished on modern instruments. What good is a performance for which an authenic oboe da caccia has been located in some out-of-the-way place in Europe, when everything else about the performance is wrong? Unfortunately there were no recordings in Bach's time; they would have given us considerably better insights. As it is, we can only resort to speculation. Technical perfection in the modern sense, especially in ensembles, was probably unknown, nor was its absence noticed. Yet the individual musician often was of high caliber. In Köthen there was probably a large group of very capable musicians—another reason Bach felt comfortable there. It was different in Leipzig. Apparently the situation there was inadequate, and the level of performances would probably have been insulting to modern ears. This is apparent not only from Bach's own constant complaints; but little imagination is needed to visualize the technical ability of the singers and players (many of the latter after all were students at St. Thomas School), the limited opportunities to rehearse owing to the constant pressure, the constant demand for church music. Consider also the poor lighting, the frigid temperatures in the churches and practice rooms in the winter, and finally, the legibility of the music, which often enough was hastily written. The results cannot have been very satisfying.[137] Nevertheless, we are probably ill-advised to judge the conditions of that time by our own standards. People then had a different relationship to music. Music was played and, above all, listened to with more imagination than it is today. The imagination of the listener was more vivid, compensating for whatever deficiencies existed. Today we cannot fathom it, we simply shake our heads: why are so many of the instrumental parts in the chorus "Sind Blitze, sind Donner" of the *St. Matthew Passion* so ineffectively written? Why, for example, are the flute parts (in the passage cited in Example 43) not written an octave higher, so that they could be heard over the massive sound of the chorus (although they were doubled by the oboes, which, however cannot be heard either)? Bach had the technical means at his disposal. But we are proceeding from false premises when we make such judgments. The present-day listener wants everything to be perfect; at that time, a general indication sufficed. The rest was filled in by the listener's imagination.

Example 43. *St. Matthew Passion,* "Sind Blitze, sind Donner." m. 105–108

Considerations of this kind lead us into the realm of psychology of music and thus to the roots of the problem of "historical accuracy." Interpretations which make it their aim to be exactly as in Bach's time do not go beyond superficiality. In all their calculations regarding supposed "faithfulness to the original," they lose sight of the fact that today's musician is a different person than the musician of 250 years ago. Let us look at the situation plainly: somebody has just attended a concert of "old music," believing that it was performed exactly the way it had been centuries ago. He then leaves and climbs into his car or boards a plane—something doesn't quite fit here. His mental attitude is irrevocably different from that of the musician of Bach's time. By "different," I do not mean the cliché of the harassed urbanite; even someone who lives in a shack, wears homespun clothing and eats from earthenware pots remains a child of this century and has an absolutely different mental set than that of a contemporary of Bach.

But let us leave this consideration of external factors and move the argument to a more artistic level. A musician who has listened to Chopin or Wagner, regardless of whether he likes or dislikes them, has a different background than a musician from an epoch which had yet to experience that development. Even the most fanatical Baroque musician today cannot play as if Chopin and Wagner (other names can be substituted) had never existed. It is impossible to act as if nothing had happened in the intellectual sphere since 1720. And since this is a development from which we cannot extricate ourselves no matter how we try to seal ourselves off, a present-day performance of works by Bach can never be the same as one of his time. A person can copy everything he knows about the original as precisely as imaginable, even including all the mistakes; the result will still always be something new.

I don't mean to sit in judgment over the harpsichord or the short-necked violin. Reviving old instruments has provided a great deal of stimulation and many new tone colors have been gained. Fine: as long as it is not considered "historically correct." At one other time in the history of music, people thought they were reviving something from the past yet something new resulted, namely during the beginnings of opera in Florence at the end of the 16th century. At that time, the primary intention was merely to "correctly" perform ancient tragedies. But the result was a new form: opera. In our time, the same thing happened with the so-called Bach trumpet: people thought they were reviving the past, but the result was a new instrument. And again, when the Cologne Cathedral was completed in the 19th century: the builders thought that they were faithfully continuing the old plan, but what they created was their own era's concept of Gothic style.[138]

Such attempts at historical revivals also may serve as a deplorable alibi. People use the claim of historical accuracy to shield themselves from having to take responsibility. Here too, we can discern that need for security we spoke of in the discussion of authenticity of Bach's works. It is a need to have all bases covered because one has shied away from personally taking intellectual risks. In this we are indeed fundamentally different from people of Bach's era: they did not require any historical props to stand on firm artistic footing. They did what they thought was right. We could learn from them.

Faithfulness to musical style is a unique intellectual phenomenon, one that has been little studied. Every age creates its own concept of how the music of previous times should sound. However, if we ask ourselves just how this concept was formed, no real answer is forthcoming. Apparently there is a tacit consensus about what is acceptable in the performance of earlier music, although no one really knows what it was like at that time. This consensus is nourished by traditions, specific historical facts, and general notions of style, but also by new advances in playing techniques, by changes in the way music is performed, i.e. in large halls or using amplification, in short, by current trends in musical performance. Factors outside the field of music are probably also brought to bear. Even artists with a special sensitivity to the currents of the time may, unknowingly, be involved. Out of all these elements a paradigm is formed, and interpretations which do not conform to this paradigm are perceived as "wrong." Most importantly, however, this paradigm, this consensus, is subject to extreme fluctuations. In the 19th century, Mendelssohn and Robert Franz believed that they had found the "correct" Bach in their performances, as do modern representatives of "Bach Swing." And in the 1930's when Furtwängler conducted Bach's *5th Brandenburg Concerto,* himself playing the clavier solo, there was unanimous indignation at his arbitrary and sentimentalized rendition of the great cadenza of the 1st movement; it was replete with changes of tempo and much pedal use; it collapsed architectonically. Every listener thought to himself, "This is all wrong; Bach can never have intended this." Yet no one knew what Bach really did intend. The consensus changes with the times. What seemed right yesterday feels wrong today, and no epoch is in possession of the only vaid truth.

The whole question of "faithfulness to the original work" can only be resolved on the basis of cultural history and the psychology of music. It is hoped that one day it will be approached from this perspective, so that our contemporary performance of older music might be raised from a level of superficial imitation and half-truths to an intellectually secure basis.

Analyses

Chapter 7

Objectives

In this second part the structural component of Johann Sebastian Bach's chamber music will be analyzed. We will investigate whether the works have common characteristics and what these consist in, and whether there are general compositional procedures and basic patterns. Furthermore, we shall investigate whether such characteristics and patterns are specific to the chamber music or can also be found in other works by Bach, at least in the realm of instrumental music.

It is a known fact, and repeatedly confirmed in performance, that many of the structural constellations that we find, for example, in *The Well-Tempered Clavier* or in the great organ works are absent in the chamber music. In other words, something that Bach writes in a *Brandenburg Concerto* comes from a completely different set of assumptions than the text of a sonata for the violin or gamba and clavier. The same can be said of the compositional differences between a *partita* and a *sonata* for violin solo. As a composer, Bach familiarized himself and came to terms with the demands posed by each project. He was not a romantic, explosive personality who regarded the various genres as nothing more than fortuitous vessels to catch the musical message he felt compelled to communicate, so that it would be purely a matter of chance if a violin sonata is written one day and a passion the next.

People are fond of calling such considerations questions of *style,* hence, in our case, orchestral, concerted, sonata, suite style, and so forth. Despite our misgivings about such an overworked concept as "style," it is acceptable within certain limits. But then we would have to concern ourselves solely with questions of genre style and would have to neglect other matters, i.e., personal or period style. For our purposes, the category of "style" is simply inadequate. Even if the category were understood to refer only to what is written in the score, avoiding all background information, we would soon come to the realization that structural phenomena go beyond the matter of style. But this is more an investigation into compositional techniques, and also partly a consideration of aesthetics (insofar as it deals with substance of sound); so that, if one attempted to encompass it all with the term "style," this vague concept would become even more watered-down.

It is not really crucial how we categorize our intentions because what matters is that we gain a more precise and comprehensive knowledge of the works.

Chapter 8

The Principles of *Ablauf* and Development

Editor's note: We have found no single English word that corresponds to the German *Ablauf* in the way the author uses it frequently, particularly in the following analytical comments. It might be variously translated as "continuous motion," "continuous development," "course of a section or movement" and signifies a compositional procedure (as explained in the following paragraphs) that is representative of this period and different from the "thematic development" principle so prevalent in late 18th and early 19th-century music. We shall occasionally use the German *Ablauf* in this translation unless the context clearly suggests a simple English equivalent term.

All instrumental music has two fundamental principles that govern the organization of individual movements: the principle of *Ablauf* and the principle of development. Their relationship is antithetical.

From the beginnings of strictly instrumental music until approximately the middle of the 18th century, the time of Bach's death, the *Ablauf* principle was the sole organizational standard. After this, the principle of development was introduced as a further possibility, although it did not replace the *Ablauf* principle. Today the two principles co-exist with equal status.

The following criteria apply to the principle of *Ablauf:* the movement crystallizes around a single theme which is a self-contained structure, unchanged in the course of the movement. The shape and character of the theme are fixed and always identifiable. The theme, which is usually introduced at the beginning of the movement, is a clearly established fact which cannot be altered. Consequently, the movement consists of constant "quoting" of the theme. It does not of course merely "run" like clockwork. It is transposed into different keys, ranges are changed, contrapuntal and (more rarely) harmonic enrichment occurs, the theme is also interrupted and fragmented. But it is never manipulated, i.e. its content is not "treated," as Beethoven "treats" a theme, especially during the process of fragmenting the theme. No, the theme "runs its course," it exists unquestioned, it is a firmly established complex which resists all attempts to break it up.

Of course, an instrumental movement of any length cannot consist solely of constant repetition of the same theme. It is necessary to get away from it at regular intervals during the movement. This is achieved by insertions which are not linked to the theme, or by continuation elements. We call them 'divertimenti," adopting a term from Anglo-Saxon analytical practice. A divertimento is an episode inserted into the course of the movement which has no relation, or at least no immediate relation to the theme. It loosens the *Ablauf* and creates a "vacation" from the theme, which, when it reenters, has a new and fresh effect. Divertimenti provide release of tension in the movement, and their function is diametrically opposed to classical development technique: they serve to gain distance from the theme, rather than heightening it.

Until the middle of the 18th century an instrumental movement constructed according to the *Ablauf* principle usually was monothematic.[1] But in Bach's music we occasionally find new ideas, middle-themes, being introduced, especially in three-part movements in A-B-A form. These themes never stand in contrast to the main theme; they merely continue its idea (see Chapter 13).

If one considers, or better, listens to, a movement constructed according to the *Ablauf* principle, one notices that any attempt to achieve dramatic climaxes is totally absent. In essence, there are no climaxes, and it would be incorrect to search for them or, worse yet, to introduce them into one's interpretation in performance. There is only a constant undulating motion of tension and release, in which, to preserve the metaphor, the theme can be compared to the crest of the wave, the divertimento to the trough. The pattern of the movement is similar to the alternation between breathing in and breathing out; Goethe's ideas of "systole" and "diastole" come to mind. Thus the emotional range also is defined by the movement's structure. No additional artistic means are required to clarify them; eruptive, dramatic "climaxes" are as superfluous as "tacked on" conclusions.

But even the *Ablauf* principle requires a propelling force, lacking which any instrumental movement degenerates into a potpourri. This force lies in rhythm and meter and draws its strength from their interdependence. It ensures the vitality of the movement and gives the music the necessary drive to hold the attention of both player and listener. This is equally true for fast and slow movements. The latent rhythmic basis is always discernable, especially in Bach's "adagio" movements, and the tension they radiate is infectious, even in expansive, imaginative movements like the introduction of the G Minor Sonata for Violin Solo, BWV 1001.

Bach's shorter movements also represent the *Ablauf* principle. Since these are primarily suite movements, i.e. originally songlike dances, there are no divertimenti. Suite movements usually consist of a succession of phrases, and sometimes of only one long phrase which is extended and varied.

The antithesis of the *Ablauf* principle is the principle of development. It gradually became established after the mid-18th century; Bach did not yet know or apply it. Only in a few rare passages in his instrumental music does one sense a premonition of it, for example, during certain episodes in the 1st movement of *Brandenburg Concerto* #3 in G Major, BWV 1048. I can think of no example in the chamber music. Even in his late works, the Trio Sonata from the *Musical Offering* and in the Sonata for Flute and b.c. in E Major, BWV 1035, he holds firmly to the *Ablauf* principle.

The development principle specifies that a theme does not stand so much on its own as within a web of relationships into which it is placed. It has full validity only from a certain perspective, in a certain light. It is less a *fact* than a reference point. Thus, in the course of the movement a theme only rarely appears in its complete form (if this can be stated at all given the various guises under which it appears), but undergoes constant metamorphosis. It is broken apart, dissected into motifs, new components are grafted onto it, old ones are dropped. Its phrases are reduced or compressed until they become an amorphous sequence, or else they are expanded into an equally amorphous "endless melody." Thus development arises as the new, typical principle. And, since various reference points or perspectives are used, a movement has to be provided with a number of themes. These themes must represent antagonistic positions; there has to be tension between them. If this does not happen, if the themes are too similar, then the principle of development loses its basic function, something that can be observed in sonata movements of the Romantic period.

A movement constructed according to the principle of development (it by no means has to be a "sonata form" movement) thus exhibits a constant structural alternation between intensification and relaxation, or, to express it in musical terms: between crescendo and decrescendo.[2] These rising and falling motions always have a discernable goal, a clear culmination point which guides the development. Thus we have high and low points. It is unnecessary to emphasize that the principle itself has a formative influence on its themes, just as the *Ablauf* principle puts its stamp on its themes.

The two principles have often been brought under the rubric of *static* and *dynamic*. There are many studies[3] of this antithesis, which is undoubtedly important to the understanding of music. These studies, however, often attempt to force all of Western music into this static-dynamic dualism and to recognize it as part of the artistic individuality of a given composer. I do not see fit to follow this line of thought. Hermann Abert's deliberations convinced me that the conversion of esthetic forms from facts to reference points, or, in musical terms, the discovery that musical themes can be relativized, becomes marked only after the mid-18th century. It signifies a fundamental change in the intellectual situation in general; its inception was probably rooted less in the conscious mind than in the emotions. Its ramifications for artistic creativity, not just in the field of music, were more far-reaching than can be gathered from the current historical categories, Baroque, Classic, Romantic, etc. Based, for example, on the differences between Goethe's Leipzig and Strassburg lyric poetry, Hermann Abert has shown that similar changes also took place in poetry.[4]

The modern composer who is acquainted with the structural implications of both the *Ablauf* and the development principles has both possibilities at his disposal and will apply either depending on what a given work requires.

Chapter 9

Combinations of Movements

Chamber music works of Bach's time always had several movements. Bach did not alter this convention; his temperament was evolutionary, not revolutionary. He does not overturn the traditions and conventions of his time, but he does fill them with very individual ideas. Thus, he is not an "avant garde composer," like Johann Stamitz, a much lesser composer, but in the end Bach's works have a more far-reaching effect and are thus much "newer," as it were.

Bach encountered the sonata as it had developed both in Italy, since Corelli, and north of the Alps, for example in the mystery sonatas of Biber. It had two basic models: the "sonata da chiesa" (church sonata) and the "sonata da camera" (chamber sonata).

A "sonata da chiesa" was defined as a work in four movements with the sequence: slow-fast-slow-fast. Details of the movements could be characterized as follows: the first movement has a measured solemnity, the second (first fast) movement is predominantly contrapuntal; the third movement is usually in the relative major or minor key and is more loosely constructed than the 1st movement; and the fourth (second fast) movement shows a predominantly dancelike character, frequently showing the influence of the suite. All in all, this sequence of movements is a model of measure and proportion, and stands on equal footing with Beethoven's classic sonata model.

The "sonata da camera," being a combination of dance movements, is basically identical with the suite. Here, too, the traditional model has four movements and consists of the sequence: "Allemande" (moderately fast). "Courante" (lively), "Sarabande" (slow), "Gigue" (fast). This sequence is frequently expanded. Other dance movements are inserted between the sarabande and the gigue; for example, Bourrée, Gavotte, Menuet, Polonaise or others. Bach was fond of preceding the Allemande with a Preludio, which could be quite long. It should be noted that he never used the term 'sonata' for chamber sonatas, but called them 'Suites,' 'Partitas,' 'Partias,' etc. For him a sonata was always the church sonata or a combination of three movements, which had nothing to do with the "sonata da chiesa" or the "sonata da camera," but rather derived from the tradition of the concerto.

If one were looking for examples of these models, the Trio Sonata for Two Violins and b.c. in C Major, BWV 1037 would be the prototype of a "sonata da chiesa," the Partita in E Major for Violin solo, BWV 1006, of a "sonata da camera," and the Sonata for Gamba and Clavier in G Minor, BWV 1029, of a three movement sonata. On the other hand, we could list some noteworthy exceptions: the Sonata for Flute and Clavier in B Minor, BWV 1030, the third movement of which is divided in half and which hence could be seen as a four-movement work with the sequence fast-slow-fast-fast. Even more unconventional is the sequence of movements in the Sonata for Violin and Clavier in D Major, BWV 1019. It exists in three versions: two with five and one with six movements, none of which, however, is a dance movement. The two five-movement versions have a very clear, symmetrical order of movements: fast-slow-fast-slow-fast. We might speculate that this structure inspired Bartók to write his instrumental works in five movements; indeed, the first of the two five-movement versions of the work by Bach exhibits a true "arch form."[5] The six-movement version features an additional movement inserted between the second slow movement and the final movement. (see p. 32).

Chapter 10

Typology of Individual Movements

Within the limits set by Bach's application of the *Ablauf* principle, individual types of movements can be recognized and grouped together. Keep in mind, again, that when Bach called a work a 'sonata,' he always meant a "sonata da chiesa" or a work with three movements with the schema fast-slow-fast, whereas the "sonata da camera" group is called a suite, a partita, a partia, or the like.

Sonata Movements

Sonata movements are based on two models: the ternary movement with the A-B-A pattern and the binary, A-B plan. Three-part movements are "through-composed." In two-part movements a repetition is usually provided for A and B.

In the A-B forms it is not uncommon for B to be longer than A, sometimes significantly longer. In these cases there is usually the hint of a reprise, i.e. the return to the beginning of the movement. This would mean that two-part movements with an expanded B part are actually disguised A-B-A movements, thus, three-part movements. We cite as an example the 2nd movement of the Sonata for Violin and Clavier in F Minor, BWV 1018; it clearly has the beginning of a reprise in m. 52. This process of incorporating the reprise element into two-part movements shows that the three-part form prevails whenever a movement exceeds a certain length. If, however, A and B have the same or approximately same length, no reprise is necessary.

In all A-B-A forms the reprise is understood. Part III corresponds to Part I; not always literally, of course, but in an unmistakable inner analogy.

Other kinds of three-part structure, an A-B-C form, for example, were not developed in musical composition. The three-part form with A-B-A as the developmental principle for larger works has, on the other hand, an archetypal character. Its roots go back to a time long before the beginning of autonomous instrumental music. The basis of its organization is an arch-like symmetry: the two A sections function as the two pillars, with the B section in the middle, as the arch. We shall not go into the psycho-esthetic analogies between the temporal art of music and the spatial discipline of architecture, but simply establish that the recapitulation of something already stated, that is, the reprise, is a basic criterion of musical structure. For this reason Stravinsky said, "Form comes from identity."[6] Thus, to understand musical forms one must devote special attention to the reprises. They activate the thought-processes and the recall, without which there can be no perception of music, a transitory art-form which unfolds in time. Let us take a brief overview of music history: we find reprises in all rondo forms from early musical cultures (usually accompanied by textual reprises), i.e. in Gregorian Kyries, in Bach's motet, *Jesu, meine Freude*, BWV 227, in Monteverdi's *Orfeo*, in every da capo aria, every suite movement with Doubles, which later give rise to the Minuets or Scherzi with trio and repetition of the opening. But one must go even further: the A-B-A scheme is the basis of every sonata movement and every rondo, and likewise it dominates all the minor musical forms of the 19th century.

Evidently Bach recognized the significance of the reprise concept more clearly than his predecessors and contemporaries and proceeded accordingly. For in his time, the reprise was not "institutionalized" anywhere in instrumental music, as it was later with the classical sonata. Bach was in virgin territory. Thus the regularity with which he employs the reprise in his sonata movements is all the more striking. In some cases they can be very prominent, as, for instance, in the 1st movement of the Sonata for Gamba and Violin in G Minor, BWV 1029. In m. 95–96 the main theme returns in the tonic, in unison—for Bach an unusually obvious way of pointing to the return. It also can be found in the literal, note-for-note da capo in the 1st and 5th movements of the last version of the Sonata for Violin and Clavier in G Major, BWV 1019, in m. 70 ff. in the 1st movement, and in m. 89 ff. in the 5th movement. In other cases the reprise is hidden, at times only tentatively, still unsure of its necessity. Examples of this can be found in the Fugue of the Sonata in G Minor for Violin solo, BWV 1001, or in the Sonata for Violin and Clavier in F Minor, BWV 1018, 4th movement, in which the theme is stated in a stretto in m. 123 ff. A particularly characteristic example of experimentation with the reprise effect can be seen in the 2nd movement of the Sonata for Gamba and Clavier in G Major, BWV 1027. Bach introduces the reprise three times here: first, in m. 92 ff., where the theme appears twice in succession, but still incompletely, then again in m. 106 ff. (now it is complete); and finally, in m. 122 ff., now in canonic condensation. The three approaches to the reprise thus become progressively more intense.

A reprise is only effective if its entry also marks the reintroduction of the movement's main key, which had been abandoned for a considerable length of time. *Harmony reveals itself as a shaping force.* In this, Bach only rarely makes an exception, as he did, for example, by introducing the reprise in the Fugue (2nd movement) in the Trio Sonata for Two Violins and b.c. in C Major, BWV 1037, which is in the subdominant (m. 91 ff.)

In the literature we repeatedly find the assertion that Bach's sonata movements are in essence a translation of forms from instrumental solo concertos to chamber music.[7] What we call reprises are interpreted in these writings as "tutti" of the (imaginary) orchestra; what occurs in between is interpreted, more or less casually, as a concertante solo. There is nothing basically wrong with this interpretation, but it remains rather superficial. Recurring tutti are, after all, only one of many ways of creating reprises. The principle is also at work in instrumental concertos, and in many other places.

Suite Movements

Compared with the diversity of sonata movements, suite movements unfold with greater simplicity and unity. The A-B, or binary arrangement is always the norm. Three-part A-B-A organization is unknown in the suite. Only when a movement features a Double, followed by a return of the initial movement, can we speak of an A-B-A form going beyond the movement.

Suite movements are based on traditional dance forms, of which the following are primary:

Allemande: slow processional dance in double time, usually with a short upbeat.
Courante: lively, running dance in triple time, also usually with a short upbeat.
Sarabande: solemn processional dance in triple time, usually beginning on a downbeat.
Gigue: very lively leaping dance with a skipping rhythm, which can be in 3/8, 6/8, 12/8, or even in dotted 2/4 time; usually upbeat.

Along with these standard forms Bach also employed the following in chamber music suites:

Minuet: leisurely walking dance in ternary time, usually beginning with a downbeat in Bach's music.
Gavotte: graceful, playful walking dance in double time; the upbeat of half a measure is typical.

Bourrée: double time, very lively skipping dance, with a quarter upbeat.

Siciliano: slow, lilting dance, often of a pastoral character, for which the ♪. ♫ rhythm is typical; in 6/8 or 12/8 time and in Bach's music usually beginning with a downbeat.

Loure: related to the Siciliano, but somewhat broader, notated in 6/4 time. The only example in Bach's music is in the E Major Partita for Violin solo, BWV 1006, which begins with a 3/8 upbeat.

All these dance forms derive from a simple shape. They are based on the two-part A-B model, all the variants of which derive from a prototype consisting of two equally long parts, A and B. They have an equal number of measures, always multiples of two: 4 measures, 8 measures, 16 measures or 32 measures. "A" usually cadences on the dominant. B then first modulates to the relative major or minor and then leads back to the tonic. Traditional theory refers to this kind of structure as "binary form". Bach provides an example of this in the Sarabande of the Suite in G Major for Cello solo, BWV 1007 (see Example 60).

But he was seldom content with this ultra-simple prototype. His imagination gave shape to the phrase, lengthened the parts, complicated the development. The introductory Allemande of the B Minor Partita for Violin solo, BWV 1002, does indeed feature an A and a B of equal length, 12 measures each, but its internal structure is so asymmetrical that the phrase can scarcely be recognized. More frequently the B parts expand into multiples of A. The resulting parts are indeed no longer of equal length, but they are regularly proportioned; the relationship of A to B is 1 to 2 or even 1 to 3. An example of the former is the Sarabande from the C Major Suite for Cello solo, BWV 1009 (8 : 16 measures): of the latter, the Bourrée I from the E-Flat Major Suite for Cello solo, BWV 1010 (12 : 36 measures). Bach seems to have taken this to extremes in the Bourrée of the E Major Partita for Violin solo, BWV 1006, in which an A with 8 measures is opposed to a B with 92 measures. Here, however, the situation is completely different. The movement does not have an A-B form at all, but is a written out rondo; the first eight measures, which are to be repeated, represent the refrain. It returns four more times in the course of the movement, separated by the requisite number of couplets. If one were to construct a diagram, it would be A-B-A-C-A-D-A-E-A.

However, despite this lengthening of the B parts, the use of reprises is much rarer in the suites than in sonata movements with an A-B form. One of the few examples is the Gigue from the E-Flat Major Suite for Cello solo, BWV 1010. In measure 27 there is a clear reprise of the beginning theme (compare the analysis of this movement, p. 152). The A-B ratio in this movement (10 : 32) is notably more complicated than usual, a 5 : 16 proportion being extremely exceptional. This might lead to the conclusion that a regular proportionality excludes the reprise, whereas an irregular one demands it.

It has already been shown that the over-all form A-B-A arises when a movement has a Double followed by a da capo of the initial movement. But interestingly enough, in the B Minor Partita for Violin solo, BWV 1002, in which Bach adds a Double to each of the four movements, he does not stipulate a da capo anywhere. Was it so self-evident to him that he simply left it out? If so, this happens four times in a row. Or, more likely does he want us to consider the doubles as simple variations of the initial movements? No parallel exists, and the work is performed both ways.

The famous Chaconne which concludes the D Minor Partita for Violin solo, BWV 1004, looms above the many suite movements as a solitary achievement. It is the only variation movement in Bach's chamber music. Its dimensions are gigantic and go far beyond the scope of the Partita form. This explains why the movement is so often performed as an individual piece.

Chapter 11

Analysis of Compositional Techniques

Linearity

Bach's musical thinking is linear and polyphonic. He is a genuine contrapuntalist. To truly understand his compositional techniques in the chamber music we have to start with a consideration of linearity.

Each of his compositions is based on a clear arrangement of the number and use of required parts. This arrangement may not apply to an entire work, it can change from movement to movement, but it is the foundation of the structure and identity of a given movement. Bach was never a dogmatic systematizer. Indeed, within a movement the number of parts can vary; one cannot find out just by counting. A change in the number of parts can be seen in all the movements which are not consistently trio-like, for example, in the introductory movements of the two Sonatas for Violin and Clavier, the one in B Minor, BWV 1014, and the one in E Major, BWV 1016, in which the total polyphonic range from three to six parts is utilized. But even here we can recognize the linear structure: in the B Minor Sonata there are two parts for the violin (double stops), two parts for the right hand of the clavier, and a bass, which contains many octave leaps. In the E Major Sonata there are a violin part, three parts for the right hand of the keyboard part, and again a bass line with many octaves. The same can be seen in other cases, such as the introductory movement of the Sonata for Violin and Clavier in F Minor, BWV 1018. In general Bach allowed himself freedom in the number of parts, especially in slow movements.

Rapid movements are usually composed with exactly three parts, in trio form. But even here, Bach occasionally violates his principle, for example by writing chords for a potential b.c. An example of this is the Sonata for Viola da Gamba and Clavier in D Major, BWV 1028, 2nd movement, m. 74, 82–3, 95–8. Or he completely splits up the two clavier parts into arpeggios, as in the extraordinary episode in m. 84–96 in the 4th movement of the same sonata. But to return to the 2nd movement of this sonata: twice he jumps directly into a four and a five-part structure, in m. 36–37, and m. 92–93, respectively. Despite such exceptions, however, it is generally true that there is a clear linear arrangement within a movement. Bach is never tempted by momentary needs to jump back and forth between chordal, linear, or even one-part idioms—a process which became common, and, indeed, necessary since the Classic period, because musical perspective had changed. With the exception of the b.c., Bach did not use filling-in parts.

This in no way means that harmony was less important to Bach. Not only in his great vocal works,[9] but also in the chamber music, there are episodes which were basically harmonically conceived. As an example we refer to the Sonata for Viola da gamba and Clavier in G Major, BWV 1027. And even if harmonic processes are not so predominant as they are there, the ratio between horizontal and vertical sound is always balanced. But the path to actual composition always *begins* with the line. Sonorities are always the result of lines in Bach's work, not lines the result of sonorities.

Movements which are in a strict trio texture proceed as follows: two melody parts play above a bass. The former are fully equal to each other; neither one is exclusively the upper or lower part. This corresponds to the structure of the Baroque trio sonata. Bach was the first to apply the trio idiom to sonatas for one melody instrument and clavier, where the melody instrument takes one upper part and the right hand takes the other. This freed the keyboard instrument from the role of being merely a continuo instrument and elevated it to the status of an equal partner. Bach made no distinction between the instrumental character of the two melodic instruments: whatever the melodic instrument plays will appear literally somewhere in the clavier part, and vice versa. It is doubtful, however, whether this is reason enough to suppose that all the sonatas for a melody instrument and clavier were originally versions for two melodic instruments and b.c., i.e. true trio sonatas. Yet we always have to respect the will of the composer who left the sonatas for melodic instrument and clavier as final versions.

All the parts in movements written in the trio idiom are in principle equal. However, we must distinguish between compositions in which the bass assumes the thematic material of the upper part, and others in which it goes its own way, where there is no verbal relationship between bass and melody instrument. In the latter case, the bass not infrequently has a continuously moving line, often in the form of an ostinato. Examples to be cited are the sonatas for flute and clavier, the 3rd movement of the Sonata for Violin and Clavier in A Major, BWV 1015, or the 1st movement of the Sonata for Gamba and Clavier in G Major, BWV 1027.

The texture of movements is different in works for a melody instrument and b.c. Their structure is like that of a duet throughout; the melody instrument has one part, the bass the other, just as the works are presented in their original notation. The chordal b.c. filling does not change this. But we should not assume these compositions are "simpler" because they have only two obbligato parts. On the contrary, Bach uses the space provided him by the two-part structure to write more elaborate individual parts. This can be clearly seen in a work which exists in both duet and trio versions, the Sonata for Flute, Violin and b.c. in G Major, BWV 1038. In the duet version, (BWV 1021) the two lines are very elaborate, in typical Baroque style; in the trio they are concentrated, compact, spare. Even the finale of the two works is arranged differently; we shall speak about this later (see pp. 201, 219 ff.).

Bach did not write any works for three melody instruments and b.c.. This is surprising, since his contemporaries, such as Telemann, did. It might also have occurred to him to combine the obbligato clavier with two melodic instruments which would have resulted in true quartets. We know from a letter of Carl Philipp Emanuel Bach to Bach's first biographer, Forkel,[10] that Bach loved to improvise such things. But why he never carried out such a project, we don't know. It surpasses imagination to think what might have surfaced if Bach had been familiar with the string quartet genre, which already existed in his time.

Compositions "senza basso"

In regard to their compositional technique, the works for solo string instruments belong to a special group; this also includes Partita for Flute solo in A Minor, BWV 1013, with certain reservations. The basis of these works is the unaccompanied individual line; they embody absolute linearity. Harmony and polyphony are only implied and are sharply circumscribed by and subordinated to the technique of the instrument in question. Bach has an incomparable ability to allow the unaccompanied musical line to develop into a musical cosmos, to give an unorthodox, yet well-proportioned order to tensions, climaxes and important rhythmic aspects, all along asserting the independence of the metric formula. The study of the linear style of these works is the central theme of Ernst Kurth's book, *Foundations of Linear Counterpoint* (Grundlagen des linearen Kontrapunkts), which made a significant contribution to the understanding of Bach in our century.[11]

Despite the single-line character of these works, "background" harmony is always implied. It is expessed in cadences, broken chords and double stops. It becomes even more interesting when an individual part implies several other parts which together amount to harmony, although *de facto* there is only one line, broken up in various ways. Example 44 is intended to show this. The linear elements are extracted from the actual one-line passage, which not only clarifies the latent, background harmony, but also gives further proof of Bach's polyphonic thinking.

We have chosen eight measures from the Sarabande of the Suite in C Minor for Cello Solo, BWV 1011. There are no double stops. In our example, line (a) shows the original, line (b), its split-up into a four-part setting, line (c), a metric simplification of (b), and finally, in line (d), its reduced harmonic structure, omitting any suspensions, passing notes and other ornaments. Additions not directly substantiated by Bach's text are indicated with dotted lines; there are none in the line (d).

Bach's ability to express harmonic and polyphonic structures through a single line greatly stimulates the imagination of both the listener and the player. The listener is compelled mentally to fill in everything that is missing. This makes dealing with works of this kind an adventure and brings about what could be called "creative listening" to use a fashionable term. To be sure, an active co-creation of this nature does not always succeed. On first listening to Bach's solo works, someone who is unprepared frequently experiences a let-down. This sounds too meager, one thinks, and attention flags. The player is in a better position. As one studies the technical aspects of the works, one almost automatically comes to a more intensive understanding of their musical structures. One is increasingly challenged, not only from the standpoint of playing technique, but also intellectually and musically. When the solo sonatas are referred to as the "advanced school of string technique," this does not mean simply their immense technical difficulty. Everyone who plays a string instrument, even the average player, must expose himself to these works, must come to grips with them, even without ever intending to play them in public. They are seldom heard in the concert hall, in any case. When he wrote them, Bach himself must have thought of them more as works for private study than as performance pieces. This also explains the extraordinary dimensions of these works, which even today cause problems in public performances. The three Fugues from the solo violin sonatas and the Chaconne of the D Minor Partita have truly gigantic proportions. The Fugue of the C Major Sonata, BWV 1005, has 345 measures and the Chaconne, only one of five movements in that partita, lasted 15 minutes and 10

Example 44. Suite for Cello Solo in C Minor, BWV 1011, 4th movement,
Sarabande, m. 1–8.

seconds in Henryk Szeryng's interpretation!

We must go into greater detail about the fugues in the works for solo strings. In each of the three sonatas for solo violin the 2nd movement consists of a "major" fugue. The rapid 3/8 part of the Prelude of the C Minor Suite for Cello Solo, BWV 1011 (with the direction *très viste* in the lute version) must also be regarded as a fugue. But a fugue in any one-part composition is essentially a self-contradiction. Even with a Baroque bow, i.e. convexly curved, and with a flatter bridge, it is extremely difficult to play more than one line or voice on a string instrument. For this reason, Bach was compelled to repeat certain formulas within this Fugue, some of which are shown below (Example 45).

Example 45. (a) Sonata for Violin solo in A Minor, BWV 1003,
2nd movement, Fuga, m. 73–76
(b) Sonata for Violin solo in C Major, BWV 1005,
2nd movement, Fuga, m. 4–7
(c) Sonata for Violin solo in G Minor, BWV 1001,
2nd movement, Fuga, m. 18–20

In the cello work already mentioned there are virtually no polyphonic passages. Nevertheless, the movement is a fugue; this can be seen from its construction and is confirmed by the parallel version of the work as Suite for Lute in G Minor, BWV 995.

The difficulties of playing more than one voice on a single string instrument also explain why Bach regularly interrupts the *Ablauf* in these fugues by using complex concertante episodes of considerable length. This enabled him to free himself occasionally from the constraints of solo instrument polyphony: they are thus "divertimenti" in the true sense of the word. The result is a completely different organization than in the clavier or organ fugues. It should also be noted that the fugue themes are subject to change within the movement. As often as not such variations are a matter of playing technique.

Further Aspects of Three-Part Texture in the Chamber Works

We have found that a substantial portion of Bach's chamber music displays three-part texture. Only the few works for a melody instrument and b.c. are based on two parts.

Bach was not in the habit of presenting the three-part texture in its totality at the start. He holds back one of the parts and introduces it later. In this way the polyphony becomes more vivid. In the trio-like allegro movements he proceeds as follows: one of the two melody parts begins, accompanied by a simple b.c. Once it has introduced the theme, the second voice enters immediately, also with the theme, but this time in the key of the dominant.[12] If the structure of the theme requires it, this second entry of the theme is transformed according to the principles of a "tonal answer," i.e. the I and V degree of the tonic version (*dux*) are exchanged in the dominant version (*comes*); hence, the theme is not literally transposed. Bach takes this type of response directly from the fugue practice of his time, although the roots of the "dux-comes" changes probably go back several centuries (Example 46).

Example 46. Sonata for Viola da gamba and Clavier in G Minor, BWV 1029, 3rd movement, Allegro, m. 1–4

After a brief episode (divertimento), the bass, i.e. the left hand, brings the third introduction of the theme, again in the tonic, i.e. as "dux." As the movement develops, both "dux" and "comes" forms are employed. Occasionally other changes in the theme's intervals also occur.

This way of introducing the themes seems to correspond to the normal exposition of a fugue. Nevertheless, chamber music movements of this kind are not fugues, neither in the shape of their themes (we shall discuss this thoroughly in Chapter 12), nor in their development. Instead, Bach created his own unique form, specific to chamber music. When in his chamber music he writes true fugues, which he usually indicates by the superscript "fuga," the movements have a completely different appearance.

If we have trio structures whose bass does not take part in the thematic material as the movement develops, the third introduction of the theme is naturally omitted. Occasionally, the expositional tonic-dominant relationship is also dispensed with in favor of a freer harmonic use.

In slow movements, too, Bach only gradually develops the linear structure. Particularly beautiful results are achieved in those movements which we shall later call "fantasia movements" (see pp 113 ff.). The clavier part begins alone, often in three or even four parts, and is only later joined by the melody instrument, feeling its way as it were, tentatively. As examples we cite the 1st movements of the Sonata for Violin and Clavier in B Minor, BWV 1014 and in F Minor, BWV 1018. It may be argued that neither of the two movements has a three-part structure; nevertheless the tripartite grouping of the structure cannot be overlooked: the violin part, the complex of parts for the middle lines of the clavier, and the bass. If the slow movements correspond to the second, the "arioso" principle, we have a clear trio texture. The two melody parts then play the main theme one right after the other in imitation. Good examples of this occur where the melody parts proceed in strict canon, in the 3rd movement of the Sonata for Violin and b.c. in A Major, BWV 1015, or in the 3rd movement of the Trio Sonata for two Violins and Clavier in C Major, BWV 1037. At the opposite extreme are movements in which each of the three parts has its own, individual material. This is exemplified in the 2nd movement of the Sonata for Viola da gamba and Clavier in G Minor, BWV 1029, which departs from all conventions. A "normal" arioso movement would be something in between, perhaps the 1st movement of the Sonata for Viola da gamba and Clavier in D Major, BWV 1028, in which the two melody parts concertize with each other in an imitative manner.

There are also expositions of movements in which the two melody parts begin simultaneously with two thematic lines. The 4th movement of the Sonata for Violin and Clavier in B Minor BWV 1014 will serve as an example (Example 47).

Example 47. Sonata for Violin and Clavier in B Minor, BWV 1014, 4th movement, Allegro, m. 1–4

There could be some doubt here as to which of the two lines is dominant; either can stand on its own. The structure is similar to that of "simultaneous" fugues, i.e. fugues with two themes, double fugues, which present both themes simultaneously from the beginning. This similarity is confirmed by the fact that the beginning and the end of both lines in our example are not exactly identical. It goes without saying that in such cases the thematic lines represent double counterpoint. In trio movements, where the bass takes part in the theme, the three parts almost always form triple counterpoint; hence they all are interchangeable at will. Bach "tossed off" these things, as it were; his brain worked innately polyphonically.

Bach's ability to write contrapuntally was indeed without equal. We are continually fascinated by the linear construction of his chamber music movements. Even in the fugues of *The Well-Tempered Clavier* the individual parts do not move with such freedom, for here, as in the organ fugues, Bach was confined to that which could be played with two hands. However, many polyphonic traditions that reveal his ties to contemporary practices are discernible in the *Brandenburg Concertos,* and even more so, in the orchestral suites. Only in *The Art of Fugue* and the ricercare of the *Musical Offering* does he write as freely as he did in the chamber music. Anyone who has learned to listen attentively to one of Bach's three-part chamber music movements, to observe the articulation of each individual part is bound to be excited: this polyphony is so daring, so filled with surprises and delight at taking risks, at combining what appears to be impossible to combine. It is difficult to single out just one example, there are so many of them, but we will offer at least two (Examples 48 and 49).

With such counterpoint Bach leaves all his contemporaries far behind, Handel

Example 48. Sonata for Violin and Clavier in C Minor, BWV 1017, 2nd movement, Allegro, m. 12–16

Example 49. Sonata for Flute and Clavier in B Minor, BWV 1030, 1st movement, Andante, m. 89–91

included. It should also be noted that the upper parts in Example 49 are led canonically.

The examples cited are in three parts, in keeping with the topic of this section. Bach teaches us that all of a composer's structural needs can be met by three parts developed contrapuntally. Any additional part is not a plus, but a minus. A polyphony of four or more parts always creates a close dependence between at least two of the parts; the parts then no longer pursue independent ideas; they are not "real" parts, but instead one linear idea is split between two parts, or, in five or six-part compositions, even three parts. Bach's mastery of three-part writing reaches its zenith in his chamber music. And from that we can formulate the compositional maxim that *everything necessary can be expressed in three well-managed parts.*

But just how little such a principle expresses some kind of musical puritanism can again be seen in Bach's music. His imagination is never hemmed in by the limitation to three parts. He operates in this area with complete artistic freedom. Take, for example, the counterpoint of the main theme from the Finale of the Sonata for Viola da gamba and Clavier in G Major, BWV 1027. In the course of the movement no less than five different basses are created, constantly shedding new light on the theme. Bach begins with the following, relatively "normal" bass (Example 50):

Example 50. Sonata for Viola da gamba and Clavier in G Major, BWV 1027, 2nd movement, Allegro moderato, m. 1–8

The same measures in the corresponding version of the work, the Trio Sonata for Two Flutes and b.c., BWV 1039, contain a different bass, which does indeed behave like a preliminary study for the bass in the gamba sonata but nevertheless displays an individual profile (Example 51; the upper part is the same as in Ex. 50).

Example 51. Trio Sonata in G Major, BWV 1039, 2nd movement, Presto, m. 1–9

But to return to the gamba sonata. The bass has already changed when the second part enters (Example 52). A completely new bass line appears in m. 42–48 (Example 53), this time an agitated, nervous commentary on the theme. It is repeated several times. Bach seems to have been especially fond of it, which does not prevent him from inventing yet another bass line for the same theme. The latter does, indeed, approximate the beginning bass line (Example 50), but now it has shed all traces of "normality:" it has a much more casual relationship to the theme. It does not support it, but rather, diverts attention from it (Example 54). This bass line also appears again right afterward as a variant (Example 55).

Naturally, each new bass line also produces a change in the harmonic structure. It is absorbed by the third part, which is not included in our series of examples.

It should also be noted that the trio sonata version in Examples 52–55 also contains a slight variant in the bass line.

Example 52. Sonata for Viola da gamba and Clavier in G Major, BWV 1027, 2nd movement, Allegro moderato, m. 9–16

Example 53. Sonata for Viola da gamba and Clavier in G Major, BWV 1027, 2nd movement, Allegro moderato, m. 42–48

Example 54. Sonata for Viola da gamba and Clavier in G Major, BWV 1027, 2nd movement, Allegro moderato, m. 82–89

Example 55. Sonata for Viola da gamba and Clavier in G Major, BWV 1027, 2nd movement, Allegro moderato, m. 90–97

Chapter 12

Characteristics of the Themes

In this chapter we will attempt to find structural characteristics of Bach's chamber music themes and make ourselves fully aware of them. This should not be viewed as a comprehensive "study of themes", as desirable and even practicable as that kind of study might be. Since, however, current music theory has not yet furnished the groundwork for this vast subject, we have to limit ourselves to certain factors.

Genre-Specific Characteristics in the Theme

There is no such thing as *The* Bach chamber music theme; however, the themes of his chamber music works do exhibit traits that are not found in the themes of his other compositions, and thus seem to be chamber music-specific. These traits are not recognizable at first sight. Thus it seems reasonable to compare them with the themes of other groups of works, in order to bring our view into focus. It is the aim of this comparison to make a distinction between Bach's *personal style,* i.e. his general approach to themes, from the *genre style* of his chamber music themes.

The following groups of themes can be distinguished in his works along with those of the chamber music:

1. Themes from fugues of *The Well-Tempered Clavier*
2. Themes from organ fugues
3. Aria Preludes from cantatas, passions, etc.
4. Themes from the *Brandenburg Concertos*
5. Themes from instrumental concertos
6. Themes from two and three-part inventions

Every musician, and especially every composer, knows that the plan of a work and of an individual movement must already be laid out in the structure of its theme. A theme cannot just be transformed *arbitrarily* into anything: a sonata movement, a fugue, a rondo or a movement in song form. Likewise, the themes of a clavier concerto, a string quartet or a motet all have distinct requirements, each must have a different look. The masters of Viennese Classicism were obviously well acquainted with these requirements and proceeded in accordance with them. In subsequent epochs this knowledge seems to have become clouded; composers became stylistically unsure. That Bach was the one composer within the Baroque

Example 56.
Series I: 1. *The Well-Tempered Clavier* I, Fugue in G Minor, BWV 861
      2. Organ fugue in G Minor, BWV 535
      3. Prelude to the aria "Heil und Segen (no. 4)" from the cantata, *Gott, man lobet dich in der Stille,* BWV 120; (also in the cantata, *Gott, Beherrscher aller Dinge,* BWV 120a).
         The theme is identical with m. 1–12 from the 3rd movement of the second version of the Sonata for Violin and Clavier in G Major, BWV 1019a (see p. 34).
      4. *Brandenburg Concerto* No. 3 in G Major, BWV 1048, 1st movement
      5. Concerto in D Minor for 2 Violins and Orchestra, BWV 1043, 1st movement
      6. Three-part Sinfonia for Clavier, BWV 800

tradition who had the most comprehensive understanding of the problem and applied this to his works can be substantiated by the works themselves.

We shall now cite three series of themes from the groups of works we have listed. They are representative of their respective genre styles and were intentionally selected because their basic structures remain constant, i.e., each series proceeds from similar tempos, similar rhythms and similar ranges of expression.

The first series shows themes with mixed rhythms (Example 56). Series II contains "adagio" themes (Example 57). Series III shows "moving themes", which consist entirely, or almost entirely, of short, running figures (Example 58).

There are analogies in the chamber music for all the material in these examples. We shall select three chamber music themes which correspond to each of the series above, thus, in total, 9 themes will be compared (Examples 59a–i).

The following conclusions can be drawn from the material presented in the series of examples:

A. Characteristics of the themes of clavier fugues (Examples 56, I, 1; 57, II, 1; 58, III, 1):

    (1) Asymmetrical phrases: often expressed in an uneven number of measures, or, when the number of measures is even, feature asymmetrical groupings e.g., syncopations.

(at the places marked × there are long appogiaturas in the original)

Example 57.
Series II: 1. *The Well-Tempered Clavier* I, Fugue in C-sharp Minor, BWV 849
        2. Organ Fugue in F Minor, BWV 534
        3. *St. John Passion*, BWV 245, aria no. 58, "Es ist vollbracht"
        4. *Brandenburg Concerto* No. 1 in F Major, BWV 1046, 2nd movement
        5. Concerto in E Major for Clavier and Orchestra, BWV 1053, 2nd movement
        6. Three-part Sinfonia for Clavier, BWV 795

(2) The themes have a *contrapposto,* i.e. the idea at the beginning is complemented by a second idea as the theme develops (see I, 1; III, 1).

The contrapposto of the theme of the C-sharp Minor fugue from *The Well-Tempered Clavier* I, no. 4, is barely discernable. Such a highly concentrated theme of only four notes seems to have no room for it. I, however, see it in the ascending diminished fourth. In order to substantiate this, compare this theme with the similar B-A-C-H theme which appears in the last, unfinished fugue of *The Art of Fugue.* Bach gave the latter an additional concluding flourish, which serves as the contrapposto, for it could not be applied to the four notes B-A-C-H. In the C-sharp Minor fugue, however, such a procedure was superfluous because of the diminished fourth.

(3) The theme remains "open" at the end, i.e. it does not end with a cadence. Thereby, the "comes" and additional thematic entries are, as it were, pressed into service.

B.   Characteristics of the Themes of Organ Fugues (Examples 56 I, 2; 57, II, 2; 58, III, 2)

(1) Asymmetry and contrapposto, as in the clavier fugues. However, the rhythms and relationships are more regular than in the clavier fugues. This can be attributed to the nature of the organ, which does not permit accenting, so that shifted accents, e.g., syncopations, can only be realized in the simplest manner.

Example 58.
Series III: 1.   *The Well-Tempered Clavier* II, Fugue in G Major, BWV 884
2.   Organ Fugue in A Minor, BWV 543
3.   Cantata, *Ein feste Burg,* BWV 80, Aria No. 2, "Alles, was von Gott geboren"
4.   *Brandenburg Concerto* No. 6 in B-flat Major, BWV 1051, 3rd movement
5.   Concerto in A Minor for Violin and Orchestra, BWV 1041, 3rd movement
6.   Invention (two-part) for Clavier, BWV 775

(2) The themes are frequently drawn out longer than the themes of clavier fugues. The reason for this is not completely clear; perhaps it can only be sought in the northern German organ tradition—the long fugue themes of Buxtehude, for example.

C. Aria Themes (Examples 56 I, 3; 57 II, 3; 58 III, 3)

  (1) These are the longest of all Bach's themes. Their function is that of a prelude to the following aria, defining its range of expression. Consequently, they develop into full, and often even extended phrases. Never-

Example 59.

Series I: (a) Sonata for Violin and Clavier in C Minor, BWV 1017 2nd movement.

           (b) Sonata for Viola da gamba and Clavier in G Major, BWV 1027, 2nd movement

           (c) Sonata for Flute and b.c. in E Major, BWV 1035, 2nd movement

For Series II: (d) Trio Sonata in C Major, BWV 1037, 3rd movement

           (e) Sonata for Viola da gamba and Clavier in G Minor, BWV 1029, 2nd movement

           (f) Sonata for Violin and Clavier in G Major, BWV 1019, (3rd version), 4th movement

For Series III: (g) Sonata for Violin and Clavier in E Major, BWV 1016, 4th movement

           (h) Sonata for Violin solo in G Minor, BWV 1001, 4th movement

           (i) Sonata for Flute and Clavier in B Minor, BWV 1030, 4th movement

theless, since they lack any continuation elements they are still *themes* not *character pieces,* as one might think. This becomes evident when they are compared with suite movements. Sometimes Bach was content with only half a phrase before an aria, as in the well known soprano aria, "Ich will dir mein Herze schenken," (no. 19) from the *St. Matthew Passion.* In such cases he probably had reservations about making the introductions too long. The rest of the phrase then appears within the aria.

    (2) The *sequence technique* (see p. 132 ff) plays a more important role in aria themes than in other themes. This is obviously due to the greater length of the themes.

D. *Brandenburg Concertos* (Examples 56, I, 4; 57, II, 4; 58, III, 4)

    (1) Their themes, especially those of the 1st movements, have a more compli-cated, one might say, less clear, phrase construction than the aria themes. They contain "surplus" measures and true continuation elements. I, 4 has what amounts to an amorphous appearance.

    (2) More than other themes, they are made up of broken triads.

    (3) The rhythmic structure is homogeneous. For the most part, only a single rhythmic idea is pursued, so that no true contrapposto can occur.

    (4) Short, motif-like themes are preferred in the finales.

    (5) The themes of slow movements have more concentrated phrases than the themes of 1st movements.

The series of examples I to III intentionally include themes from a first move-ment (I, 4), a slow movement (II, 4) and a final movement (III, 4) from the *Brandenburg Concertos.*

E. Instrumental Concertos (Examples 56, I, 5; 57, II, 5; 58, III, 5)

    (1) The themes of the first movements are shorter and are more striking than their counterparts in the *Brandenburg Concertos,* as well as being more varied rhythmically. They nearly always feature regular phrases and clear cadences.

    (2) In slow movements extensive song phrases are employed more frequently as themes than in the *Brandenburg Concertos;* they resemble the aria themes.

    (3) The themes of final movements approximate those of first movements; this also is not the case in the *Brandenburg Concertos.*

F. Themes of Inventions

    (1) The thematic idea of an invention rarely goes beyond the scope of one motif.

It should be noted that the idea of the contrapposto, so important for fugue themes, is poorly developed in the aria themes and is not pursued at all in the themes of the Brandenburg and instrumental concertos. In the inventions there would not be enough room for it.

The next item on the agenda is to seek out the traits that distinguish Bach's chamber music themes from theme groups A to F above. We can list the following:

(1) In contrast to the fugue themes, the phrase construction of the chamber music theme is more regular and symmetrical.

(2) The contrapposto idea is only developed sketchily or not at all.

(3) The end of the theme has a clear cadential conclusion; hence, unlike that of the fugue, it is not "open."

(4) The rhythmic structure exhibits extreme variety. Bach obviously recognized that the small scoring and the intimate scope can render even quite complex rhythms intelligible.

(5) The themes in the slow movements are incomparably more imaginative than in any other class of themes.

This last thesis, which taken alone may seem somewhat of a generalization, needs further substantiation. There is a certain striking similarity—one could even say, uniformity—in the slow movements of Bach's other instrumental works. In contrast to this there are at least three distinct types of slow movements in the chamber music, which, of course, is reflected in the themes. These three types can be named and described as follows:

(1) The "Fantasia" type. Its themes are wide-ranging extending in great melodic curves. They are often richly provided with figurations, and one frequently detects hints of Baroque exuberance. An example is the Sonata in G Minor for Violin Solo, BWV 1001, 1st movement.

(2) The "Arioso" type. Its themes are not as extended as those of the "fantasia" group; they are more compactly constructed, arising out of repeatedly stated motifs. Their foundation is frequently a "running" bass line in equal note values. In contrast to the heightened expressiveness of the "fantasia" themes they have a relaxed, occasionally playful, serenadelike effect. Example: Sonata in D Major for Gamba and Clavier, BWV 1028, 1st movement.

(3) The "Intermezzo" type. Its theme is no more than a short, motif-like impression. Its phrasing and rhythm are virtually without contours. Example: Sonata for Viola da gamba and Clavier in G Major, BWV 1027, 3rd movement, or Sonata for Violin and Clavier in F Minor, BWV 1018, 3rd movement.

So much for the adagio themes. In the case of rapid movements, the distinction must be made, as in other genres too, between rhythmically profiled themes and themes of motion, (see series I and III). The former can be further subdivided into those with the character of a folk song and the more "artistically" constructed ones. Folk themes have simple diatonic intervals and uncomplicated phrases (Example 59b). "Artistic" themes have complexly interwoven phrases, a rhythm scheme full of contrasts, and in many cases are chromatic. Apart from this, they feature components which approximate fragmentation, shortening and dividing, in short, which come close to treatment as a development. This is unique in Bach's catalog of themes. It is most often encountered when there is a strong emphasis on sequences within the theme. The theme of the 1st movement of the Flute Sonata in B Minor, BWV 1030 (cited and analyzed on p. 116 ff.) may serve as an example.

Fundamental distinctions between the themes of first and second allegro movements of a church sonata cannot be made, with the exception of the three violin solo sonatas, which, as we know, always have a fugue as the 2nd movement. On the other hand, in sonatas with the movement sequence fast-slow-fast, the themes of concluding allegros are always substantially more compact than those of the opening movements—in the flute sonatas, for example.

Phrasing of the Chamber Music Themes

Themes are not simply "inspirations." Indeed, their creation presupposes a conscious, intellectual effort. For this reason, an even smaller unit, the motif, has been introduced in order to clarify the initial elements of a theme. It is said that a theme is made up of motifs. We shall not get into the pros and cons of such an approach, which does only superficial justice to the facts. However, even a motif does not simply fall from the sky in its final form; it too requires deliberation. Nor is it true that a few motifs strung together constitute a theme. Additional components are needed. One of the most important of these is the articulation of the line: phrasing. Before we go into detail, let us recall some of the principles of musical phrase construction. We are not often conscious of the formal aspects of music; yet this conscious awareness is needed to fully appreciate Bach's thematic art.

Musical themes are organized like the stanzas and verses of a poem. They are grouped according to lines, or, in musical terms, phrases (periods). Instead of *phrase,* the term 'song-form' is occasionally used. But this term is not clear enough, because it gives rise to incorrect associations. This phenomenon is related to "song," or even "folk song," only to the extent that folk songs also have phrase structures (and much less regular ones than is usually assumed). The "phrase" is the higher level, one might say archetypal, concept.

The basic model of the musical phrase consists of four lines. It rests on the principle of duality; both the individual line and the phrase as a whole consist of units of time based on the number 2 or multiples thereof. A model phrase would appear as following:

1st line = 2, 4 or 8 measures
2nd line = 2, 4 or 8 measures
3rd line = 2, 4 or 8 measures
4th line = 2, 4 or 8 measures

Accordingly, the sum of a regular phrase is 8 or 16 or 32 measures. There are also lines which consist of only one measure. In this case, the single measure is usually clearly divided into two halves; the sum of such a phrase would thus be 4 measures.

Every second line of a phrase concludes with a cadence or a half cadence. For this reason the first and second lines are occasionally called the antecendent phrase, the 3rd and 4th lines, the consequent phrase. Those readers who want a graphic illustration of this situation are referred to the simple example of the well-known song, "Kommt ein Vogel geflogen" (A Bird Comes Flying). It is a clear eight-measure phrase with 4 lines of two measures each.

A phrase construction of this kind is closely related to the organization of lines in a poem. The same archetypal structures are probably operating in both cases. To carry the analogy further, musical cadences would correspond to the end-rhymes in poetry. Likewise, the rhymeless verse of modern poetry would be analogous to the cadenceless phrases of contemporary music. In general, though, the phrases in poetry are more varied than musical phrases. Compare, for example, the musical with the poetic phrases in Schubert's song, "Meine Ruh ist hin, mein Herz ist schwer," from Goethe's *Faust*: Schubert declaims in a uniform manner; Goethe, however, is always variable.

However, our outline of musical phrases with 4 lines of two, four, or eight measures each is no more than a basic norm. It rarely appears in its pure form. One of the few examples is the Sarabande from the Suite in G Major for Cello solo, BWV 1007 (Example 60).

Example 60.
Suite for Cello solo in G Major, BWV 1007, 4th movement, Sarabande, (complete)

Phrases are usually significantly altered. The number of measures in an individual line is varied, lines are omitted or added; sometimes only parts of a phrase are considered sufficient. The distribution of motifs within the phrase is also important and critical to the final effect. We can only give a rough idea of the process here, but the phrases can have one, two, three, four or even more motifs. This makes possible an almost unlimited number of variants which composers have used as they saw fit. Schubert, for example, is tireless in his invention of new groupings; Verdi, on the other hand, uses almost nothing but the basic model. Although we did state that in comparison with poetry, musical phrasing tended to be less varied, it is anything but impoverished.

Bach's imagination in this respect is extraordinarily rich. He continually invents lengthenings, shortenings, re-arrangements, and other variants; his goal is to make the phrases more asymmetrical. In this he went farther than any of his contemporaries. To illustrate this, we present a few characteristic examples, the first of which is the theme of the 4th movement of the Sonata for Violin and Clavier in A Major, BWV 1015 (Example 61).

Example 61.
Sonata for Violin and Clavier in A Major, BWV 1015, 4th movement, Presto, m. 1–6

The theme is composed of 6 measures. The bracketed notes in the last measure are part of a transitional passage rather than belonging to the theme, but measure 6 itself belongs entirely to the phrase. The latter consists of 3 times 2 measures; thus, each line has 2 measures. Hence, 2 measures are lacking to make a regular phrase. If we ask which 2 measures Bach removed, we see that he deleted the 2nd line; the phrase consists only of the first, 3rd and 4th lines. To prove this we present the theme, adding the 2nd line (Example 62). Now it is indeed regular, but at the same time, it is so inane that it is obvious why Bach shortened it.

Example 62.

The following example is likewise taken from the sonatas for violin and clavier; this time, from the C Minor Sonata, BWV 1017, 4th movement (Example 63).

Example 63.
Sonata for Violin and Clavier in C Minor, BWV 1017, 4th movement, Allegro, m. 1–4, 9–16

Here the phrase of 8 (4 times 2) measures is not shortened, but lengthened from 4 to 6 lines. Bach achieves this by repeating the 3rd line (m. 9–10) twice; the first time as a direct sequence, (m. 11–12), the second by abbreviating the continuation of the motif (m. 13–14). The 4th line does not appear until m. 15–16. Moreover, Bach employs an additional artistic trick: at first he begins the movement with only half of the phrase, the antecedent phrase. He then allows the second melody part to begin with the same material in G Minor (m. 5–8), adding the continuation, the consequent phrase, only after this second entry. (This is the reason for skipping from m. 4 to m. 9 in our example, and likewise, for the transposition to C minor from m. 9 on.) Below we also give a corrected "regular" form for this theme; it is just as inadequate as the construction in Example 62. A third-rate Baroque composer might have written the theme this way—provided he had been inspired enough to come up with the beginning (Example 64).

Example 64.

One of the more interesting themes in all of Bach's chamber music is the main theme of the Sonata for Flute and Clavier in B Minor, BWV 1030, the last example we shall analyze. Its phrase is so asymmetrical, it deviates so very much from any norm or customary practice, that on first hearing it it almost seems to have come apart. First, we present the original form (Example 65):

Example 65.
Sonata for Flute and Clavier in B Minor, BWV 1030, 1st movement, Andante, m. 1–20. In order to facilitate this explanation, a special nomenclature was used. The 8 basic measures of the phrase are marked with Roman numerals, from I to VIII. Their repeated variants have the same numbers plus a superscript, i.e. I', II', etc. Inserted measures which do not belong to the phrase are marked with lower case letters a, b, c, etc.

The theme is composed of 20 measures in *andante,* hence very broadly conceived. The first 4 measures, to be sure, do not belong to the actual theme; they are immediately recognizable as a prelude. The real theme only begins in m. 5. The 1st and 2nd measures do contain the main idea, but it is interrupted in m. 3 in favor of simply continuing the accompaniment figure of the clavier (a, b). Bach probably did this to bring to the listener's attention the great importance this accompaniment figure was to have in the course of the movement (see the complete analysis of the movement, p. 143 ff.). But the first 4 measures of the sonata do not belong to the phrase of the main theme.

The real theme phrase thus does not begin until m. 5 with the repetition of I–II, after which it extends for 16 measures. However, these 16 measures are by no means grouped in the normal 4 by 4 order. The half cadence on the dominant which separates the antecedent from the consequent phrase is not in m. 12, but already in m. 10. Thus, we have an antecedent phrase with only 6 (instead of 8) measures. It is followed by a consequent phrase of 10 (instead of 8) measures, i.e. it is asymmetrical. The 6 measures of the antecedent phrase result from expanding the four-measure basic model: III (m. 7) is followed by a sequential variant, III' (m.

8), which, in turn, is followed by an interpolated measure (m. 9). It introduces a new, chromatic idea (c). IV, the actual conclusion of the antecedent phrase, does not enter until m. 10. Example 66, which is a reconstruction of the "original form" of the theme, will help clarify this arrangement.

The consequent phrase begins in m. 11. Its 10 measures likewise prove to be derived from a four-measure basic model (V, VI, VII, VIII), which first extends from m. 11 to m. 14, and then concludes with a full cadence in the tonic. This four-measure consequent phrase is then repeated in m. 17–20 (V', VI', VII', VIII'), although significantly altered and with new ideas. But as far as the phrase construction is concerned, these 4 measures constitute a repetition of the consequent phrase. Between these two four-measure passages of the consequent phrase and its repetition, there are two inserted measures, (d, e, m. 15–16).

The following outline gives us an overview of this complicated phrase construction:

Measure number	1	2	3	4			Prelude
Position in the phrase	I	II	a	b			
Measure number	5	6	7	8	9	10	antecedent
Position in the phrase	I	II	III	III'	c	IV	phrase
Measure number	11	12	13	14	15	16	
Position in the phrase	V	VI	VII	VIII	d	e	consequent phrase & repetition
	17	18	19	20			
	V'	VI'	VII'	VIII'			

This classification scheme shows that the 16 central measures of the phrase (m. 5–20) must be viewed not as 4 × 4 measures, but rather as 4 × 2 measures, supplemented by 5 repetition measures and 3 inserted measures. The following reduction of the theme to its basic form will help clarify this (see below, Example 66).

Example 66

The interpretation of m. 17–20 as a repetition and variant of m. 11–14 may seem odd, since they do contain some new material. But there is a total congruence between these 2 × 4 measures with regard to their phrasing; the structure of their internal rhythm is the same, and the full cadence in the main key B minor which appears twice, in m. 14 and 20, emphasizes the parallelism. Only a small experiment is needed to make the repetition character of these measures absolutely clear: all one has to do is to append m. 17–20 directly to the full cadence of m. 14. Moreover, the fact that the motif-idea in m. 7–8 is recapitulated in m. 17–18, gives this apparently "free" variant a firm anchor in the overall thematic structure.

One more thing: the phrase organization of the theme, already complicated, is further encumbered by the abundance of ideas with which Bach infuses it, making it even more difficult to gain a view of the whole. A second table, addressing the individual ideas, shows how rich they are: Example 67. Thus, within *one* theme complex we have no less than *five* clearly defined ideas, without including the variations. Neither the purely cadential measures nor the inserted measures a and b (m. 3–4) were taken into consideration. In the above table they are not yet given the status of independent ideas. We have already indicated that they become important as the movement develops.

Idea A (two measures); m. 1–2, 5–6

Idea B (one measure); m. 7, 8, 17, 18

Idea C (one measure); m. 9, 13 (inversion), 19 (sixteenth-note variation)

Idea D (one measure); m. 11, 12

Idea E (one measure); m. 15, 16

Example 67

The manner in which this largesse is tied together, how a dissolution of the theme has been avoided, can be seen in the distribution of the ideas in the individual measures. B and C appear in various places and function as brackets. By virtue of its two starts, A tends to lead the way. D and E are the only ones to be simply repeated.

In Chapter 16 the reader will find an overall analysis of this extraordinary movement (pp. 143 ff.) which contains even more inspirations than the ones enumerated in Example 67 under A–E. This piece simply cannot be studied enough. Philipp Spitta was one of the first to recognize that it had a special status in Bach's chamber music, stimulating, as it does, both the players' and listeners' intellect and imagination. Spitta wrote:

" . . . the greatest flute sonata in existence. . . . An imaginative structure that moves us like a great elegy. . . . The development unfurls from measure to measure, but it takes many unexpected turns, is more richly embellished, expanded when need be, especially by means of splendid canonic imitations which erupt as if impelled by the forces of nature. Especially stimulating is the effect brought about by the repositioning of individual phrases. . . . The form, modelled after that of an Italian aria, can be discerned at the beginning by the way Bach introduces the melody, tentatively then interrupts it after two measures, only to take it up again in the fourth measure. This is the way in which Bach frequently arranged his sacred arias."[13]

Linear Thematic Development

In addition to the time components of meter, rhythm and phrase, the theme also has a vertical component: the rising and falling of the line. These two dimensions are the primary determinants of the shape of the theme. Sonority and harmony recede into the background and are not genuine thematic elements, at least not in traditional music. In order to understand the linear element of a theme, its development in the lower and upper registers as well as the connecting of intervals must be isolated from all the other components. The method for doing this has been furnished by both the *cantus-firmus* theory and the twelve-tone system, both of which present the line in indefinite note values. The fugue theme of the 2nd movement of the Trio Sonata in C Major, BWV 1037, would, for instance, have the following appearance (Example 68): Of course, this is a purely theoretical proce-

Example 68.

dure which distorts the music; but it is useful for understanding themes as interval-skeletons of this kind, because the rise and fall and the quality of interval combinations are easier to identify. We see the alternation between stepwise progressions and larger intervals; we can see how one time the chordal principle derived from the third defines the linear development, another time it is stepwise progression, a third time, fifths, fourths, or sevenths or octaves. Diatonicism and chromaticism receive their full due. More importantly, the distribution of the culmination points and the balance between ascending and descending movement become clear.

Themes whose linear development is derived predominantly from triads and seventh chords are frequently found in the music of Classicism and Romanticism, but relatively rarely in Bach's music. But the 1st movement of the Sonata for Violin and Clavier in C Minor, BWV 1017, a Siciliano, has such a theme (Example 69). The beginning of the 1st movement of the E Major Sonata for Violin and Clavier, BWV 1016, was also derived from the triad.

Example 69. Sonata for Violin and Clavier in C Minor, BWV 1017, 1st movement, Largo, m. 1–6.

More typical are themes which only consist of stepwise progressions. The fugue theme from the Sonata in C Major for Violin Solo, BWV 1005, consists exclusively of steps except for the descending fourth between the 7th and the 8th notes. (Example 70).

Example 70. Sonata for Violin Solo in C Major, BWV 1005, 2nd movement, Alla breve, m. 1–3

A similar situation is found in the theme of the slow movement of the Sonata in A Major for Flute and Clavier, BWV 1032, in which the continuous stepwise motion is interrupted only once by the ascending third. (The sixth between m. 1 and 2 is insignificant, since it falls on the caesura of the repetition of the motif; Example 71.)

Example 71. Sonata for Flute and Clavier in A Major, BWV 1032, 2nd movement, Largo e dolce, m. 1–2

However, principles of formation are rarely encountered in such a clearly defined form (and indeed the traditional *cantus-firmus* doctrine prohibits it). Usually, they are broken up in some way, as in the ornamental embellishment of a strictly stepwise progression in the following example (Example 72). In this example the brackets indicate the run of seconds reduced to the basic line. Similarly, in the Siciliano of the Violin/Clavier Sonata in C Minor (see Example 69), stepwise progressions can be detected in between the chord notes.

Example 72. Sonata for Violin and Clavier in E Major, BWV 1016, 3rd movement, Allegro, m. 1–4 (K = Culmination)

More common and more interesting are occasions on which the various principles are intermingled. In the following example from the 4th movement of the Sonata for Violin and Clavier in A Major, BWV 1015, we recognize that the basic line ascends stepwise, then descends again starting with measure 4; (upper bracket); it is combined with skips of a fourth, fifth and sixth which have absorbed the chordal content. Finally, the example shows the limited extent of the lower line which is fixed first at e′, then at a′ (Example 73).

Example 73. Sonata for Violin and Clavier in A Major, BWV 1015, 4th movement, Presto, m. 1–5

Likewise, the highly interesting theme from the C Minor Sonata for Violin and Clavier, BWV 1017, 2nd movement, includes at least two lines as shown in Example 74. The upper line can be traced to a step progression (upper bracket). The lower line (lower bracket) has almost a bass character, although the theme does have a separate bass line, shown in small print. Thus we could speak here of an upper scale-like contour and a lower chordal contour, but this by no means exhausts the content of the theme. It has a number of additional intervals which have a constructive character:
(1) the ascending sixth (m. 3, 4, 5, dotted brackets);

Example 74. Sonata for Violin and Clavier in C Minor, BWV 1017, 2nd movement, Allegro, m. 1–5

(2) the corresponding thirds, C-E-flat ascending (m. 1) and F-D descending (m. 2, ties);

(3) the emphatically descending sevenths, G-A-flat and F-G (m. 3) from which is derived the descending seventh A-flat-B (m. 4, dotted ties), filled by a scale;

(4) the striking interval augmentation in m. 1: descending fifth, descending octave, ascending tenth (pointed bracket).

But the above examples, especially the last three, point to another factor which is of crucial importance for creating a theme: the establishing of a *culmination point.* By this we mean a note at the outer limit of the theme's range that usually occurs only once. In the examples above, such notes are marked with a K (=Kulmination); in Example 72, it is the C-sharp^3, in Example 73, the E^2, in Example 74, the A-flat^2. Culmination points can also appear as low points. Example 75, the theme of the fugue from the Trio Sonata C Major, BWV 1037, shows just such a case.

Example 75. Trio Sonata in C Major, BWV 1037, 2nd movement, Alla breve, m. 1–6

In the second movement of the Sonata for Flute and b.c. in E Major, BWV 1035, we also find a culmination point in the lower register (m. 4, 2nd eighth). And even in slow tempos there are examples of low points, thus, for example, in the beautiful Siciliano of the Gamba Sonata in D Major, BWV 1028 (m. 1, last sixteenth). The value of a culmination point depends on its correct placement. It must satisfy the balance of tension required by thematic development, which generally means the culmination note has to be in the second half of the theme. It can be the last note of the theme, or at the earliest, the middle note. A culmination note introduced too early dissolves the tension of the lines too soon; the theme loses its interest because it contains an unintentional asymmetry (in contrast to a resolved, deliberate asymmetry). Musical symmetry develops differently than architectonic symmetry. In music, the rise to the culmination must be longer than the descent from it, otherwise the structure will have an inadequate foundation (see illustration, Example 76).

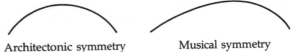

Example 76.   Architectonic symmetry   Musical symmetry

This can be explained by the way we hear things. As a temporal art-form, music obeys different laws than static architecture. A completely balanced line, perfected by its increasing rhythmic concentration, can be found in the following theme from the third version of the Violin–Clavier Sonata in G Major, BWV 1019, 4th movement (Example 77):

Example 77. Sonata for Violin and Clavier in G Major, BWV 1019, 4th movement, Adagio, m. 1

Interestingly enough, a culmination note which appears early, i.e. in the middle of the theme, frequently calls forth a second, contrasting culmination note. Consider the following example from the Sonata for Viola da gamba and Clavier in G Minor, BWV 1029, 1st movement: the low point, F-sharp, in the middle, is followed by a high point, A^1, shortly before the conclusion (Example 78):

Example 78. Sonata for Viola da gamba and Clavier in G Minor, BWV 1029, 1st movement, Vivace, m. 1–2

I have no doubt that Bach was familiar with these requirements for the construction of a theme and proceeded in accordance with them. After all, he was one of the most prolific inventors of themes of all time; thus, it was inevitable that he gather and apply the experiences of his craft, even if they were never set down in writing. But in any case, theoretical foundations in art always come after the fact.

A similar rule of the craft also exists for balancing the ascending and descending movement within a theme. It is evident in almost all of Bach's themes that these two directions are kept in balance. If the line ascends for a time, it is "intercepted" and immediately inverted by a descending motion. The two thrusts are complementary, interdependent and exist in a subtle balance which would be difficult to systematize. The rhythm of these alternating directions can be long or short. There also can be a general direction with many small ups and downs. In order to train the listener's ear for this balance of direction, we shall cite a passage written by Bach, but not from the chamber music. We are referring to the famous tenor aria with obbligato oboe and chorus from the *St. Matthew Passion,* "Ich will bei meinem Jesu wachen" (No. 26). Introduced first by the oboe, its principal theme is as follows (Example 79a): When the tenor takes over the theme, its second half is altered (Example 79b). Thus, during the descent after the culmination note G, a brief ascending counter-movement is interpolated: B^1 in the oboe part, A^1 in the tenor part. Now, it would be conceivable for Bach to alternate and intermingle the two versions, to apply variants, since the theme appears quite often. However, this does not happen; both versions remain neatly separated. It would have been impossible anyway. This can be confirmed by examining a hypothetical version containing B^2 and A^2, or another with A^1 and B^1, (Examples 79c and 79d);—both of them are much worse. Version (c), which lacks a counter-movement, is insipid; and version (d), with two counter-movements, is overloaded.

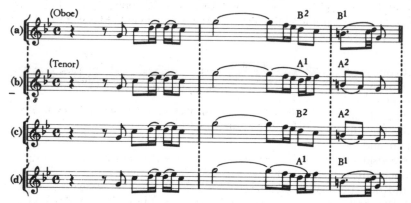

Example 79. Aria No. 26, "Ich will bei meinem Jesu wachen," from the *St. Matthew Passion*

A close study of Bach's thematic developments shows that Bach regularly applied this technique and that he had an unerring sense for the balance, the weight of these counter-movements. What we observed earlier; namely, that an early culmination note gives rise to another, opposing one, is thoroughly grounded in the principle of directional balance.

We could easily produce a long series of examples to confirm the principles of the culmination note and directional balance. However, we shall limit ourselves to one characteristic example which not only demonstrates the principles as such, but also shows how two themes, very different in form, still belong together; both of them follow the same structural concept, one "recto," the other, "inverso." We are referring to the two main themes of the two-part concluding movement of the Sonata for Flute and Clavier in B Minor, BWV 1030,—two themes whose relationship has often been suspected, but which has been difficult to prove. As we recall, the movement begins with a fugal Presto (a), followed "attaca" by a Gigue (b). We present both themes one below the other (Example 80):

From the second measure on, theme (b) descends to a low point (m. 4), then ascends again in m. 5 and 6. Theme (b) proceeds in the opposite direction: from the second half of the first measure it rises to a high point (m. 2, 3rd eighth), and then descends in the following measure. As regards the length, two measures of (a) cor-

Example 80. Sonata for Flute and Clavier in B Minor, BWV 1030,
(a) 3rd movement, Presto, m. 1–8; (b) 4th movement, Gigue,
m. 1–4

respond to one measure of (b); there is thus an exact correspondence between the phrases. However, this correspondence between upward and downward movement goes even further: within the thematic structures, both (a) and (b) exhibit the same rising and falling of short motifs, indicated by the dotted lines in the example. And finally, the culmination note in both themes appears twice: the low point F-sharp^1 in (a), and the high point G^2 in (b). Hence, the congruency between the two themes is considerable; (b) is, to a great extent, an inversion of (a).

In conclusion, we shall introduce two negative examples: themes which in my opinion did not succeed because the principles we have mentioned were not observed. We shall discuss elsewhere the problems of the last movement of the Sonata for Violin and Clavier in F Minor, BWV 1018. Its theme (Example 81) rises steadily, obviously lacking the balance afforded by a descending movement. This does indeed give it a rather excited quality, and Bach had to compensate for this one-sidedness with continually descending counterpoint (compare p. 140 ff.). Nonetheless, the movement still appears unbalanced. The second example is that of the Sonata for Violin and Clavier in E Major, BWV 1016, specifically the theme of its second movement (Example 82). Although its initial inspiration has the appealing quality of a folk song, as the movement develops it remains somewhat tepid and indecisive. The repeated C#^{2} cannot be viewed as a high point, nor the unimportant E^1 as a low point. I have often found that after the splendid beginning movement of this sonata, probably one of the greatest ever written, the 2nd movement is strangely colorless. The reason for this seems to lie in its thematic imperfection.

Example 81. Sonata for Violin and Clavier in F Minor, BWV
1018, 4th movement, Vivace, m. 1–4

Example 82. Sonata for Violin and Clavier in E Major, BWV 1016, 2nd movement, m. 1–7

Rhythm

Bach had an elemental sense of rhythm. The richness and variety of his rhythmic inventions have no parallel among his contemporaries or later. This can be sensed in a comparison with composers who came after him. Especially after about 1830, after the deaths of Beethoven and Schubert, the rhythmic inventiveness of most musicians became confined to a few formulas; the rhythmic palette did not begin to expand again until the 20th century, notable due to the work of Bartók, Stravinsky, and the early Hindemith. But it is an easier matter in this century; we are free in our choice of meters, whereas Bach, who never indulged in a change of time signature within an individual movement, was bound to a regular meter.

It is outside the scope of this book to develop a comprehensive system of rhythmics. The terrain is largely unexplored; our theory of rhythm is even less developed than our theory of melody. However, in order not to completely neglect this important field, we will at least attempt to point out some typical characteristics of Bach's rhythmic structure as they relate to his themes.

We can omit isorhythmic themes, i.e. themes which consist of absolutely equal values. In Bach's music they occur only in lively tempos and we have already referred to those as themes of motion. Normally, one of Bach's themes includes rhythmic values of differing lengths. In most cases, he begins with larger values which become progressively smaller. A good example is the theme of the 2nd movement from the Sonata for Violin and Clavier in F Minor, BWV 1018 (Example 83).

Example 83. Sonata for Violin and Clavier in F Minor, BWV 1018, 2nd movement, Allegro, m. 1–4

The same process is less tangible, but still evident in the 3/8 theme of the Prelude of the C Minor Suite for Cello solo, BWV 1011 (Example 84).

Example 84. Suite for Cello solo in C Minor, BWV 1011, 1st movement, Prelude, m. 28–35

The themes of slow movements show the same tendency (Example 85).

Here as elsewhere, the smaller values are first introduced on a weak beat, which, incidentally, meets a requirement of the "stilus floribus" according to strict contrapuntal theory. If, on the other hand, a larger note value falls on a weak beat, preceded by smaller values, the irregular flow of the syncopation is immediately noted (Example 86).

Only when there is clear cadencing can the rhythmic values at the conclusion be increased without bringing about such an effect. An example of this is the above theme from the 4th movement of the same sonata (Example 77), with the sixteenths entering at the end of the measure after being preceded by thirty-seconds. If we try the opposite, we are convinced: if thirty-seconds are also used in the last eighth of the measure, the theme immediately loses its concentration.

Example 85. Sonata for Flute and Clavier in B Minor, BWV 1030, 2nd movement, Largo e dolce, m. 1–2

Example 86. Sonata for Violin and Clavier in G Major, BWV 1019, 3rd movement, Allegro, m. 1–4

In the following theme from the 2nd movement of the Sonata for Violin and Clavier in A Major, BWV 1015, is it desirable to move into sixteenths in the 5th measure? The formula ♪♫♪♫ was rather severely overworked during the last three measures of the theme. But Bach's solution is surely the better one; for the following sixteenth-note counterpoint would be lose its effectiveness by more sixteenths (Example 87).

Example 87. Sonata for Violin and Clavier in A Major, BWV 1015, 2nd movement, Allegro, m. 1–5

The Sarabande of the Partita in B Minor for Violin solo, BWV 1002, twice progresses from large to small values, the second time with one of the quarter-notes in diminution (Example 88).

Example 88. Partita for Violin solo in B Minor, BWV 1002, 3rd movement, Sarabande, m. 1–8

The opposite direction, from a smaller to a larger value, is more difficult for the composer to master. The best way to control it is by adding small-value counterpoints to the large values. We have such a case in the theme of the fugue from the Partita in C Minor for Lute, BWV 997: from the moment the theme switches to dotted quarters, the counterpoint in eighth-notes is a virtual necessity (Example 89).

Example 89. Partita for Lute in C Minor, BWV 997, 2nd movement, Fugue, m. 1–3

Example 90. *The Well-Tempered Clavier* II, Fugue No. 6, BWV 875, m. 1–2

This kind of contrapuntal "smoothing out" is possible mainly in polyphonic works. This may explain why Bach preferred themes of this type in *The Well-Tempered Clavier;* he may have found them to challenge his skill (Example 90).[14]

The rhythmic balance that Bach employs in the 3rd movement of the Violin-Clavier Sonata in E Major, BWV 1016, is truly extraordinary (Example 91).

Example 91. Sonata for Violin and Clavier in E Major, BWV 1016, 3rd movement, Adagio ma non tanto, m. 5–8

After the sustained opening note he immediately begins with sixteenth-note triplets, which start with the lightest part of the measure in 3/4 time, the fourth eighth. Following a caesura, these sixteenths are advanced by two eights in m. 3; this increases their intensity, especially since there are two further triplets. After the second quarter in m. 4, the last measure of the theme, the urgency of the triplets is intercepted by a transition to simple sixteenths, and the syncopation acts as a brake.

It is plausible to argue that this example seems a little too calculated, too artificial. On the other hand, the rhythmic shape of the melodic line of the introductory movement of the E Major Sonata for Flute and b.c., BWV 1035, exhibits perfect balance, despite its diversity (Example 92). Yet another illustration is provided by the next example from the 1st movement of the Sonata for Flute and b.c. in E Minor, BWV 1034. Here the phrase and the rhythm are intimately interwoven (Example 93).

Example 92. Sonata for Flute and b.c. in E Major, BWV 1035, 1st movement, Adagio ma non tanto, m. 1–3

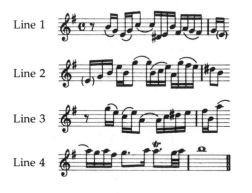

Line 1

Line 2

Line 3

Line 4

Example 93. Sonata for Flute and b.c. in E Minor, BWV 1034, 1st movement, Adagio ma non tanto, m. 1–5

Each of the four lines of the phrase has a different rhythm. The connection between them is preserved by the fact that the first three lines are based on the same shape. The 1st and 2nd lines are rhythmically almost congruent, with the exception of the feminine two-eighth ending of the 2nd line. The 3rd line shifts the rhythm by a quarter note, so that the syncopated figure ♫ now falls on strong beats. Moreover, the rhythm is condensed, so it can appear twice—the beginnings of the development principle. Only the 4th, the concluding line, goes its own way, cadencing and therefore in larger note values.

We have mentioned the feminine line ending, which falls on the unstressed, light beat. Its opposite, the masculine ending, falls on the stressed, heavy beat. Normally, these endings alternate within the phrase, but, as in poetic verse, there are many variations.[15] It is sometimes hard to realize how strong an impact changes in ending have on structure. Yet errors in the endings can directly affect quality.

We conclude our brief glimpse into the subject of rhythm with an example which illustrates this last point, the theme of the 2nd movement of the Sonata for Violin and Clavier in B Minor, BWV 1014 (Example 94a). If one of the line endings in this theme is altered so that *both* lines are either masculine (Example 94b) or feminine (Example 94c), the theme changes for the worse in both cases. Another alternative would be to switch the two endings, i.e. 1st line masculine, 2nd line, feminine (Example 94d); while this is workable, Bach's solution is unquestionably better.

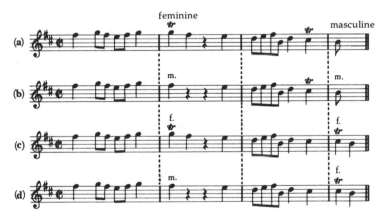

Example 94. Sonata for Violin and Clavier in B Minor, BWV 1014, 2nd movement, Allegro, m. 1–3

Chapter 13

The Middle Themes

In Bach's music there are also themes which only appear during the course of a movement, rather than beginning it. They are most frequently encountered in the middle (B) part of three-part movements. It is here that they show their most characteristic profile and draw the most attention. However, they can also appear in other places, within expositions or in the development of A parts.

When Bach introduces these middle themes, he is not concerned with thematic contrast in the Classical sense, as expressed, for example, in the themes of a Beethoven sonata. Bach is not trying to contrast them sharply with the opening theme. On the contrary, the middle theme is related to the opening theme and develops organically from it.

There are two reasons for introducing a middle theme. The first is that the main theme, after having been thoroughly explored, needs to be left for a while. The middle theme also provides the necessary distance from the main theme, which, when resumed, will have renewed vigor. This usually occurs in three-part movements. Examples can be found in the Sonata in A Major for Violin and Clavier, BWV 1015, 2nd movement, m. 30 ff., where a new idea in two voices introduces the B part (Example 95).

Example 95. Sonata for Violin and Clavier in A Major, BWV 1015, 2nd movement, Allegro, m. 30–33

In the last movement of the Sonata for Flute and Clavier in A Major, BWV 1032, there are several middle themes. This is more like a Bach rondo than a three-part movement and may be the reason for its abundance of themes (Example 96).

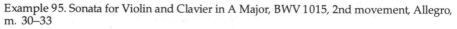

Example 96. Sonata for Flute and Clavier in A Major, BWV 1032, 3rd movement, Allegro, m. 53–54, 128–129, 136–139

In the B part of the 2nd movement of the Sonata for Viola da gamba and Clavier in G Major, BWV 1027, the middle theme is the inversion of the main theme, though shortened by a half. The middle theme of the Sonata for Violin and Clavier in G Major, BWV 1019, shows more profile (Example 97).

The second reason for a middle theme exists when the main theme itself does not have enough material to support an entire movement, or even part of one. In

Example 97. Sonata for Violin and Clavier in G Major, BWV 1019, 1st movement, Allegro, m. 22–25

this case, the main theme is supplemented by a middle theme. The process might be called an "emancipated contrapposto." We find this when main themes consist of purely triadic motion. Bach was undoubtedly aware that the material in the main theme was inadequate, and thus supplemented it with additional ideas. We shall cite two cases which are surprisingly similar, the Sonata for Violin and Clavier in G Major, BWV 1019 and the Sonata for Viola da gamba and Clavier in G Minor, BWV 1029, first movements. The two sonatas begin with a theme that consists of broken chords, and both times Bach adds an additional motif to the opening idea. The similarity between these two middle themes is striking (Example 98).

Example 98. (a) Sonata for Violin and Clavier in G Major, BWV 1019, 1st movement, Allegro, m. 9
            (b) Sonata for Viola da gamba and Clavier in G Minor, BWV 1029, 1st movement, Vivace, m. 9

These similarities could lead to the assumption that the two sonatas were written at very nearly the same time. Likewise, the 6th *Brandenburg Concerto* could be considered in this context, although the structural relationships between its main theme and the development of the movement are completely different. However, for the purposes of our study this question can be disregarded. In any case, a composer can obviously deal with the same problems over a period of years while at the same time working on other projects and challenges.

A special case is that of the middle theme of the last movement of the above-mentioned gamba sonata in G minor. Here Bach opposes the driving rhythmic main theme to a totally contrasting, true arioso theme, whose importance is emphasized even more by the fact that all polyphony suddenly ceases and the Clavier becomes a real "accompaniment" (Example 99).

Example 99. Sonata for Viola da gamba and Clavier in G Minor, BWV 1029, 3rd movement, Allegro, m. 19–22

We have here two diametrically opposed thematic positions in one move-ment; this would correspond exactly to the situation in the classical sonata. Still, we should not overlook the fact that the movement as a whole remains static in its con-tinuous motion. This is confirmed by the manner in which Bach handles his "arioso theme" in the rest of the movement, subordinating it to static principles. The counter subjects of double and triple fugues cannot be considered middle themes. Such themes always stand in conscious opposition to the theme which opens the fugue and comment on it in accordance with the rules of rhythmic complementation.

Chapter 14

Sequence Technique

Bach's frequent use of sequences, i.e. repetition of a phrase or a motif on a dif-ferent scale step, is obvious at first glance. He employs this technique not only in developing a movement, but often also within the theme. This technique was common practice in Baroque music; many composers used it to the point of becoming tiresome. Bach, however, avoids stereotyped, mindless sequences. Every situation in which he uses a sequence is different; he always seeks new points of departure. We also have the impression that he tested each idea he intended to use as a sequence, making sure in advance that it could support it and, when necessary, altered it so that a sequence had to occur as a logical development.
Bach usually used a sequence for the following reasons:
(1) Clarification of the congruence of adjoining parts of phrases (Example 100);
(2) To lengthen the regular phrase (Example 101);
(3) To create a contrapposto (Example 102);
(4) As a means of continuation or extension in the course of the movement (Example 103).
The reasons cited in (2) and (3) can coincide. Reason (4) is extremely common. If sequences already occur in the theme (reasons (1), (2) and (3)), they are always used outside the theme in the course of the movement. There are, of course, other reasons for using sequences apart from the four cited.

Structurally, sequences have the following characteristics:

(1) Their development is not simply horizontal, i.e. thematically linear, they are usually also paired with a vertical, harmonic sequence.
(2) Descending sequences are more common than ascending ones.

Without too much difficulty we can determine that a combination of the two characteristics can be found in those secondary seventh-chord sequences which are typical not only of Bach, but which, Brahms for example, was still fond of using and

Example 100. Partita for Violin solo in D Minor, BWV 1004, 4th movement, Gigue, m. 3–4

Example 101. Sonata for Flute and Clavier in A Major, BWV 1032, 1st movement, Vivace, m. 3–5

Example 102. Sonata for Violin and Clavier in A Major, BWV 1015, 2nd movement, Allegro, m. 1–5

Example 103. Trio Sonata in C Minor, BWV 1079, 2nd movement, Allegro, m. 59–63

Example 104. Harmonic plan

Bruckner made one of his main subjects in his lectures on harmony at the University of Vienna.[16] We shall now give a reconstructed example of a chord sequence derived from Example 100: the implied chords are the harmonic content of Bach's linear sequence (Example 104).

Descending sequences express a leveling, at times also a relaxation of tension. Ascending sequences, on the other hand, are always associated with progressively increasing intensity (see Example 102). This observation seems to support those theoreticians who speak of the "gravitational force" of music.

Of all the means available to the composer, sequences are most easily and immediately accessible. They confirm Stravinsky's insight into the importance of identity for musical development.

Chapter 15

Harmony

A comprehensive study of Bach's harmony would fill an entire book, as would a full description of his contrapuntal techniques. For this reason we shall have to be satisfied here with a reference to certain facts which are relevant to the chamber music. However, we should make it clear right from the outset that there is no such thing as harmonic usage found only in Bach's chamber music. What we are doing is merely using certain examples from the chamber music to provide an especially clear illustration of certain harmonic principles which are characteristic for Bach.

Over and above its intrinsic sound value, Bach's harmony has a second, decisive function: it clarifies the form, i.e. the course and the structure of a movement. Its individual parts are set off from each other by cadences; this gives both players and listeners an overview, so that they can orient themselves to the course of a work. Take as an example any very simple suite movement and follow the course of its harmony. Sarabande movements are especially well-suited because of their limited range and their simple phrase structure. Hence we select for our study the Sarabande from the first Suite for Cello solo in G Major, BWV 1007, which was reproduced in full in Example 60 (p. 115). It consists of two times 8 measures, thus it is a simple phrase with an antecedent and a consequent part. The harmonic course of this movement is as follows:

M. 1–4: Fixing of the tonic, G Major, by means of an excursion to the subdominant (m. 3) and a half cadence on the dominant (m. 4).

M. 5–8: Modulation to the dominant, D Major, and cadence in this key (m. 8). (Repetition of m. 1–8).

M. 9–12: Modulation to the relative minor, E Minor, and cadence in this key.

M. 13–16: Return to the tonic, touching on the subdominant (m. 13) and its relative minor, A Minor (m. 14); the latter is reinterpreted as the subdominant representative of the main key and introduces the final, concluding cadence in the tonic, G Major (m. 15–16).
(Repetition of m. 9–16).

This overall view shows us that every fourth measure there is a cadence, giving it a regular macro-rhythm, proportionate to the phrase, which thereby is rendered clearly audible and understandable. The keys employed are all closely related to the tonic, whose predominance is confirmed by the fact that equal weight is given to both dominant areas.

This procedure is fairly standard for the construction of all Bach's movements. Naturally, the sequence of keys in relation to the main key is not always the same. In movements in minor, the relative major may appear in place of the dominant. In long movements, more distant keys are employed. To be sure, a prominent place is always reserved for the relative major or minor. The harmonic balance in relation to the principal key is always maintained, indeed, with an intuitive sense of harmonic balance.

When the movements are longer and the proportions more difficult to comprehend, the harmonic cadences clarify the picture. They help distinguish between individual sections. We shall now give three examples of how the cadence is used in more extensive movements with a more complicated structure.

Trio Sonata for Two Violins and b.c. in C Major, BWV 1037, 2nd movement (Fugue)

Key: C Major.
M. 34–35: Cadence to the dominant, G Major.
M. 56–57: final cadence to the dominant (the cadence in 34–35 proved to be of a tentative nature).
M. 81–82: cadence to the relative minor, A Minor.
M. 90–91: cadence to the subdominant, F Major (beginning of the reprise).
M. 112–113: cadence to the main key.
    (M. 121–130: pedal point on the dominant.)
M. 140–141: final cadence in the tonic.

Sonata for Violin and Clavier in E Major, BWV 1016, 1st movement

Key: E Major.
M. 9–10: cadence to the dominant, B Major.
M. 13–14: cadence to the subdominant parallel, F-sharp Minor.
M. 19: cadence to the relative minor, C-sharp Minor.
M. 24–25: cadence to the tonic.
M. 33–34: final cadence in the tonic (before that, in m. 26–27, the subdominant, A Major, was also touched upon).

In direct relationship to the harmonic development of this movement is the bass part, whose measured majesty lends solemnity and calm.

    Even movements like the following one, interspersed with numerous modulations and touching on chromatically distant keys, is given structure by its primary cadences, a structure that can be readily heard.

Trio Sonata from the **Musical Offering** *for Flute, Violin and b.c. in C Minor, BWV 1079, 3rd movement*

Key: E-flat Major.
M. 7: cadence to the dominant, B-flat Major.
M. 10–11: cadence to the relative minor, C Minor
M. 17–18: cadence to the subdominant, A-flat Major.
M. 25–26: half-cadence on the dominant of the main key, B-flat Major.
M. 27–28: cadence to the tonic, E-flat Major.

    On rare occasions, Bach abandoned this principle. There are cases where the harmonies are free and rambling, in which the morphology of development is therefore difficult to trace. The 3rd movement of the Sonata for Gamba and Clavier in G Major, BWV 1027, can serve as an example. The material of its motifs consists of a relatively contourless sixteenth-note figure in both upper parts. Beneath them is a bass line of broken octaves in eighth-note motion. The entire movement consists of only 18 measures. The path of the harmony in the first 12 measures leads rapidly by means of chromatic modulation from the opening key of E Minor to F-sharp Minor, C-sharp Minor, G Major (V⁷), E Minor, F Major (V⁷), D Minor (cadence), G Major (V⁷), E Minor (cadence). This seems variegated indeed, but even here we can recognize a structural principle. The harmonies of m. 1–4 are transposed a fourth down in m. 8–11 and repeated. A comparison of the corresponding measures 5 and 12 is interesting. Bach uses the same linear material in both, but in m. 12 he has a Neapolitan sixth chord over the pedal point of the dominant: F Major over the bass B.

The remaining measures serve to confirm the E Minor tonic; the end brings a half-cadence on the dominant. The example shows the sequence of the harmonies of this movement reduced to pure chords. This structural plan clearly shows that Bach already knew and was able to apply what theoreticians later called *chromatic modulation,* something thought to have been first used as a means of modulation by Romantic composers. The bass lines in our example, however, are indistinguishable from the typical, chromatically descending "Tristan basses" (Example 105).

Example 105. Harmonic scheme of the 3rd movement, Andante, of the Sonata for Viola da gamba and Clavier in G Major, BWV 1027

The harmonic development of the famous Chaconne from the D Minor Partita for Violin solo, BWV 1004, is worthy of our attention for different reasons. Here Bach was unable to indulge in harmonic expansiveness; after all, the usual definition of "chaconne" is a sequence of variations on the basis of an unaltered harmonic scheme. The series of examples (Example 106) shows, however, that Bach by no means intended to hold strictly to the harmonic scheme. He changes it in almost every variation. For our example, 13 of these changes of harmony were selected. In setting them down, supplementary harmonic parts were added when it seemed necessary; they are not found in the original for reasons related to violin playing technique (Example 106).

Example 106. Harmonic scheme of the 5th movement, Chaconne, from the Partita for Violin solo in D Minor, BWV 1004

This series reveals something that one is barely aware of while listening: the constant harmonic fluctuation of the movement. The following should be noted:[17]

M. 32 ff.: An originally diatonic bass becomes a chromatically descending line. This kind of bass line occurs in many of Bach's other works.

M. 56 ff.: The stepwise bass line becomes a sequence of thirds. This idea is picked up again with the entry of the variations in major (m. 132).

M. 96 ff.: The descending bass becomes an ascending one. Later (m. 110–111), it likewise changes from diatonic to chromatic.

M. 104 ff.: From here on the progression of modulations is substantially expanded, in part by the chromatization of the upper part.

M. 116 ff.: New bass idea with a descending fourth.

M. 200 ff.: brand new chord sequence; the harmonic framework seems to be static, only the bass remains active. But having reached the lowest note on the violin in m. 202, Bach had to avoid the perhaps anticipated continuation (it is outlined in Example 107), arriving instead at a highly original solution which enabled him to lead the bass upward again.

M. 240 ff.: Now the bass has been reduced to no more than a cadence bass: fifths and fourths. For the first time in the entire movement, the harmonies change from eighth-note to eighth-note (m. 243), thus anticipating the imminent conclusion.

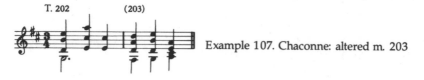

Example 107. Chaconne: altered m. 203

It is worth mentioning that the Neapolitan, i.e. the triad of the lowered second degree as a substitute for the subdominant, is used repeatedly, although it is not included in the scheme. However, Bach does not always employ it in the "textbook", i.e. sixth-chord form.

A good deal of the fascination with this chaconne comes from these harmonic metamorphoses. Every violinist who values an exciting rendition of this great piece must incorporate them into his or her interpretive strategy. Also, it would have been impossible for Bach to have built such a long movement on a stereotyped ground plan. Just to write endless variations of mere embellishments, which his contemporaries did for pages on end, was not Bach's style. The chaconne does have the simple cadence pattern, T-S-D-T-rel.m—S-D-T.[18] But Bach thought further ahead than all the theories of "functional substitution" (or whatever we call these terms that plague harmony students) could suggest. He developed a richness of harmony that could not have been foreseen.

In conclusion we should mention an example of harmonic daring which makes it clear that Bach's thinking was primarily linear. In measure 22 of the 1st movement of the Sonata for Violin and Clavier in E Major, BWV 1016, he does not hestiate to write a D in the violin part against the D-sharp of the bass. Thus we hear simultaneously d^2 plus d-sharp and (low) D-sharp. In order to avoid the tritone in the violin part, he accepts not only the "impure" chord, but also (in the violin part itself) the diminished octave d^2—d-sharp^1. There are many such cases in Bach's music, the most extreme probably being m. 9–10, 20–21 and 31–32 in the 2nd movement of the 1st *Brandenburg Concerto* in F Major, BWV 1046. When A-flat and A, B and B-flat, E-flat and E are heard simultaneously, many a listener has taken it to be a mistake by the players.

Chapter 16

Development and Use of the Material in Rapid Sonata Movements

Rapid sonata movements offer the most varied examples showing interesting uses of the kind of material we have become familiar with. We already know that, along with thematic quotations, these movements contain divertimento-like interludes, whose task it is to create distance from the themes. The material of such divertimenti can come from various sources. Bach often takes it from the theme itself, as, for example, in the last movement of the Sonata in B Minor for Violin and Clavier, BWV 1014 (Example 108).

Example 108. Sonata for Violin and Clavier in B Minor, BWV 1014, 4th movement, Allegro, m. 13–15

The part which carries this episode, the bass, comes from the fourth measure of the theme. The relationships, however, are not always so direct. In the 2nd movement of the same sonata the material for the divertimento is taken from the inversion of the fourth measure of the theme, a measure which appears to be quite insignificant within the theme (Example 109).

Example 109. Sonata for Violin and Clavier in B Minor, BWV 1014, 2nd movement, Allegro, (a) m. 4, (b) m. 19–20

Elsewhere Bach creates something completely new that cannot be detected in the theme or its counterpoints. The divertimenti from the last movement of the G Major Sonata for Viola da gamba and Clavier, BWV 1027 are an example of this (Example 110). This divertimento involves no more than simple broken chords. The divertimenti in the 2nd movement of the E Minor Sonata for Flute and b.c., BWV 1034, come about in the same way. There are also examples in other movements of how the divertimento's purpose of providing release and distance is reduced to mere chordal motion. But Bach still makes such situations more interesting by exchanging parts when they are used repeatedly.

Example 110. Sonata for Viola da gamba and Clavier in G Major, BWV 1027, 4th movement, Allegro moderato, m. 26–29

The situation is entirely different when the divertimenti contain new ideas. We have an instructive example of this in the 4th movement of the Sonata for Violin and Clavier in F Minor, BWV 1018. Here Bach needs numerous divertimenti. He first proceeds from the counterpoint of the main theme, which consists of a descending scale (Example 111).

In the first divertimento he fashions the scale into intertwined runs using contrary motion (Example 112).

Here we recognize yet another connection between the rhythm of the right hand of the clavier and the first measure of the thematic counterpoint (see Example 111). On the other hand, the violin figure from m. 9–10 (see Example 112) becomes independent and provides material for a new divertimento (Example 113). But

Violin (counterpoint)

Clavier (theme)

Example 111. Sonata for Violin and Clavier in F Minor, BWV 1018, 4th movement, Vivace, m. 5–8

Example 112. Sonata for Violin and Clavier in F Minor, BWV 1018, 4th movement, Vivace, m. 9–12

Example 113. Sonata for Violin and Clavier in F Minor, BWV 1018, 4th movement, Vivace, m. 43–48

Example 114. Sonata for Violin and Clavier in F Minor, BWV 1018, 4th movement, Vivace, m. 29–32

Example 115. Sonata for Violin and Clavier in F Minor, BWV 1018, 4th movement, Vivace, m. 33–38

Example 116. Sonata for Violin and Clavier in F Major, BWV 1018, 4th movement, Vivace, m. 61–66

before that there was yet another divertimento motif (Example 114). Immediately after this, beginning with m. 33, it continues as follows (Example 115).

After the theme is quoted again in C Minor, m. 55–58, a new divertimento appears in m. 61–62 (Example 116):

Such an abundance of ideas within a relatively short movement seems like almost too much of a good thing. The result is a confusing combination of contrapuntal lines, which all but overwhelms both players and listeners. Perhaps Bach felt that the main theme of the movement (we might call it resolutely syncopated and twisted, struggling upward without relief—see p. 125) was too artificial and inflexible; hence he tried to loosen it up with a number of new divertimento ideas.[19]

In these sonata da chiesa allegros the themes themselves always have a focusing effect. The *Ablauf* is concentrated in them and decisive stages are reached. A theme may indeed take us by surprise at times, but we always understand why it is there. It does not sound haphazard, but rather serves as a guidepost which leads us through the movement. This guidepost feature is also seen in the choice of keys for individual thematic quotations. This corresponds to the disposition of cadences dealt with in Chapter 15 and guarantees that the movement will be logical and balanced.

It may come as a surprise that, apart from the alternation between themes and divertimenti, almost nothing happens in these movements. With the exception of a couple of cadential measures, there are virtually no free episodes. Bach handles his material with extraordinary economy. Even when placed in constantly changing relationships, the themes and divertimenti seldom are materially changed. An exception is the contrapuntal exchange of voices. In chamber music, Bach's poly-phonic three-part texture actually always appears as three-part counterpoint. Moreover, he varies the lengths of both the divertimenti and the themes; an idea that originally had six measures may be reduced to four or three measures, or, con-versely a motif can, in the course of the movement, grow into a theme and be extended in length.

Yet it would be wrong to view Bach's construction of movements as merely arranging and rearranging its parts, like moving men on a chessboard. This is con-tradicted by the vitality and energy radiating from the various units and by the fact that they arouse immediate interest in every listener, even the naive and the unprepared. It is also contradicted by the fact that no two situations are ever the same. The themes and divertimenti are constantly cast in a new light; Bach manages it so that we hear them from different perspectives. This lends the movements their powerful, impelling energy, their sense of necessity. If a major portion of the art of musical composition consists in knowing how much can be yielded by the material one is working with, how much can be extracted from it, how much space it needs to unfold, but also when it is exhausted and cannot be forced any further—then, in this respect, Bach is one of the greatest of composers. When a Bach movement comes to an end, everyone knows that the possibilities have been exhausted; nothing more can be said. For this reason, too, Bach never found it necessary to write grandiose conclusions.

To prove Bach's use of economic and concentrated compositional techniques, we shall next present a complete analysis of two allegro movements. We have selected a simple movement for melody instrument and b.c. with little composi-tional material, and a more complicated movement with a trio structure and an abundance of material.

Table 1
Analysis of the 4th Movement of the Sonata for Flute and b.c. in E Minor, BWV 1034

The top line gives the measure numbers. The two lower lines contain the analytical tabulation of the musical material, flute above, b.c. below. If there is only one lower line, the bass line belongs to the flute part and requires no separate analysis.

Roman numerals I, II, and III, etc., indicate the measures of the thematic phrase. The lower case letters, a, b, c, etc., denote divertimento measures. Superscript Arabic numbers (for example, 1^1) denote variants of the measures in question. A superscript lower case 'i' (for example, I^i) denotes an inversion of a measure. Measures marked with a 'K' are pure cadence measures with no apparent relationship to the motifs.

If there is a line and a '2' beneath a signature (i.e. $\frac{1}{2}$), this means that only half of the material is being used, i.e. only one part of a two-part structure.

1	2	3	4	5	6	7	8	9	10	11	12	13
I	I	II	III	IV	V	VI	VI^1	VII	VIII	IX	X	a

cadence (canon:) [spanning 10–12]

14	15	16	17	18	19	20	21	22	23	24	25	26
b	a	b	a	b	I^1	I^1	I^1	I^1	I^2	I^2	I^2	I^2
a	b	a	b	a	b	b	b	b	I^2	I^2	I^2	I^2

27	28	29	30	31	32	33	34	35	36	37	38	39
V^1	V^1	V^1	continu. V^1, last quarter				K	K	I	I^3	V^2	V^2
I^3	I^3	I^3	b augmented								I^4	I^4

40	41	42 :‖	: 43	44	45	46	47	48	49	50	51	52
V^2	K	K :‖	: I^i	VIII^1	VIII^1	I^i	VIII^1	VIII^1	II	II	II	II
I^4									I	I	I	I

53	54	55	56	57	58	59	60	61	62	63	64	65
I^2	I^2	I^2	I^2	b	a	b	a	b	a	b	a	b
I^2	I^2	I^2	I^2	a	b	a	b	a	b	a	b	I^2
	exchange of parts											2

66	67	68	69	70	71	72	73	74	75	76	77	78
b	b	b	I^2	I^2	I^2	I^2	V^1	V^1	V^1	continu. V^1, last quarter		
I^2	I^2	I^2	I^2	I^2	I^2	I^2	I^3	I^3	I^3	b augmented		
2	2	2		as m. 23–26								

79	80	81	82	83	84	85	86	87	88 :‖
. . . . .	K	K	I	I^3	V^2	V^2	V^2	K	K :‖
. . . . .					I	I	I^4		
					2	2			

There may be some differences about how the thematic phrases are analyzed. IV might be seen as a recapitulation of I. On the other hand, the last quarter of IV already anticipates V. VII and VIII could also be continuations of VI; in that case, IX and X would have to be marked 'VII' and 'VIII,' and we would then have an eight-measure phrase as the basic structure of the theme. However, for interpreting the movement as a whole, these distinctions are insignificant.

Table 2
Analysis of the 1st Movement of the Sonata for Flute and Clavier in B Minor, BWV 1030

This movement is one of the richest and most interesting movements in Bach's chamber music.

M. 1–20 in the table correspond to the thematic analysis on pp. 117 ff. Everything else corresponds to the legend for Table 1. Only the dual division of the analysis line has a different meaning here: it refers to the two *melody* parts; top line = flute, bottom line = right hand of clavier part. If there is only one analytic line, the two melody parts form a unit (exchange of parts is not taken into account). There is no need for a separate bass line, since the bass takes no part in the thematic work, with the exception of two measures, which are specially marked in the table.

The length of the sections being analyzed should be noted. They do not always correspond to the lengths of the measures; this identifies the various lengths of the motifs. The capital letters A, B or A¹, B¹ found above the measure number at the beginning, middle and end refer to the overall developmental scheme, depending on whether it is based on a three-part (A-B-A) of a two-part (A¹–B¹) structure.

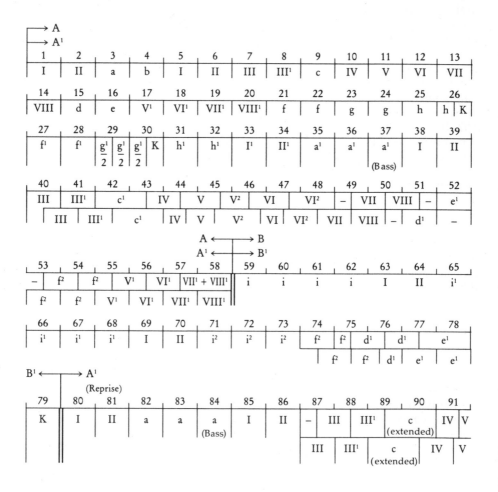

| → A | | | | | | | | | | | | |
| → A¹ | | | | | | | | | | | | |
1	2	3	4	5	6	7	8	9	10	11	12	13
I	II	a	b	I	II	III	III¹	c	IV	V	VI	VII

14	15	16	17	18	19	20	21	22	23	24	25	26
VIII	d	e	V¹	VI¹	VII¹	VIII¹	f	f	g	g	h	h ǀ K

27	28	29	30	31	32	33	34	35	36	37	38	39
f¹	f¹	$\frac{g^1}{2}$ ǀ $\frac{g^1}{2}$ ǀ $\frac{g^1}{2}$ ǀ K		h¹	h¹	I¹	II¹	a¹	a¹	a¹ (Bass)	I	II

40	41	42	43	44	45	46	47	48	49	50	51	52
III	III¹	c¹	IV	V	V²	VI	VI²	–	VII	VIII	–	e¹
	III	III¹	c¹	IV	V	V²	VI	VI²	VII	VIII	– ǀ d¹	–

| A ←——→ B |
| A¹ ←——→ B¹ |

53	54	55	56	57	58	59	60	61	62	63	64	65
–	f²	f²	V¹	VI¹	VII¹ + VIII¹	i	i	i	i	I	II	i¹
f²	f²	V¹	VI¹	VII¹	VIII¹							

66	67	68	69	70	71	72	73	74	75	76	77	78
i¹	i¹	i¹	I	II	i²	i²	i²	f²	f²	d¹	d¹	e¹
								f²	f²	d¹	e¹	e¹

| B¹ ←——→ A¹ |
| (Reprise) |

79	80	81	82	83	84	85	86	87	88	89	90	91
K	I	II	a	a	a (Bass)	I	II	–	III	III¹	c (extended)	IV ǀ V
								III	III¹	c (extended)	IV	V

92	93	94	95	96	97	98	99	100	101	102	103	104
V	V²	VI	VI²	VII	VIII	–	d	–	f	f	i³	i³	i³
V	V²	VI	VI²	–	VII	VIII	–	e	–	f	f		

105	106	107	108	109	110	111	112	113	114	115	116	117
i³	i²	i²	i²	V¹	VI¹	VII¹	VIII¹	d¹	e¹	e¹ Variant	V¹	VI¹
				V¹	VI¹	VII¹+VIII¹	d	e		e¹ Variant	V¹	VI¹

B ←
A¹ ←

118	119
VI¹	VII¹ + VIII¹
VII¹	VIII¹ ‖ Fine

A mere tabulation of such a richly imaginative movement may seem strange—nothing more than a systematization of data. But it is indispensable if one wants to see at a glance how each individual measure is part of an overall idea, even in such a long movement. We shall give a few more particulars.

Our last statement seems to be contradicted by m. 59–62. The flute triplets become merely mechanical, the clavier is reduced to a contourless b.c. accompaniment, and the three-voice texture is abandoned: all in all, the measures seem like empty filler. Such a view, however, is superficial. First, it should be noted that the same episode appears two more times, slightly altered each time, in m. 65–68 and 102–105. Thus, the measures in question have an architectonic significance and are certainly not used as fillers. Their motivation had already been furnished before m. 59, having been set up in m. 25–26 and 31–32. Nevertheless, the sense of absolute "newness" of this triplet idea in m. 59–62 can be explained as follows: in the middle of the movement there is a distinct caesura, the cadence in F-sharp Minor, m. 58. It divides the movement into two nearly equal halves, 58: 61 measures. Overwhelmed by such an abundance of ideas in the first half of the movement, the listener needs relief as the second half begins. Hence Bach puts in here the inconsequential "filler" measures. Only after these are finished are we ready to hear the main theme again, this time in the submediant G Major. The same procedure is repeated again: the four triplet measures, 65–68, followed again by the main theme, this time in the subdominant (E Minor). The trio episode thus plays a true divertimento role. To emphasize this, Bach eschews polyphony when this divertimento begins. At this moment he bows to psychological necessity: he allows the listener to relax for a few measures. Later on, when the divertimento appears for the second and third times, this need is not so pressing. He can indulge in a bit of counterpoint again, although it is rather modest in comparison to the polyphony in the rest of the movement.

Apart from the five main ideas shown on p. 119, which come from the basic theme, Bach now offers another highly interesting idea. The first is the divertimento, which takes over in m. 21 after the main theme has been completed (Example 117).

For a divertimento theme, the idea is almost too individualized. In fact, it becomes increasingly significant as the movement progresses. After entering in m.

Example 117. Sonata for Flute and Clavier in B Minor, BWV 1030. 1st movement, Andante, m. 21–22

21–22, it is continued by a motif we already know: it is the "accompaniment" of the main theme, all that was left when the flute suddenly paused in m. 3 and 4. This accompaniment is now elevated to the status of a thematic component. Thereafter, it easily gives rise to the first motivation of the triplet divertimento, namely in the 4th quarter of m. 23, in the 4th quarter of m. 24, and in m. 25–26.

Especially striking is the frequent canonic writing in both upper parts. Canonic voice leading always intensifies the material. The divertimento cited in Example 117 is treated twice as a canon, in m. 53–54 and in m. 100–101; in both places a pedal point is written beneath. M. 11 and 12 of the main theme also appear as a canon, in m. 44–48 and m. 91–95. In so doing, Bach proceeds with special artistry: he gives alternate precedence to the parts, so that there is not a continuous canonic structure, as one might expect, but a continuing overlapping (Example 118).

Example 118. Sonata for Flute and Clavier in B Minor, BWV 1030, 1st movement, Andante, m. 44–48

The chromatic components of the main theme are also included in this canonic treatment, for example in m. 42–44. Bach provides a certain fascination here by keeping each part in its "real" key rather than making use of a half-tone, "tonal," freedom, with the result that each part cadences in a different key (Example 119).

Example 119. Sonata for Flute and Clavier in B Minor, BWV 1030, 1st movement, Andante, m. 42–44

One might think that these canonic structures sufficiently demonstrate Bach's contrapuntal skill, but his imagination in this area is inexhaustible. He changes the temporal distance between the two canonic parts from theme to theme and from situation to situation. At times they are separated by a full measure, for example, in m. 48–50; at times, the interval is only a half measure, as in m. 42–44; indeed, there is even an interval of a single quarter note (compare Example 118). He avoids any uniformity in the polyphony.

The only motif that Bach incorporates into the bass line is the idea that consists of groups of two sixteenths connected by legato ties; we already made its acquaintance during our study of the main theme (m. 19 from Example 65, p. 117). There we recognized it as a variant of the ninth measure of the theme. Indeed, the idea of pairs of tied sixteenths can be found even earlier, namely, in the "accompaniment figure" in m. 3, although here Bach neglected to write in the ties. In the version of m. 3, the idea appears for the first time in the bass line (Example 120), and it is from this that all the related bass lines, which we perceive both before and afterwards, derive their significance: m. 16, 43–44, 48–52, 76–78, 84, and so on. This sixteenth-note pattern is a Bach "archetype;" we know it well from the cantatas and the passions.

Example 120. Sonata for Flute and Clavier in B Minor, BWV 1030, 1st movement, andante, m. 37 (phrasing added)

It is a wonder that the movement does not collapse beneath its extraordinary abundance of ideas. Although on first hearing or playing it one may feel confused, afraid of losing the thread, Bach easily leads us back to the main idea. He disposes of his material with a light touch, tying it all together in a straightforward, comprehensible developmental scheme. As we have seen, the movement has two parts, with a caesura clearly dividing the two halves in m. 58 (cadence in F-sharp minor).

The second half, beginning with m. 59, is only 3 measures longer than the first part of the movement, which is comprised of 119 measures in all. But this second part is in turn divided in two. The caesura is in m. 79, where we find a half cadence to the tonic, which completely interrupts the motion. (Of course, this half-cadence in the first two quarter notes of the flute part has to be imagined as ornamented.) After that an unmistakable reprise ensues. It is 21 measures shorter than the 58 measure exposition (A). Obviously its material has to be compressed in the reprise. Bach accomplishes this by not adopting the very first presentation of the theme (m. 1–20), but rather the second, from m. 38–54, and transposing it back from F-sharp minor into B minor. This is the genesis of measures 85–100. In the process the important divertimento theme from m. 21 ff. is inserted into the theme at m. 100–101, in place of the repetition of the consequent phrase of the theme (compare the thematic analysis of m. 17–20). Having thus been elevated to the status of a component of the main theme, its divertimento function disappears. However, the variant of the consequent part of the theme (m. 17–20), which was skipped over, has not been forgotten. We have already encountered these measures (55–58) a second time. When they have all but vanished from our memory, they appear suddenly in the reprise as m. 109–112. This makes their powers of recapitulation all the stronger.

But again things turn out differently than they did before. In m. 102 Bach abruptly had left the main theme complex and for 7 measures turned to the triplet divertimento. The effect of this extends into the consequent phrase variant which begins in m. 109.

One is tempted to see in this last, extremely artful interweaving of ideas starting with m. 102, which could be called a *coda*, a highly concentrated retrospective of the entire second half of the movement (B). But Bach retracts this artfulness again in an admirably simple manner. Once more he brings in the variation of the consequent phrase, this time without triplets, but still in canon and finally leads into the last measures of the main theme. Here the powerful movement ends in a touchingly unpretentious manner.

We can see from the following developmental scheme that the movement combines a two and three-part structure. The two-part form, indicated by 'A' and 'B', proceeds from the caesura in m. 58; the three-part form, indicated by 'A¹', 'B¹', and A¹, comes from the reprise, which begins in m. 80.

Developmental Scheme

M. 1–58: A^1 = A (58 measures)
M. 59–79: B^1 ⎫
M. 80–119: A^1 (reprise)   ⎬ = B (61 measures)

From our modern perspective, Bach's technique of constantly arranging his compositional material into new groupings appears to be a "manipulation" of the listener. Bach plays with his partners psychologically, he wants to constantly reawaken their interest so that they will continue to pay attention. The craftsman-like methods of the techniques with which he accomplishes this can be seen in the Flute Sonata in B Minor and summarized as follows:

(1) Bach extracts individual parts and measures of phrases from the *Ablauf.*
(2) New phrases often come from this, individual parts of which derive from different ideas.
(3) The phrase is preserved as a whole, but is varied by the displacement of individual parts.

Other compositional means, independent of the development of the phrases:

(4) The material is contrapuntally condensed.
(5) Ideas already familiar are supplemented by new counterpoints, new bass lines, new subordinate parts.
(6) The harmonic structure is varied (the use of pedal points belongs here).

Techniques (5) and (6) could only be hinted at in our table, if considered at all. But they can be easily found by comparing the tables with the score.

This concludes our analysis of the movement. One might come away with the impression that this is an unusually complicated movement. On the contrary, the flow of the music is always completely unconstrained, with no trace of any constructivistic effort. The greatness of this music overpowers by its naturalness.

Chapter 17

Other Structures of Movements

Slow Sonata Movements

In slow sonata movements, it is more difficult to recognize the distinction between thematic and divertimento material than in fast sonata movements. The former have the tendency to continuously develop their beginning themes, so that we might speak of *endless melodies,* broken up only by cadences. But our earlier division of slow movements into the "fantasia," the "arioso" and the "intermezzo" types (see pp. 113 ff.) can help us recognize the differences in the way their *Ablauf* is structured.

The "fantasia" type essentially has no divertimenti at all. It thrives on the further development of its opening theme, which Bach cultivates into large, vaulting melodies with an extensive range. He was fond of elaborating such structures with Baroque figuration, which makes them seem boundless. However, the total picture is never lost sight of and the direction of the basic melodic line remains concentrated, its contours preserved. A good example of this would be the opening movement of the Sonata in G Minor for Solo Violin, BWV 1001.

In "arioso" movements, the connection to the opening theme can be looser. They have measures and groups of measures which could be considered divertimenti, although they do not have the obvious function of breaking things up to which we are accustomed in rapid movements. To give one example: in the 3rd movement (Andante) of the Sonata for Gamba and Clavier in D Major, BWV 1028, m. 6, 12, 17 and 21 show a tendency to withdraw from the theme (which then always returns with renewed intensity), so that the above measures have a true divertimento function.

There is no analogous procedural plan for "intermezzo" movements: they employ only a single idea which is generally not diverged from. It is possible to view the two interruptions of the dotted eighth note motion in m. 12 and 39–42 in the 1st movement of the Sonata in C Major for Violin solo, BWV 1005, which can be classified as an "intermezzo" movement, as a divertimento.

If the absence of characteristic divertimentos causes slow movements to lack contrast, Bach makes up for this in other ways. Individual phrase lines vary greatly in length. This is a structural element of which the average listener and player is hardly aware. For Bach, however, it is an indispensable means of creating internal tension. Scarcely any of the phrase lines are alike. The result is a constant change in the flow of energy. Both listener and player must pay constant attention, because what they encounter is never exactly what they might expect. A line-by-line analysis of a slow movement from a violin—clavier sonata will serve as an example: the 3rd movement of the Sonata in A Major, BWV 1015. Here the incongruity of the individual lines has another specific reason: the two melody parts, the violin and the keyboard right hand, form a real canon at the unison and distance of a full measure. Thus Bach imposed a special limitation on himself; it compelled him to use any in means possible to diversify the inner tension of melodic development, and this opportunity was provided by the varied length of the line.

As far as the technical aspects of our analysis are concerned (Example 121), it is necessary in this case to use a time unit other than the numbering of measures. We restrict ourselves to strong and weak beats, which roughly corresponds to the unit of half a measure. This allows us to pick up the shift of half a measure which Bach initiates in measure 11, and we can devote our full attention to the constantly changing upbeats, the rhythmic structures, i.e. the syncopations, and the shifts in the rising and falling course of the melody. If the unit of measurement 'heavy beat—light beat' seems impracticable we can test them by repeating the individual lines; that is, we imagine the end of a line followed by its beginning. Then there can be no more doubt about the length of the line.

We can observe the following: the entire line is divided into two unequal halves. The first comprises 4 lines (prototype of the phrase), the second, a transposed repetition of the first, is lengthened by a tripling of the third line to 6 lines. None of the four phrase lines resembles any of the others. Only the corresponding lines of the first and second halves (labeled in each case as line 1,2,3,4) are identical, with the exception of line 3, which is shortened in the second half, but, as we

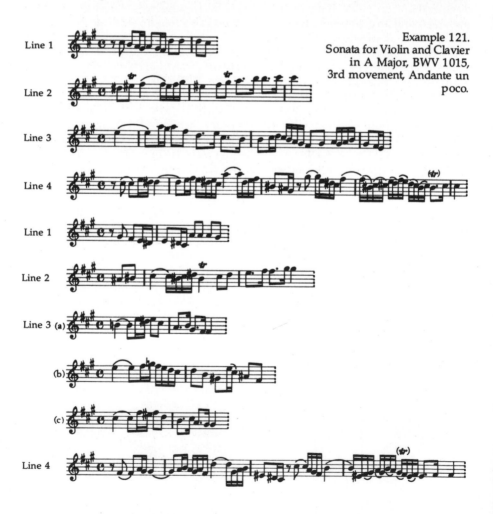

Example 121.
Sonata for Violin and Clavier
in A Major, BWV 1015,
3rd movement, Andante un
poco.

pointed out, is used three times in this shortened form. Of these three forms of line 3 in the second half, the middle one proves to be a rather remote variant of the original line 3. The vitality of the phrase, taken as a whole, rests on the constant change of its upbeats and endings, in the shifting of the rhythmic center of gravity caused by syncopation and the shifting of the culmination points from line to line.[20]

Suite Movements

The development of suite movements—with the exception of preludes—was noted earlier as an expansion or sequence of phrases or parts of phrases. Virtually without exception there are no continuation or divertimento elements. Even if it seems like the development of the movement approaches such a procedure, closer scrutiny reveals that variants of phrases are involved, which can be derived from the opening theme. Thus, even in the case of long and apparently complicated movements, the proximity to the dance model remains. Bach gives free rein to his imagination in the Allemandes, without, however, adding anything substantial to the opening theme. This results in their strange lack of tension. On the one hand, this makes it hard to get an overall grasp on them; on the other hand, it explains their particular fascination.

In the other rapid suite movements, the Courante, Gigue, Bourrée, Gavotte, etc., it is easier to orient oneself. The transformations of the phrases are visible at a glance. Finally, the slow Sarabandes almost always offer clear phrasal relationships, since, based on the number of measures, they have the least scope of any of the suite movements. Consequently they are very easy to understand.

Sequences are employed, in many suite movements, both as a means to extend the phrase or as the germ of new secondary phrases. Example 122, the Bourrée from the Partita in B Minor for Violin solo, BWV 1002 illustrates this procedure. We

Example 122. Partita for Violin solo in B Minor, BWV 1002, Bourrée I, (shortened and original phrase)

first present a version reduced to the normal phrase of 8 measures, which consists of the original m. 1–6 and 19–20. This is followed by Bach's original version of 20 measures. By comparing the two versions we can see where Bach interrupts the phrase and where he introduces the sequences. We should also note the abundance of rhythmic variants which Bach has to offer, despite the pre-programmed Bourrée rhythm.

In the Gigue of the Suite in E-flat Major for Cello solo we have an extreme case of phrase extension (Example 123).

Example 123. Suite for Cello solo in E-flat Major, BWV 1010, 6th movement, Gigue, m. 1–2

Cellists consider this movement to be unusually difficult and strenuous. This is probably due not only to its "perpetuum mobile" quality and its very rapid tempo, but also to the fact that the movement provides no pause, no chance to catch one's breath. The disposition of its first part is still relatively clear, although sequences are employed in two places. They are grouped as follows: 4 × 1 measure (m. 3–6), then 4 × ½ measure (m. 7–8). Then in the second part the relationships become increasingly assymetrical. This goes so far that Bach is finally compelled to introduce a regular reprise (m. 27 ff.) in order to maintain a clear perspective. In suite movements reprises are very rare.

An analysis of the motif relationships within the movement shows that, with the exception of three or perhaps four cadence measures (m. 10, 18 (?), 26 and 42), its course is related only to phrases. They are as follows:

(1) the two measures of the opening motif (m. 1–2); they also appear in m. 11–12 (B-flat Major), 19–20 (C Minor) and as the above-mentioned reprise in m. 27–28 (E-flat Major). It should be noted that in m. 20 (C Minor version) the characteristic concluding note of the motif is omitted, which deprives us of another breather;

(2) the sequences derived from the continuation of the main theme: m. 3–6, 7–8, 13–14, 15–17, 22–23 (here, as in m. 7–8, we have the sequence of 4 × ½ measure), m. 24–25, 29–32, 33–34, 35–38 and 39–40 (again, 4 × ½ measures).

M. 9, 18, 21 and 41 still are unaccounted for in our analysis. Of these, m. 9 and 41, both of which precede a cadence, belong to the main phrase, which began with m. 1–2, i.e. the opening theme. That leaves two measures, 18 and 21, which cannot be clearly traced to any source, since they cannot be viewed as either phrases or sequences. They might be considered "excess" or filler measures. Based on this analysis, only two measures out of a total of 42 (namely, m. 18 and 21), are considered unconnected.

In performing this extraordinary movement, players understandably resort to the echo effect. This dynamic gradation facilitates the division of the sequences, especially where there are literal repetitions. Bach, however, did not provide any directions for this.

The Fugues

In chamber music fugues are rare. The first ones to be cited are the three great fugues in the three Sonatas for Violin solo, BWV 1001, 1003 and 1005. Bach's motivation for writing an extensive fugue as the 2nd movement in each of these sonatas was probably not solely the desire to write especially difficult, virtuoso pieces. Obviously he was following a specific formal plan, according to which the 2nd movement of a sonata da chiesa, which traditionally features rich polyphony, receives special emphasis. All three fugues exhibit similar architectonic characteristics. In addition to the developments of the themes, which are more numerous in these fugues than in those of, say, *The Well-Tempered Clavier,* they contain long interludes which can easily be recognized as divertimenti. These parts simply reflect a love of violin playing. In contrast to the arduous polyphony of the themes, they provide a welcome relief—for the listener as well. Even the development of the themes themselves is carried out with brief divertimento-like passages, which mostly consist of continuous sequences.

Let us take the fugue from the C Major solo Sonata, BWV 1005, and create a 'topography", something indispensable in a movement of 354 measures. The fugue theme (see Example 149, p. 176), resembles the chorale, "Komm heiliger Geist, Herre Gott," and comprises four measures; this must be kept in mind so that the following analysis will show whether themes are introduced in close succession, whether interludes are blended in or whether strettos occur.

Space precludes reproducing the entire movement, but the reader can refer to any edition of the work, either the "NBA," VI, 1 or the edition by Carl Flesch (Ed. Peters, No. 4308); the latter contains both the original text and a practical version. Our numbering of the measures will follow the practice of these two editions, i.e. m. 1 is the first full measure; the upbeat of half a measure is not counted.

1st Thematic Exposition, m. 1–66 (original theme)
(the measure and the key at the entry of the theme are given)

m. 1 C	m. 25 F
m. 5 G	m. 31 C
m. 11 C	m. 45 C
m. 17 G	

Cadence in C, m. 65–66

1st Divertimento, m. 66–92

Half-cadence in A, m. 92

2nd Thematic exposition, m. 93–165 (only occurrence of themes in minor)

m. 93 A minor ⎱ Stretto	m. 136 C (false reprise)
m. 94 E ⎰	m. 148 G ⎱ Stretto
m. 99 D minor	m. 149 D ⎰
m. 110 G	m. 153 C
m. 114 C	m. 158 E minor
m. 122 G	

Cadence in E minor, m. 164–165

2nd Divertimento, m. 165–201

Cadence in G, m. 200–201

3rd Thematic exposition, m. 201–245 (inversions)

m. 202 C inv.	m. 228 G* inv. ⎫
m. 206 G inv.	m. 229 C* inv. ⎬ Stretto
m. 210 F inv.	m. 236 chromatic* ⎭
m. 214 C inv.	

Note: In the entries marked with a *, the key cannot be clearly established, since the note from which the inversion proceeds has been changed.

Cadence in C, m. 244–245

3rd Divertimento, m. 245–288

Half-cadence in C, m. 287–288

4th Thematic exposition, m. 289–354 (original themes)

m. 289 C (definitive reprise)	m. 313 F
m. 293 G	m. 319 C
m. 299 C	m. 333 C
m. 305 G	

Cadence in C, m. 353–354

Thus, there are 32 thematic entries in all, not counting some questionable references to the theme. There is no known fugue with such a high number. Although the themes move in closely related keys, (the extreme case is the double dominant D, which occurs only once, and E as dominant of the relative minor, in stretto; other than that, only the three primary functions, C, G and F and their relative minors are employed), and in spite of its great length, this fugue does not tire the listener. This can be attributed to its eminently logical disposition and the harmony of its proportions.

Chapter 18

Interrelations of Themes and Motifs

The Idea as the Germ Determining the Course of the Movement

Whereas up to now we have considered the development of movements based on the relationship between theme, divertimento, phrase and similar groupings, we now turn to other details of treatment. We have seen that Bach constantly rearranges his material in the course of a movement. This economical procedure is applied right down to the level of the individual measure. Virtually no note sequences are written which are not related to existing themes or motives, or to material of the divertimenti. One is always surprised at the intensive organization of the musical text and at how little is left to chance. One constantly finds new clues and discovers previously overlooked correspondences.[21]

Let us consider the triple fugue of the Trio Sonata in C Major for Two Violins and b.c., BWV 1037. Its numerous eighth-note figures appear to derive from the standard repertory of Baroque formulas that are found in any instrumental work written by lesser composers of the period; at first glance they are scarcely worthy of note. But a second glance reveals that there is nothing routine here, nothing that smacks of empty mechanical motion or chance. Rather the movement's entire course can be traced back to the last measure of the first theme (bracket). Let us first consider the theme itself (Example 124), followed by some passages from later measures; their relationship is evident (Example 125).

Example 124. Trio Sonata in C Major, BWV 1037, 2nd movement, Alla breve, m. 1–6

Example 125. Trio Sonata in C Major, BWV 1037, 2nd movement, Alla breve

Another example is the last movement of the Sonata in G Minor for Violin solo, BWV 1001. The movement consists solely of sixteenth-note motion. But we did not need the piano adaptations of Brahms (this movement inspired him to write two piano etudes) to recognize that this is not an etude to be reeled off. The lapidary main theme (Example 126), no more than a broken chord, gives rise to endless metamorphoses of chordal figurations.

Example 126. Sonata for Violin solo in G Minor, BWV 1001, 4th movement, Presto, m. 1–3

In the next series of examples we follow the transformations made possible first by the broken triad then by the seventh chord. We also see the inexhaustibility of Bach's imagination, which, indeed, gives us the impression that he was especially challenged by such primitive material. The variants become increasingly demanding in the course of the movement, both player and listener are subjected to a growing tension; and yet the musical connection to the beginning idea of the broken G Minor triad is not left to question for a moment (Example 127).

Details about Example 127: m. 17–20, the inversion of the main idea, reappears numerous times; as at the beginning of the second part, m. 55 ff.; the expansion to the broken seventh chord in m. 9–11; the new form of the broken seventh chord in m. 43–45; the combination of broken triad and seventh chord in m. 60–62; intensification by means of both narrower and wider spacing of the broken chords in m.

Example 127. Sonata for Violin solo in G Minor, BWV 1001, 4th movement, Presto

75–79; a free inversion of the forms occurring in m. 43 ff. in m. 89–93; and the ever new and increasingly daring combinations of broken chords in m. 95–100, 113–116, 117–120 and 121–127. Two further phenomena can be observed in the analysis of the figurations of this movement: if one of the arpeggio figures is tied into a descending sequence, then inevitably an ascending sequence will arise in the inversion of the arpeggio. Furthermore, Bach was keenly aware that broken chords occasionally had to be interrupted by other material if they were not to wear thin. For this reason, he enlivens the *Ablauf* in several places with stepwise progressions, the most interesting of which is found in m. 33–39 (Example 128).

Example 128. Sonata for Violin solo in G Minor, BWV 1001, 4th movement, Presto, m. 33–39

Not only is the meter broken up here, but in some measures a latent two-part structure emerges (m. 36, 38 ff.).

Earlier we dealt with the final movement of the Sonata for Violin and Clavier in F Minor, BWV 1018. There we showed that its numerous divertimenti present new ideas independent of the main theme. But this claim has to be somewhat amended. It will not escape the alert player or listener that the divertimenti continue to show the strong influence of the theme. The motifs dovetail even more intensively in the 1st movement of the same sonata. The dominating third motif must be regarded as the "moving force" behind the entire movement. It already appears in the opening measures of the bass part, even though at that point our attention is focused on the expressive, supple motif of the upper parts. But beginning at the very latest in m. 3, the bass thirds clearly become the focus (Example 129). Through diminution they

Example 129. Sonata for Violin and Clavier in F Minor, BWV 1018, 1st movement, Largo, m. 3–5

have gained intensity. Soon they become an important component of the violin line (Example 130; note the double diminution in m. 22) and are condensed into a new, expressive gesture (Example 131). New forms are garnered from the last, simply

Example 130. Sonata for Violin and Clavier in F Minor, BWV 1018, 1st movement, Largo, m. 18–22

Example 131. Sonata for Violin and Clavier in F Minor, BWV 1018, 1st movement, Largo. m. 26–28

diminished phrase, which Bach uses to reach, through cadencing, the relative major key, A-flat Major, and rounds off the first section. The eighth-note figure of the violin in m. 45 and 49 is carefully planned, as is the rising broken chord in m. 56. This is the place where the supple motif in the upper keyboard part is finally taken over by the violin (m. 55, 56 and 65). The very close combination of these ideas brings about a kind of climax. But the energy of the succession of thirds is not yet spent. In m. 68 there is an inversion of the descending thirds from m. 26; measure by measure it builds into an oscillating ebb and flow of thirds in which the substance achieves its maximum concentration (Example 132). M. 68 and 71 are so similar to a vocal phrase from Cantata No. 56 that it cannot be dismissed as mere coincidence. In the

Example 132. Sonata for Violin and Clavier in F Minor, BWV 1018, 1st movement, Largo, m. 68–78

cantata the melody is found in m. 35, 38 and 40 of the aria, "Ich will den Kreuzstab gerne tragen," and later, even more impressively, in m. 91–96 (Example 133). We should likewise mention that an interesting similarity exists between our thirds motif and Beethoven and Brahms. In Beethoven, we find the idea in the Adagio sostenuto of the *Hammerklavier* Sonata; in Brahms, it forms the main theme of the opening movement of the Fourth Symphony, in the Song, "O Tod, wie bitter bist du" from the *Vier ernste Gesänge,* opus 121, and in several other works.

Example 133. *Kreuzstab* Cantata, No. 56, Aria I, m. 91–96

We could undoubtedly go on and on. We could consider not only the chamber music, but Bach's entire oeuvre, from the standpoint of how themes and motifs intermesh, and in so doing would constantly encounter new and indeed unexpected facts. But the further one goes, the greater our skepticism as to whether this kind of analysis can yield results of any essential or even material value. It does serve to confirm the foresight and concentration with which Bach worked. But only one factor has validity as a criterion of the quality of his work: the frequently repeated use of the same idea. However, we might well ask ourselves whether the fact that a theme or a motif can be applied again and again is in itself any guarantee of quality. True, one experiences the pleasure of recognizing the theme, transformed and in a new environment. But does something increase in value because a composer presents it two or three times, or even more than that? Nearly all the usual analytical methods rest on this belief. On the other hand, one of the fundamental experiences of a composer is that some ideas may be used only once if they are not to suffer a loss of importance and effect. Bach's familiarity with this experience can be seen, among other things, in the spontaneity of his work which, even today, retains its freshness. One does not do Bach justice to view him as a cold structuralist or even as an assiduous drudge. And with this observation we shall leave the discussion of thematic and motivic intermeshing and pursue it no further.[22]

Techniques of Compression or Condensation

Another way of handling musical ideas is the technique of compression or condensation. In order to illustrate this, we refer again to the 1st movement of the Sonata in F Minor for Violin and Clavier, BWV 1018. In Example 130, m. 18–22 of the violin part were cited. Here the idea of a descending third appears a total of three times, twice in half-notes, the third time in eighth-notes (m. 22). Thus it is compressed into a smaller space (time). We referred to this process as double diminution, but this was only a superficial characterization. A more important consideration is that this compression causes the idea to gain intensity. It becomes charged with tension and acquires an urgent quality.

However, such heightening of intensity is not achieved solely by reduction of note values or diminution. We have already observed that ascending sequences can be employed with comparable success. More important and having wider ramifications is the technique of extracting a particularly striking motif from a theme and treating it individually. This process is like distilling an increasingly concentrated essence from the thematic substance.

Historically speaking, Bach's use of this procedure opened the way to the Classic period, in that the procedures described correspond to the practice of "development" in the classic sonata, especially in Beethoven.[23] Even though the specific concept of development in the manner of Viennese classicism was certainly alien to him, the compositional means for it were available to him. Let us cite three examples.

The first is the final movement of the Sonata for Violin and Clavier in C Minor, BWV 1017. As we have already seen (see p. 116), the phrase of the theme is not immediately presented in its entirety. At the beginning, only the first part of the phrase appears in m. 1–4, while the second part is not heard until m. 9–16. On closer inspection we see that this consequent phrase (we know that it is twice as long as the antecedent phrase) is the result of condensation. In the antecedent phrase, the opening motif gives impetus to a group of four measures (Example 134). In the consequent phrase, the grouping is first compressed into two × two measures (Example 135), after which it is further concentrated into two individual measures (Example 136). In the interest of uniformity, the music in Example 135 and 136 was transposed back to C Minor. In the original these measures are in G minor.

Example 134. Sonata for Violin and Clavier in C Minor, BWV 1017, 4th movement, Allegro, m. 1–4

Example 135. Sonata for Violin and Clavier in C Minor, BWV 1017, 4th movement, Allegro, m. 9–12 (transposed)

Example 136. Sonata for Violin and Clavier in C Minor, BWV 1017, 4th movement, Allegro, m. 13–14 (transposed)

Bach uses a similar method in the 3rd movement of the Sonata for Gamba and Clavier in D Major, BWV 1028. The eminently expressive main idea of this movement (m. 1–2) has a length of two 12/8 measures. But very soon, Bach settles on the first of the two measures (see m. 7 and 8: the first measure of the theme is quoted twice in A Major). That is not enough, however; in m. 15, the main theme is condensed into two half-measures, and in the following measure all that is left of the entire theme-complex is the sixteenth-note figure, compressed into one quarter beat (Example 137). We can thus trace how the idea is intensified and its essence crystallized.

Example 137. Sonata for Gamba and Clavier in D Major, BWV 1028, 3rd movement, Andante, m. 15–16

Entire phrases or parts of phrases are also compressed. In the 2nd movement of the Sonata for Viola da gamba and Clavier in G Major, BWV 1027, the theme appears as an inversion in the middle part of the movement (m. 63 ff.). In the process, the original four-measure phrase has been reduced to two measures. Elsewhere, phrases which had been asymmetrically expanded by the insertion of "surplus" measures are reduced to their normal dimension and thereby condensed. An especially attractive case of phrase compression can be found in the last movement of the Trio Sonata from the *Musical Offering*, BWV 1079. Its main theme, modelled after the "royal theme" and expanded accordingly, has an opening motif of two and a half 6/8 measures (Example 138). Later it becomes so compressed that the original grouping of two and a half measures becomes one measure of real 9/8 time, i.e. although it is not noted as such, a change of meter has taken place (Example 139).

Example 138. Trio Sonata in C Minor, BWV 1079, 4th movement, Allegro, m. 1–3

Example 139. Trio Sonata in C Minor, BWV 1079, 4th movement, Allegro, m. 39–42 (changed meter)

Even though it is not a chamber music work, for the purposes of comparison we shall cite the following episode from the 1st movement of *Brandenburg Concerto No. 3*, BWV 1048. In m. 97–100 of this movement, its main idea, shown at the beginning of Example 140, undergoes a concentration that corresponds exactly to Beethoven's technique.

Example 140. *Brandenburg Concerto* No. 3 in G Major, BWV 1048, 1st movement, (a) m. 1–2, (b) m. 97–99

Inversions

The importance that Bach attached to the inversion of a theme can be seen above all in the fugues. But he also made use of this method in other forms. It enabled him to take an idea that is already familiar and put it into new perspective, thus gaining new interest for it. We regularly encounter the procedure in the Gigue movements of suites, whose second part nearly always begins with the inversion of the opening idea. The inversion of the main theme of the 2nd movement of the Sonata for Gamba and Clavier in G Major, BWV 1027, has already been mentioned. Likewise, in the 2nd movement of the B Minor Sonata for Violin and Clavier, BWV 1014, a significant inversion occurs. Using an inversion, Bach extracts a new figure from the last measure of the theme and this has a decisive effect on the further development of the movement (Example 141).

Example 141. Sonata for Violin and Clavier in B Minor, BWV 1014, 2nd movement, Allegro, (a) m. 4, (b) m. 10–11

Finally, "recto" and "inverso" forms are intermingled, out of which come entire concertante divertimenti (Example 142).

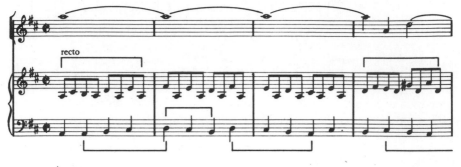

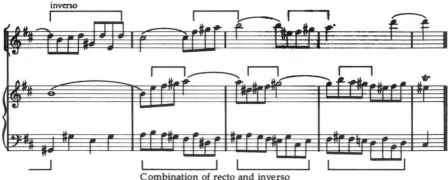

Combination of recto and inverso

Example 142. Sonata for Violin and Clavier in B Minor, BWV 1014, 2nd movement, Allegro, m. 80–87

Anybody is free to detect other derivatives of the first three notes of our motif, sometimes in augmentation, in the bracketed notes.

There are myriad examples of inversions, even in places where they would be least expected. Thus, for example, in the Sarabande from the Suite for Cello solo in C Minor, BWV 1011, one of the greatest movements to issue from Bach's pen, the melodic forms beginning in m. 5 are derived from the inversion of the preceding measures (Example 143).

Example 143. Suite for Cello solo in C Minor, BWV 1011, 4th movement, Sarabande, (a) m. 1–2, (b) m. 5–6

Chapter 19

Analytical Results

Musical analysis often leaves behind an uncomfortable feeling. No matter what method is used, it tempts, indeed, even forces the analyst into a one-sided position, into a narrowing perspective, and it seldom does justice to the phenomenological complexity of a work of art. If the analyst regularly checks his methods against the reality of living music, every step of the way he will have to acknowledge exceptions which cast doubt on his results. However, if he wants to "prove" his thesis at any price, he is likely to take into account only that which confirms his thesis; everything else falls by the wayside. The tangible artwork itself seems to slip through his fingers.

Nevertheless, it is confirmed over and over again that we neither can nor should forgo the intellectual penetration of a work of art. We know only too well that we go astray when we rely only on "feelings", "instinct", or whatever we wish to call it, in our reaction to music. Feelings and instinct are undependable, some control is necessary.

A fundamental reason for the discomfiture that sets in at the end of every analysis of an artwork is the mountain of details, indeed, of shards, with which one is faced. Synthesizing the sum of the individual insights gained was impossible, or simply forgotten. But anyone who studies art cannot stop once the facts have been gathered. Rather—and this is the decisive step—one must incorporate this knowledge into the ensemble of all the other aspects of the work in question. One must become aware of its organic unity. Only then will the detailed knowledge gained by the analysis, which in and of itself can only remain fragmentary, have achieved its own value and its true meaning. Let us take an example. A certain harmonic turn which has drawn our attention achieves its effect only because it coincided with a specific linear constellation. Perhaps the latter was the culmination, perhaps the end of a contrapuntal climax, which, however, was only interesting because of its key position in the development of the movement, the beginning of a reprise, for example. But this combination of all the aforementioned parameters has specific acoustic results; they are possible only at this unique moment and would be meaningless anywhere else. In addition to the above requirements, one would also have to add a certain thematic treatment that is appropriate only at this moment— say, a specific stretto or inversion. This enumeration could be continued almost *ad libitum*. In a musical work, everything is mutually contingent. It is not so much *what* happens, but when, in what context and to what extent. Only from the totality does each detail derive its meaning.

Unfortunately, so far as I can see, scarcely any practicable analytical procedures have been made available that would give us such a total view. The work as an organic unit "is a mystery to most". And yet we have to take the entirety of the artistic *gestalt* as a point of departure if we are to expect analytic results.

For Bach, the entirety of the artistic *gestalt*, or in musical terms, the unity of the movement, was never a subject for debate. He viewed his compositional task as accomplished only when he had created a *gestalt* that was thoroughly organic, a movement that was complete in itself, "worthy of posterity". That was the only way in which he was capable of expressing himself. "Open forms" or "intentional fragments" were not his style. This was the viewpoint not only of his entire epoch, but of composers at least until the time of Schönberg. But, then, as soon as Bach's work is compared with that of his contemporaries, clear distinctions arise precisely in the area of unity. In the realm of sacred music, to be sure, there were secure traditions. The various formal prototypes for motets, cantatas and oratorios had evolved over a period of centuries; their individual movements were largely programmed types. And within this context Bach only had to carry on the tradition and bring it to its apex and its temporary final stage. The same can be said, *cum grano salis,* even of his organ works and a large portion of his keyboard music, with the exception of *The Well-Tempered Clavier* and a few other works, e.g. the four duets, BWV 802–805.

The situation of instrumental ensemble music was different. Here the traditions that Bach encountered were not strong, the genre itself was still young. The models he had observed (Couperin le Grand in Celle, Vivaldi in Weimar) were at best starting points, but never a solid foundation for his own personal achievement. Naturally he had contemporaries who were working along similar lines, and naturally there were already certain "norms" in orchestral music. But all one has to do is compare one of the typical concerti grossi of the early 18th century to a *Brandenburg Concerto,* or one of the innumerable dance suites of the time to his four orchestral overtures: the difference is astronomical, and one gathers that he must have been somewhat critical of the output of his contemporaries.

And in this regard, chamber music was absolute *terra incognita.* Bach's achievement lay in his immediate grasp of the advantages and musical possibilities offered by an ensemble of two, three or four musicians. We have already mentioned elsewhere that in the early 18th century one cannot really speak of any tradition of larger instrumental ensembles. This is confirmed by the great stir caused by such formations as the *16 petits violons* which Lully had trained into a disciplined ensemble at the court in Paris. For the most part, people were probably satisfied if everybody played together fairly well. But in chamber music there was no concert master who competed for leadership against the harpsichordist (the winner usually being the one able to stamp out the beat loudest). In chamber music, musicians played together by listening to each other. They were the best musicians available. Bach made use of this subtle way of cooperating. Other factors also came into play: Chamber music was (and still is today) an "unofficial", unpretentious genre. It was not subject to social obligations. There was no prescribed text, no dramatic plot that had to be followed. All efforts benefited the common cause; it was possible to be musically creative, on the spot, as nowhere else. But as a consequence, chamber music also makes the greatest demands on the composer. Anything that even faintly resembles "coasting along" or routine is promptly exposed as such. Every sound has to fit, every line evolve from structural necessity, every *Ablauf* must be well proportioned. Something that would be barely perceptible as a casual nuance in the broad flow of colorful orchestral writing acquires a perilous immediacy in chamber music, and it has to hold its own in this immediacy. Dimensions are smaller, the paths to effectiveness more direct.

Above all, Bach was aware of the great breadth of expression possible in chamber music. For here, despite the restrictions of the medium, there is tension, climax, and eruptiveness; there is meditative contemplation as well as passionate ecstasy, there is lyric fluidity, the solemnity of nature, playfulness, rhythm, the joy of making music—and whatever other qualities may be accessible to the range of musical expression. And everything is more immediate in its impact. Bach was the first to impart real substance to this genre. His standards are still valid today, and it is no exaggeration to state that it was he who gave to chamber music its true meaning.

The extent of his achievement can be measured when one compares him with his contemporaries. Whereas in their chamber music they complacently string along one minor inspiration after another, Bach consciously employs the development of the movement as a formative element. His proportions reveal his unerring sense for the significance of structures within time whose proportions are not merely a matter of measurement, but rather draw their vitality from the expansion and concentration of the material. While others busied themselves in the sheltered preserve of contrapuntal devices that had been used hundreds of times, Bach risked the sound of daring, tension-filled three-part constructions. His themes have the hardness of a "forged feature,"[24] where his contemporaries are content with the innocuous, though at times (in Telemann, for example) this may indeed advance into the realm of *esprit*, but which never stirs, unsettles the listener. With their music it is possible to let one's attention stray for a few moments, whereas it is unthinkable not to concentrate fully on Bach's chamber music. Even a movement as successful as the famous B Minor Larghetto from Handel's Violin Sonata, Opus 1, No. 13[25] evokes the impression of a theater aria transcribed for violin, when compared with a corresponding piece by Bach.

In setting up such antitheses we do not mean to lionize Bach or to downgrade his contemporaries. They had their merits and their artistic function, and they did indeed have moments of genius. What we are trying to do is to acknowledge the way Bach intensified and enriched the genre of chamber music in a way considered impossible by his contemporaries. It is in steadfast awareness of this "total situation" that all the analytical details should be understood.

On the other hand, one must beware of utopian thinking, of believing that in Bach's world everything always is safe and sound. The following, from a letter written by Hans Carossa, pertains more to Bach than to any other composer of his time: ". . . what I want to feel in a poem is danger:—the danger which affected the poet's spirit at the time he wrote it! Of course, I want the first line of the poem to give me a sense of assurance that the spirit is not going to perish in this danger; but danger I must feel, even in the simplest love song or landscape."[26] Surely Bach composed with the sovereignty of someone who is sure of his craft and at peace with himself. His creativity was not that of the exalted, high-strung genius, but neither must he be pictured as an honorable, "petit bourgeois"[27] artisan. This is contradicted by his oft-confirmed human vulnerability, his sensitivity in matters of justice and, moreover, the intensity of many of his personal utterances. Intimate details of his life fortunately do not contribute to our knowledge of the artist. Bach cannot be pictured as a celebrated idol of the public or as a brooding introvert. Though he probably viewed his mission as a composer to be "to delight the spirit", and everything which went beyond that as "Soli Deo Gloria,"[28] this does not mean that his music (and the chamber music no less than any of the rest, since its speaks the same language) does not have multiple layers of meaning. To be sure, nothing is added to our understanding of the music by attempting to formulate the contents of these layers. "Background illuminations" of this sort are usually extremely questionable intellectually, for in this matter, words are simply too imprecise.[29] When applied to Bach's music, all eloquence is thread-bare; it does not need any context.[30]

Even the overworked concept of "absolute music" is of no help here, however many aesthetic systems, ideologies or intuited contents might be brought to bear on it.[31]

From time to time one reads that Bach was already considered "old-fashioned" in his own lifetime. If this is true at all, at the most it applies to his church cantatas, and even at that, only to those written in the last decade of his life. The reason why he was forgotten so soon after his death was probably simply that he had never been a popular celebrity. The complexity of Bach's work then was accessible to only a few. The label "old-fashioned" was never appropriate for the chamber music. Nevertheless, it took more than a hundred years after his death for people to realize its artistic importance.

Part III

Individual Works

In Part II, we analyzed the characteristics that apply to Bach's Chamber music in general, that are specific to its genre and composition. In Part III, each work will be considered individually. We will now be looking at those aspects which identify a sonata or a suite as a particular work. This method necessarily entails the emphasis of details. Hence, the respective discussions should not be considered comprehensive "introductions to the works," which would only result in excessive repetition, but should be read and used together with Parts I and II. However, I avoided making constant reference to these earlier parts so that the text would not be too cumbersome. For this purpose, therefore, the reader is advised to make use of the index of works on page 257.

Chapter 20

Sonatas and Partitas for Violin Solo

The *Sei Solo a Violino senza Basso accompagnato,* as Bach entitled this group of works on the autograph title page, have always been considered the apex—a summing up of violin playing. We have reason to believe that Bach gave little or no thought to the public performance of these pieces, but rather intended them as works for study or, at most, be be played in a small circle of friends. Still, it is very difficult for a violinist to resist the temptation to play them in public. This is understandable, for these works are much more than mere "etudes". The music of both the sonatas and the partitas has an elemental power, often of symphonic dimensions, and even taken in the context of Bach's work as a whole it occupies an exclusive position. Bach's approach involves contrast: three four-movement sonatas which follow the "sonata da chiesa" scheme are countered by three multiple-movement partitas (suites) of the "sonata da camera" type. The sonatas are consistent in the sequence of their movements: 1. a slow, "fantasia-"like introductory movement; 2. fugue; 3. arioso in the relative major or minor key (the subdominant in the third sonata); 4. playful, fast finale. The movements of the partitas, on the

Figure 7. Autograph of the Sonata for Violin solo in G Minor, BWV 1001, 1st page.

other hand, are variously combined, although the basic "Allemande-Courante-Sarabande-Gigue" model is usually discernable. The middle partita supplements this model with the colossal structure of the "Chaconne," the first partita adds a "Double" to each movement, the last one precedes the series of dances with a Prelude. We shall follow the sequence of Bach's autograph manuscript, according to which each sonata alternates with a partita.

Sonata No. 1 in G Minor, BWV 1001

1. The Adagio opens the sonata and thereby the entire cycle with a stirring gesture. The Baroque extravagance of the figuration is effortlessly subordinated to the basic proportions of the movement; despite the eruptiveness Bach remains in control and does not allow the whole to be overwhelmed by detail. One senses a parallel with both the rich detail and the rigor of Roman Baroque facades. In this respect the movement serves as a counterpart to the organ fantasy in the same key, G minor, BWV 542, which likewise originated in Köthen. But despite its more restricted instrumental medium, the violin work seems more extensive; it is precisely this restriction that can greatly affect the listener's imagination.

2. The wandering quality of the introduction is countered with the rhythmic solidity of the Fugue. Its theme is concentrated in a single measure. This brevity forms a necessary contrast to the broad curve of the introductory movement. The fugue is more closely bound to its theme than the fugues of the other two sonatas. Divertimenti occupy relatively little space and have less architectonic significance than the divertimenti of the A minor and C major fugues. This, along with other historical developments in fugue construction, may be the reason for the metamorphoses of the theme itself in the course of the movement: its second half is modified several times (m. 53–54, 58–59, 61–63, et al.). To resolve the arpeggio passage noted by Bach as a simple chord sequence (m. 35–41), Carl Flesch makes the following convincing proposal (Example 144). The unusual sequence of

Example 144. Sonata for Violin solo in G Minor, BWV 1001, 2nd movement, Fugue, m. 35–36, 38

seventh chords (m. 45, 4th quarter–m. 46) should be noted; it has parallels elsewhere (m. 9–11, m. 89–93) and in the Siciliano (m. 14).

3. The Siciliano offers real technical challenges to the violinist and is therefore difficult to interpret satisfactorily. It is basically a three-voice movement: two high parts and a "bassetto". For technical reasons, these lines must be constantly interrupted, otherwise such a polyphonic structure cannot be played, even with a Baroque bow. The lines must be followed in the mind and filled in wherever they

are not actually present. The result of this limitation is a movement showing a peculiar interruptive technique in which Bach anticipates practices used in the 20th century. As an illustration we offer m. 7–8 in a reconstructed score (notes that have been added are circled). The craftmanship of the run of 32nd-notes in m. 8 deserves special mention: it begins as the continuation of the bass line and connects smoothly with the melody line (Example 145). In view of this latent polyphony, it is

Example 145.
Sonata for Violin solo in G Minor, BWV 1001, 3rd movement, Siciliano, m. 7–8 (circled notes were added)

understandable that Robert Schumann added a keyboard accompaniment to the solo sonatas—a procedure that seems barbaric to us, but which can be legitimized by a verified tradition, according to which Bach himself occasionally accompanied the violin solo works on the clavichord indicating the harmonies—a fact of which Schumann probably was not aware.[1]

4. The concluding Presto, a movement which flows in uninterrupted, rapid 16th-note motion, is a virtuoso piece of extraordinary brilliance, not in the style of Paganini, but rather, brusque, unconciliatory, not catering to the public. Bach writes an abundance of imaginative broken chord figurations. This leads to alternating points of culmination and relaxation despite the continuous motion; they must be sought out and understood (cf. pp 155 ff.).

Partita No. 1 in B Minor, BWV 1002

Of the three partitas, the first one seems to be the simplest. It has only the four classical suite movements (a Bourrée instead of a Gigue), to each of which, however, a Double is added. Bach frequently used this type of variation in individual movements, but never in an entire work. In the B Minor Partita, the Doubles all have a common arrangement: they consist of continuous, uniform motion (observe how Bach always phrases such motion unconventionally), so that compared with the original the Double seems to be a simplification. This is particularly pronounced in the Allemande. In the first version it is awkward, both rhythmically and in regard to violin technique; in order to interpret it effectively, one must think of a moderately flowing eighth-note pulse. Just how crucial it is to adapt the numerous ♫ rhythms to the 16th triplets, i.e., to replace them with ♪♪ , is a matter of opinion. I do not believe that this procedure is always appropriate in an unaccompanied solo work, and I am supported in this view by both Carl Philipp Emanuel Bach and Quantz, both of whom expressly made the distinction between dotted values and triplets (cf. Chapter 6). The Double of the Allemande should undoubtedly be played more rapidly, the beat now being the quarter note.

The Corrente and its Double are movements with a lively pace and should be played briskly. To prevent them from becoming mere busywork, one should pay attention to the consistent asymmetry of the corner notes, i.e., the high and low points of the motion; they seldom coincide with the strong beats of the measure.

The noble proportions of the juxtaposed groups of eight measures constitute the appeal of the Sarabande. They inspire Bach to lovely melodic turns. Although it, too, consists only of consecutive eighths (triplets), the Double must be conceived melodically, not mechanically.

We have already discussed the splendid construction of the principal idea of the Bourrée. Here we shall call attention to the interesting periodic and sequential irregularity of m. 33–38, which infuses new energy into the movement's course, as well as to the aperiodic, coda-like continuation technique of m. 54–64. This irregularity is abandoned in the four final measures when Bach again quotes the principal motif. The Double of the Bourrée is unfortunately somewhat weak in comparison with the main part of the movement and is not a satisfying conclusion to the partita. Various solutions were tried in order to overcome this: a da capo of the Bourrée, without any repetitions, or interweaving the first part and the double in the following manner: Bourrée, part one, Double, part one; Bourrée, part two, Double, part two.

Sonata No. 2 in A Minor, BWV 1003

1. *Grave*. The introductory movement is related to that of the G Minor Sonata, although it is more intimate in its overall arrangement. The bass line of the two opening measures (Example 146) is used several times as the fundament of a motif, for example, in m. 14–15 in G minor, in which the absent but latent 'g' must be supplemented on the 1st quarter of m. 15. The movement also features several unusual harmonic sequences (cf. m. 9–11); the cadences are not carried through to the tonic, but rather modulate into other keys before that (m. 9–11).

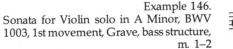
Example 146.
Sonata for Violin solo in A Minor, BWV
1003, 1st movement, Grave, bass structure,
m. 1–2

2. The Fugue has a relatively simple theme which sounds as if it were derived from Italian violin music. Bach also employs it extensively in its inversion. The unusual length of the piece (289 measures) gives both player and listener problems at first . Its length confirms our suspicion that no thought was given to performing fugues like this. The violinist is meant to play them for himself; today the non-violinist can come to grips with a work like this in his own home through record-ings. The best way to gain an overview is to target the principal cadences, which provide the necessary formal clarification and clearly distinguish between thematic

blocks and divertimenti. However, any attempt to shorten the fugue on that basis would soon present problems, for wherever something is cut, the proportions are thrown out of balance—proof of how firmly established they are.

3. The bass line and the melody line are so clearly differentiated, and the compositional indication for violin accompaniment in the lower eighth part is so painstaking that the two-part, arioso Andante could originally have been a movement for melody instrument and b.c. There is even a two part duet over the b.c. in one place (Example 147). Bach may have enjoyed creating a "violin reduction" of an imaginary work and playing it himself, which, among other things, would confirm his skill as a violinist. But if someone who enjoyed its melodic beauty attempted to adapt the movement, say, for violin and keyboard b.c., the result would perhaps be more justifiable than many other reconstructions of a supposed "original version" of a Bach work.

Example 147. Sonata for Violin solo in A Minor, BWV 1003, 3rd movement, Andante, m. 6–7

4. In this Allegro finale, as in the first sonata, Bach dispenses with all double stops and writes a movement whose substance is derived predominantly from broken chords. It is playful and capricious rather than a dashing virtuoso piece. The original phrasing is unconventional as usual, and for this reason it offers considerable difficulty for the player, especially using the modern bow. This may have been the reason why Flesch undertook several changes in his practical edition, although in so doing a certain Paganini-like sound unfortunately slips in and leaves the true Bach by the wayside. Bach later rewrote this sonata as a clavier sonata in D minor, BWV 964.

Partita No. 2 in D Minor, BWV 1004

Since, like the partita in B minor, this partita lacks a prelude, it opens with the traditional Allemande, an austere, introverted piece. Here Bach foregoes all Baroque ornamentation, although in other allemandes he often generously uses it, but this makes the movement much clearer. The most appropriate tempo is a moderately-paced quarter, rather than an eighth-note pulse which is called for by the corresponding movement of the first partita. Here, however, a quarter-note pulse gives the 16th-triplets and the more relaxed 32nd-notes enough time to be heard and be clearly distinguished from each other. The following detail may serve as a characteristic example of the movement's imagination: the preparation of the Neapolitan sixth chord at the end of each part (m. 12, 3rd quarter—m. 13, and m. 30, 4th quarter—m. 31, 3rd quarter). In the first part, this is preceded by a sequence of quarter notes of descending triad inversions (m. 11–12, 3rd quarter); in the second part, by a likewise descending sequence of complete measures with four chords each (m. 28–30, 3rd quarter). The first, *short* sequence leads perforce to the broad Neapolitan harmony of one and a half measures, while the second, *long* sequence cuts its Neapolitan chord by half.

The Courante should not be played too hurriedly. It, too, has a somewhat brooding quality. An adjustment of the ♩♪ values to the triplets, i.e., their approximating ♩♪ will probably take care of itself; but it is possible, or at least conceivable, to go only halfway and allow the dotted notes to retain a certain edge. In this way the movement can gain additional charm.

The Sarabande gives the impression of a preparatory study for the later Chaconne theme. After the austerity of the preceding movements it projects a mood of irreconcilability. The clarity of its *Ablauf* is admirable. It consists only of regular, symmetrical phrases: first part, eight measures; second part 8 + 8 measures. It ends with an epilogue of 4 measures—a rarity in Bach's suite movements.

If the Sarabande is seen as a link between the measured introductory movements and the Chaconne, the following Gigue, a wild, forceful piece, leads directly to the culmination of the suite provided by the Chaconne. It now becomes evident that the whole partita builds up to the final movement, just as there are symphonies in later periods which reach their climax in the finale. Although it could just as well have been written in 6/8 time, Bach wrote the Gigue in 12/8 time; this results in a broader sweep of the overall rhythm, and the movement is controlled despite its impetuous disposition. There is tension between this movement and the two earlier movements in more restrained motion: we are thus prepared for an extraordinary conclusion to the work.

This conclusion is found in the Ciaccona, which is the crowning feature not only of the partita but the violin solo repertory in general. In duration alone, it last longer than any other movement, not excluding the great fugues of the A Minor and C Major sonatas; and if one were to omit some repeats in the preceding movements of the D Minor sonata, it is longer than all these movements combined. Its exceptional status is evident from this fact alone. But this is also true from a musical standpoint: no other chamber music work contains a variation movement.

The overall organization of the variations (excluding the theme and its recapitulation at the end, we count 34 variations, the arrangement of which will be established later) is far removed from a mere concatenation of sets of embellishments. We showed earlier that the harmonic scheme itself changes in the course of the movement (cf. pp 136 ff). Bach provided a long-range plan for the various types of motion and cleverly balanced the incidences of tension and relaxation against each other. The first thing to note is its division into three parts: a minor section, a major section, and again a minor section. Thus, the A-B-A principle also applies here, although the second minor section cannot be called a reprise. It should also be noted that the sections differ in length. The first minor section is 131 measures long, the major section, 76 measures, the second minor section, 49 measures.[2] Thus we have an asymmetry of reduced proportions. But the movement seems balanced: proof of the distinction between mere numerical measurement and the perception of time in music. If we disregard the theme (m. 1–7), which stands by itself as a "motto" and strikes an ambitious pose that arouses our expectations (Example 148), all three sections begin in a relaxed, normal disposition: the first minor section in moderate, dotted motion; the major section with tranquil lyricism; the second

Example 148. Partita for Violin solo in D Minor, BWV 1004, 5th movement, Ciacona, m. 1–7

minor section with a reduction of the thematic material to a descending chord sequence, into which simple ornaments are interpolated. In the following variations, Bach allows gradual intensifications to arise from these respective "zero points." These evolutions develop at different rates, depending on the length of the section in which they are located. For the most part, they are expressed as intensifications of the elements of motion: quarter notes become eighths, eighths become sixteenths, sixteenths, thirty-seconds. Corresponding to the structure of the theme (it has 2 × 4 measures and already contains a repeat), Bach usually proceeds in such a manner that the same figuration formula occurs twice in succession. In the process, it often happens that the second group of four measures is developed from the inversion of the first group; for example, m. 48 ff., its inversion, m. 52 ff.; m. 64 ff., inversion, m. 68 ff.; m. 152 ff., inversion m. 156 ff.; m. 216 f., inversion m. 220 ff. Two other ways of creating tension are to alternate single-line and chordal writing, (extensive arpeggio episodes like m. 88–119 have to be considered as chordal), and the other, to contrast homogeneous and heterogeneous rhythms, i.e., allowing a variation to develop continuously in eighths, sixteenths or thirty-seconds or a combination thereof. Thus m. 56 ff., where eighth-notes and sixteenth-notes alternate, or m. 64 ff., where the same process occurs with 16ths and 32nds, have a more intensifying effect than the exclusively 16th-note passages in m. 76 ff. or the continuous 16th-triplets in m. 240 ff.

Having recognized the technical means by which Bach creates tensions, we can now point to the broad curves of development: the first intensification, beginning in m. 56, continuing until m. 75. After this, a brief, meditative interruption in m. 76–83, followed by a renewed, direct eruption of tension with the 32nd notes in m. 84–87. (M. 86 contains the highest note that Bach wrote for the violin, g^3.) A long passage of 32nd arpeggios ensues, which maintains the high intensity. There are numerous possible solutions and suggestions for playing these arpeggios, which Bach wrote only chordally; but all the editors are unanimous in insisting that the 32nd-notes be retained up to the point where the arpeggios end and the tension eases (m. 119). The two subsequent variations, numbers 16 and 17, quickly produce a calming effect, lead back to the theme and bring the first minor section to a close (m. 131). Bach has the ensuing D Major section begin like an Adagio. Even the four measures 148–151 fit into this calmness. The movement does not begin to free itself from this atmosphere until m. 152, at first by means of simple 16th-note arpeggios. However, these arpeggios intensify rapidly and escalate to an "energico" rhythm, the "battle motif" (m. 168–171) with which we are familiar from Albert Schweitzer's writing about Bach. The motion suddenly subsides in m. 176; immediately thereafter (m. 184, var. 25), a new structure is initiated, this time based on chords and with the principal rhythm of the theme. Then in m. 200–207 we have yet another climax which concludes the major section. The 28th variation, which begins the second minor section, is itself quite colorful, with its alternations of chords, one-voice figuration and diverging rhythms; yet it always remains somewhat reserved. This restraint is maintained throughout the next two variations (m. 216–227); their featured 16th-note and, later, 32nd-note passages continue to evoke an expansive "espressivo". The extreme tension of the two preceding sections is then resumed in the following, virtuoso episode using *Bariolage* (m. 228–239). But it is clear that we are nearing the end; the circle is closing, what must be said has been said; there is no need for another dramatic climax. The last two variations beginning in m. 240 do introduce a new element, the 16th-triplets, but no new fuel is added to the fire. On the contrary, from m. 244 on the action coasts to a halt, as it were. The quotation of the theme closes the circle in the last eight measures. However, this is not simply a repetition of the "motto;" rather, m. 252–256 contain a completion of the thematic phrase previously withheld from us—as if it were a natural outgrowth of the theme, the product of the 34 variations, of a process of thesis and antithesis.

The number of variations which we have established for the Chaconne, 34, evokes comparable numbers in other great variation works: 32 Goldberg variations, 33 Diabelli variations by Beethoven. It may well be that this is something like a key number. But this was scarcely our motive in dividing the Chaconne into 34 variations. This division is grounded in the development of this movement, or more precisely, in the fact that Bach did not completely transfer the dual nature that we have noted in the theme to the variations. There are several variations based not on 2×4 measures, but, rather, on 1×4 measures, making them half as long as "normal" variations. We shall enumerate them now, so that whoever is interested may make a complete count of the variations. These are the short variations: in the first minor section, m. 72–75 (var. 9), m. 84–87 (var. 11); m. 120–123 (var. 16); in the major section, m. 148–151 (var. 20); in the second minor section, m. 224–227 (var. 30), m. 236–239 (var. 32), m. 240–243 (var. 33); m. 244–247 (var. 34). The accumulation of short variations near the conclusion is striking and creates an intensification by using the formal device of compression.

We conclude with a noteworthy phenomenon: although the Chaconne seems to exemplify classical equilibrium, in its details it is thoroughly asymmetrical. It is tempting to think of the design of ancient temples, which also give the viewer a sense of complete harmony, but which are not symmetrical in every detail, as measurements made at the Parthenon have shown. (A similar study could be made of the Chaconne.) We might further ask whether the impression of monumentality the Chaconne gives might have its basis in the discrepancy between its compositional aims and the medium being used, that of the solo violin. In any case, arrangements of the work for large orchestra, which have occasionally been attempted, have diminished rather than heightened its power.[3] Its extraordinary quality is realized only by the solo violin. But despite this exclusive status, the rest of Bach's work for violin solo should not be relegated to the shadows of the Chaconne. That would amount to both an unjustified devaluation and the setting of an unrealistic standard.

Sonata No. 3 in C Major, BWV 1005

D Major is Bach's "official" ceremonial key; the trumpets sound, the drums roll, and he composes with the dimensions of a large canvas. C Major, on the other hand, could be called his "personal" key of joy. In both works for solo strings in C Major (apart from this violin sonata there is the No. 3 cello suite), the radiant quality of the music is based not on a colorful arrangement, but emanates directly from its structural substance. Perhaps another reason for the felicitous effect of the C Major sonata is the fact that the four preceding solos are in minor keys. The ratio of minor to major in the violin solos is 2:1, emphasizing their seriousness more than in the works for cello solo, in which this ratio is inverted, 1:2. Observations of this kind are not romanticizations, but are based on the oft-cited fact that in Bach's work the idea, the themes, the structure and the key are all directly related. He has a typical B minor mood that does not occur in any other key; the situation is similar in other keys.

1. The C Major Sonata begins with a somewhat tentative Adagio. Using the classification we established earlier, it would belong to the intermezzo type: the elaboration of a single short motif, in this case, in moderately paced, dotted rhythm. Note how the movement expands from one-part to four-part texture within the first four measures. Bach extracted amazing results from the restricted possibilities of playing double stops on the violin. From then on, three-voice writing dominates. Several daring enharmonic chord sequences catch one's attention (m. 7–11); they amount to a romantic treatment of the diminished seventh chord. In two places Bach interrupts the course of the movement by inserting improvisatory passage work, first brief, then more broadly at the end of the movement. He concludes with a half cadence on the dominant, which, as it were, places a colon before the following movement, the powerful fugue, by far the most substantial movement of the sonata.[4]

2. As we know, the theme of this Fuga is derived from the beginning of the chorale, "Komm heiliger Geist, Herre Gott." Bach must have been fond of it because he used it so often (Example 149). We have already thoroughly discussed the struc-

Komm, hei-li-ger___ Geist,Her-re Gott.

Example 149. (a) Sonata for Violin solo in G Major, BWV 1005,
                 2nd movement, Fuga, m. 1–3
           (b) Chorale, "Komm heiliger Geist, Herre Gott,"
                 beginning

ture of this gigantic movement of 354 measures, mainly in regard to the planning of the exposition of the five themes. But the divertimenti also demand attention. Ernst Kurth established that they do not consist merely of mechanical running passages, but that these sections gain an inner expansion from the distribution of the culmination points;[5] this results in heightened tension at the end of each divertimento and gives weight to the implied polyphony that is in effect for several measures. Special note should be made of the two pedal-points, d^1 in m. 186–200 and g in m. 273–288, from which are derived sequences proceeding from the theme which heighten its intensity. More than one seminar on composition could be devoted to a thorough analysis of this fugue, but here we need make only one more observation: it is admirable how Bach negotiates the broad dimensions of this structure with only a single theme. In other fugues of comparable length, for example, *The Art of Fugue* (the fugues in *The Well-Tempered Clavier* are mostly shorter), he introduces second or even third themes. Here, *one* idea suffices to carry the monumental structure.[6]

3. After the intensity of the fugue a period of relaxation is needed. This Bach provides in the ensuing Largo. The tempo indication should not influence us to let the music move toward a "grave" tempo. The movement is really closer to an "andante amabile." The lovely melody seems almost too innocuous after the preceding music. A surprising preference for feminine endings in the melody lines lend the music a sentimental quality. This gives an inordinate emphasis to the few lines that do have masculine endings. In a deviation from his usual practice, Bach chose the subdominant key for this movement rather than the relative minor; this, too, underscores its idyllic character.

4. The concluding Allegro assai is a high-spirited piece; fun for the musician. Its capriciousness and turbulence do not let up for a moment; except for the 2 × 2 eighth notes of the theme, the entire movement seems to consist only of 16ths. It is tempting to play the movement as fast as possible, and it does, indeed, withstand a furious tempo. The high point of its brilliance is m. 88–93; with a sweeping approach, Bach again (as he did in the Chaconne) reaches the highest notes attainable by a violin at that time, when the instruments had shorter necks.

Partita No. 3 in E Major, BWV 1006

From the very beginning, the last in the cycle of works for violin solo has most quickly and directly captured the favor of the public. And in fact, Bach seldom composed with the freedom and ease he shows here. The partita is a unique, felicitous venture. It is a perfect place to start learning about Bach's literature for solo strings. It poses no problems of interpretation; whatever the imagination has to supply is clear and easily understood. One might quote Nietzsche and say that here "the depths lie on the surface." Bach himself seems to have been fond of the composition, as evidenced by his many adaptations of it.

It is the only one of the partitas to have a Preludio, whereas all the suites for cello solo have one; a violin show piece par excellence. The 16th-note figures, derived mainly from broken chords, ascend and descend with a nimbleness that suggests Vivaldi. Here, Bach writes his passage work entirely within the meter. The culmination points are symmetrically placed and coincide with the strong beats of each measure, giving the movement immediate comprehensibility. The *bariolage* effect is used twice, first with the open E-string, later with the A-string. The echo effects in m. 5–12, 45–51, and 61–67 are authentic and can be supplied in the other corresponding places. In order to orient oneself to the overall organization of the movement, one should realize that something akin to a reprise of the beginning, in the subdominant, takes place beginning in m. 59. One need only supply mentally the opening bars, transposed into A Major, before m. 59, and the matter will be perfectly clear. However, this reprise is longer than the exposition.

The following Loure, a dance in fluid 6/4 time (unusual for Bach), has a rather intricate rhythm. Here one must understand the eighth-note quarter-note upbeat,

Example 150. Partita for Violin solo in E Major, BWV 1006, 2nd movement, Loure, m. 1–4

so that the shape of the opening idea becomes clear (Example 150). The Loure is a kind of swaying dance step; any trace of hurriedness is inappropriate, and yet the half-measure pulse must be perceptible. The small note values in m. 10 and 20 should not obscure it.

The following Gavotte en rondeau again radiates high spirits. Bach did not write all that many rondeaus: the last movement of the violin concerto in E Major, the last movement of the clavier partita in C Minor. They appeal by virtue of their concise, forceful themes. Some of the flavor of the original "round" can still be felt.

Since the partita conspicuously lacks a Sarabande, i.e. a slow movement, the two Minuets, I and II, will have to be played in a comfortable, leisurely manner; otherwise there would be too little differentiation in the sequence of movements. One attractive detail should be pointed out: the extension of the second part of Minuet I from the customary 8 measures to 10 in m. 9–18.

As in the Prelude, there are authentic dynamic indications in the next movement, a Bourrée. It is interesting that Bach twice writes only *forte,* but not the *piano* that is needed 2 measures before. The two notations do not appear until m. 23 and 25, thereby correcting the stylistically indefensible hypothesis that since only the *forte* was indicated, the movement would have to be played basically *piano.*

Finally, the Gigue returns to the character of the Preludio which it strongly resembles in figuration and playing technique. Thus, the last partita and the entire cycle are brought to a close with a light touch.[7]

Chapter 21

Suites for Cello Solo

It is generally assumed that Bach wrote the six solo suites for cello *after* the solo works for violin, because he wanted to create a complementary group for the latter. But this cannot be substantiated. In fact, Eppstein believes that it was the other way around: first came the rather modestly conceived cello works, then the boldly fashioned violin pieces—although this characterization should not be taken as a value judgment. It is beyond doubt that the two cycles were written at very nearly the same time and this is confirmed by the music. With all due caution, it might be ventured that, like the keyboard inventions, the cello suites are informed by a certain didactic intent, more so than the sonatas and partitas for violin. This impression, however, may only be due to the fact that Bach evidently had to acquire a knowledge of cello technique. We know that he played the violin and the viola, but nothing is mentioned about his playing the cello. Be that as it may, the six suites are high points in the cellist's repertory, just as the corresponding violin solo works are for the violinist.

Suite No. 1 in G Major, BWV 1007

When we spoke of the didactic intent of the suites we were thinking primarily of the first suite. It has all the qualities of an "introductory work"; every player who studies the suite cycle will tackle this work first. Nevertheless, one will realize very quickly that the piece is considerably more than a preparatory study. The conclusion of the Prelude, the *bariolage* section and the ensuing passage on the pedal point, D, effect a tension-filled escalation and transcend the boundaries of a simple prelude using broken chords, with which the piece began.

Next comes an Allemande which is appealing because of its symmetrical proportions; any Baroque excesses which occasionally characterize Bach's Allemandes are suppressed.

The same is true of the Courante; its principal idea is expressed nonchalantly and directly. Both movements, the Allemande and the Courante, can be played at a rather lively tempo because of their clarity.

The classically rounded Sarabande, with its phrase of twice eight measures, has already been discussed.

Regarding the two Minuets, I and II, we call attention to the fact that in all the cello suites, Bach interrupts the traditional sequence of movements by inserting a pair of lighter dance movements in penultimate position, between the Sarabande and the Gigue. In the first two suites the two interpolated movements are Minuets, in suites 3 and 4 they are Bourrées, in the last two suites, they are Gavottes. These movements are all characterized by elemental rhythm and dance qualities; they are replete with the joy of making music, as if Bach took particular pleasure in working outside the "official" sequence of suite movements. The high-spirited quality of these movements should be reflected in any performance. Indeed, the two minuets of the D Major Suite are good examples of this principle of relaxation; of course, the leisurely quality peculiar to every Baroque minuet should not be forgotten.

The concluding Gigue contains interesting examples of how phrases can be compressed. Example 151[8] shows a sample of this procedure. Within the first ten measures, bowing to the necessity of intensification, long and short particles (= sequences) are lined up, one after the other. Disregarding the inevitable cadence formulas, these units become progressively shorter. Then, in part two of the Gigue, there is a charming detail. To agree with part 1, part 2 should actually end in m. 28. But Bach introduces yet another conclusion in m. 28 ff. Again, note the intensification by means of compression into the second half of the idea; it still is complete in m. 29; its second half appears in m. 31, and in m. 32 it is reduced. This gives the movement and the work a kind of *underscored* conclusion.

Example 151. Suite for Cello solo in G Major, BWV 1007, 6th movement, Gigue, m. 1–10.

Suite No. 2 in D Minor, BWV 1008

The lines of the Prelude are more intertwined than those of the introductory movement of the first suite. Now the substance carries a heavier emotional load, although Bach does not lose his control over it. The inner agitation of the piece can be seen by the asymmetrical placing of the stresses and culmination points. There are seldom any identical sequences long enough to help understand the work. With this in mind, we can recognize what an abundance of disparate ideas are found in m. 22–39. The last measures of the movement, 59–62 (not including the final measure), must be played as arpeggios. In this, solutions that are too conventional must be avoided; in Chapter 5 (Example 7) I gave some suggestions which could be the basis for further development.

The Allemande makes extensive use of double stops, especially in its first part. This emphasizes a certain severity, which is generally associated with the key of D minor.

The Courante provides a glimpse into Bach's artistry by showing how he makes an important structural element out of a formula that at first appears incidental. Example 152 demonstrates this development. August Wenzinger showed convincingly in his edition that the characteristic phrasing, with its slurring of pairs of sixteenth-notes, derived from the only two original phrase marks that appear in m. 10, 3rd quarter, and m. 6, 3rd quarter (designated by the sign § in Example 152). In the example, Wenzinger's additions are printed like the original phrasings. I myself would like to go even further and place the slurs in a number of other places which are structurally dependent on the element in question. This would clarify the musical structure. My additions are shown with dotted lines.

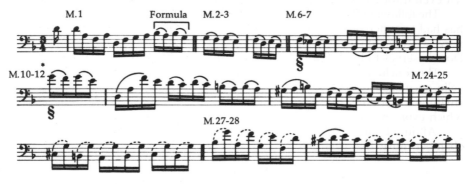

Example 152. Suite for Cello solo in D Minor, BWV 1008, 3rd movement, Courante.

The Sarabande features a regular alternation between chordal and linear parts. The chordal measures always have the classical Sarabande rhythm: quarter-note, dotted quarter, eighth-note, with a syncopated accent on the second, weak beat of triple time, i.e., the dotted quarter-note. The linear measures, then, contain the cadences. M. 17–20 deviate from this structure. They are linear all the way through. This irregularity gives the movement its tension.

The first of the two minuets sounds almost too defiant for a gallant dance movement. Only the alternative Minuet, which is in the parallel major, introduces a little more levity into the proceedings.

The concluding Gigue also has an air of "going against the grain" and its angularity occasionally projects an "appassionato" mood. It should not be played too rapidly lest the accents lose their weight.

Suite No. 3 in C Major, BWV 1009

C Major, the richest and most resonant key for the cello, inspired Bach to veritable cascades of sound in the Prelude. Even in the first measure we sense a broad gesture, as if he is saying, "Let me offer you this." Then, in the second half of the movement, the composer constructs an extensive arch of arpeggios over a pedal-point, G. Bach was fond of using pedal points as means of intensification, especially within his Preludes. At the conclusion, dramatic double-stop strokes energetically bring the (so far uninterrupted) 16th-notes to a halt. Just how unconventionally Bach invented double stops for strings can be seen in the chords of measures 77, 79 and 80. He seems to have known something about the cello, after all.

The Allemande appears complicated, but is only capricious to the point of exuberance, and the many 32nd-notes do not disrupt the balance.

The Courante is characterized by dazzling virtuosity and can stand a lively tempo.

The Sarabande, on the other hand, is proud and solemn; it is far removed from the meditative introversion we find in other Bach Sarabandes. This movement represents a measured, courtly step,—what Busoni later called a "cortège." This is felt even throughout the more complicated parts, such as m. 13–14.

The following Bourrée is one of Bach's best-known suite movements and thus has had to suffer numerous arrangements. It is, indeed, an inspired venture. Its verve extends into the C minor Double, and the more modest appearance of this Double serves to lend more luminosity to the first Bourrée.

The concluding Gigue is a true skipping dance, spirited, almost acrobatic. The cello once again "pulls out all the stops" and unfolds a variegated spectrum of rhythms and sounds. In the process, episodes like m. 33–40 use pedal point effects which evoke some early 20th-century music.

All in all, this suite is perhaps the most beautiful piece of "representative" chamber music that Bach wrote.

Suite No. 4 in E-flat Major, BWV 1010

Many cellists seem to give this work a wide berth. The suite is considered especially difficult, and this is probably why it is seldom heard. Indeed, a key that includes three flats is hardly idiomatic for the instrument. Yet the E-flat Major suite richly rewards the effort put into it; it is not a work that should be kept in the closet.

The broad chords which open the Prelude are progressively broken up into smaller units in the course of the second half of the movement, so that it is difficult to establish the continuity. However, with the F-flat Major Neapolitan sixth chord that enters in m. 80, Bach again ties everything together; the musical action is rounded off and brought to a conclusion in 10 measures which once again sum up this great movement.

The relatively simple Allemande has surprising sequence forms in several measures; note the leaps of ascending sevenths (m. 9–12). A relatively fast tempo for an Allemande seems to be called for.

The Courante, on the other hand, is much too complex to be played with excessive speed. Eighth-notes, 16th-notes and eighth-triplets are interspersed, combinations seldom met in Bach's suite music. In this movement, too, the sequences occasionally seem "willful," as if Bach were trying to get a better grasp, to make the sheer abundance of ideas more comprehensible by frequently repeating the individual elements.

The dancelike feeling exuded by the Sarabande is rare for a work of this genre; its gracefulness is unmistakable. The classic Sarabande rhythm is consistently avoided and replaced by elegant dotted rhythms which dominate the motion. Even the quarter-note chords of part two (m. 15 and 17) are incorporated into this rhythm.

The two following Bourrées are appealing because of the charm of their ideas. The long, drawn out (48 measures) first Bourrée with its joyful 16th-note runs is countered by a second one of only 12 measures; it comes close to being comical by virtue of its "rumbling" quality.

Finally the Gigue, the most exuberant virtuoso movement in all six cello suites, is worked out with extreme concentration, and yet it seems to have been jotted down in a spirit of great fun. We have already pointed out its exceedingly concentrated thematic work (pp. 152 ff), virtually unparalleled in the suites. The movement demands the ultimate in concentration on the part of the cellist, allowing no time to catch a breath. A masterful interpretation can really inspire an audience.

Suite No. 5 in C Minor, BWV 1011

This suite requires a "violoncello discordato," the a-string having to be tuned a whole step lower, to 'g' (cf. Figure 8). Bach requires this to facilitate the use of chords which are not playable in normal tuning, for example, the four-part ones (Example 153a), in which the upper 'g' is allowed to sound as an open string. However, cellists do not like to change the tuning of their instruments, fearing that both scordatura and normal tuning will suffer. Thus they will have to change several chords and play the chord cited in Example 153a, for example, only as it appears in Example 153b. That might be acceptable. It is regrettable, however, that the quiet sound peculiar to this suite is lost without scordatura, which changes the resonance of the instrument when the a-string is tuned lower. Since such a less brilliant timbre is characteristic of this suite one is reluctant to dispense with it.

Example 153.
Suite for Cello solo in C Minor, BWV 1011

The two-part Prelude with a broad, serious introduction followed by a lively section with a polyphonic effect (it is given the dynamic direction "très viste" in the

Figure 8. Suite for Cello solo in C Minor, BWV 1011, manuscript by Anna Magdalena Bach, 1st page

lute adaptation of the work), is an extended movement. Traditionally, the scheme of the so-called French overture, after which it is modelled, would demand a repeat of the slow introductory section at the end (cf. the introductory movements of the four orchestral overtures or suites). Here Bach dispensed with it as the movement was apparently long enough for him. The rapid section has the structure of a fugue, but it is only its appearance that evokes this impression; there is no actual polyphony. Its formal organization, at least, with thematic expositions and divertimentos, corresponds roughly to that of the fugues in the violin solo sonatas. Thematic expositions can be found in the following measures: m. 28–63 (exposition), m. 72–79 (variation); m. 88–94 (pseudo-entrance, variation); m. 102–109, 151–157, 176–183 and 197–204. Upbeats are not included in the numbering of measures. Of the total length of 196 measures in "très viste," the thematic quotations take up only two-fifths, or exactly 78 measures, of the section. This is probably due to the fact that, with the exception of the exposition, in which there are four thematic entrances in the sequence tonic-dominant-tonic-dominant, the theme each time is quoted only once and is immediately followed by divertimenti. Despite this preponderance of divertimenti, the themes remain the formal supporting elements of the movement. In order to understand their latent polyphony, one has to bear clearly in mind that the theme consists of two lines; in other words, it is accompanied by an obbligato counterpoint. These two lines are interchanged several times and thus represent double counterpoint at the octave (Example 154). The theme, which itself consists of eight measures, enters repeatedly but remains the same only during the first four measures; its second half is subject to considerable variation. In one place, m. 72–79, even the beginning of the theme is dissolved into 16th-notes. In the lute version, on the other hand, Bach constantly varies the entire theme after m. 56.

Example 154. Suite for Cello solo in C Minor, BWV 1011, 1st movement, Prelude, (a) m. 27–31, (b) m. 149–153

The very measured, almost solemn Allemande seems to many players to be in danger of falling apart structurally; many listeners also lose the thread. But despite its expansiveness it is effective when played with a steady pulse; if one holds to this the movement loses its tendency to dissolve.

The Courante also perpetuates the rigorous severity of the piece. It is one of Bach's Courantes in 3/2 time, many of which can be found in his keyboard music. Such movements tend to have a ceremonious quality. Only the concluding measures of both sections (m. 12 and 24) convert the 3/2 meter into 6/4, thus injecting some relaxation.

I do not hesitate to count the Sarabande of this suite among Bach's masterpieces in any category. The way he conjures a total musical cosmos into a single line (the movement has no double-stops at all) is absolutely incomparable. Earlier we attempted an analysis of the linear and harmonic structure of the first half of this movement (pp. 100).

The two Gavottes, I and II, finally ease the tension that had been hanging over the previous movements of the suite. It is fascinating to observe how Bach varies the principal rhythm itself within the first Gavotte. The process extends through the entire course of the work. The second Gavotte draws its vigor from a triplet motion and, deviating from the customary scheme of the suite, has a rondo-like arrangement.

Finally, the Gigue: as a concluding movement to this suite, it is almost too light, too terse, compact. In Bach's music its ♩♪♪ rhythm seems to be closely linked to the key of C minor; it can be found in many other of his C minor works. On listening to m. 61–67, I cannot resist associating them with the first movement of Brahms' C Minor Symphony. Could he have been acquainted with the solo suite?

Suite No. 6 in D Major, BWV 1012

This work was written for a five-string cello. Instruments of this kind are documented, and it is known that the Köthen court orchestra had them when Bach was there. The fifth string was located above the normal a-string and was likewise tuned at a distance of a fifth, i.e., e^1. The composition is intended for this kind of instrument and not, as is occasionally thought, for a violoncello piccolo or a viola pomposa (cf. p. 49). Since five-string cellos are no longer in use today, this poses considerable problems for performance. In the higher registers Bach requires a significantly greater range, g^2 in contrast to g^1 in the other works (the fifth suite in C minor uses scordatura; the highest note is lowered accordingly to f^1). Moreover, Bach requires *bariolage* effects, for which an open e^1-string was indispensable (m. 23–32 of the Prelude). The latter problem can be resolved on the regular four-string cello by using the thumb position; Bach was not yet familiar with this technique. Since Haydn and Beethoven the upper registers have ceased to be "terra incognita." Also, some of the chords in the movements following the Prelude can be rearranged. Such efforts are more than handsomely rewarded by the beauty of the work.

Prelude: The movement has an unusually far-reaching architectonic span, which helps one forget its considerable length. Although it consists merely of a regular motion of eighth-note triplets, which do not let up for a moment and are only intensified toward the end by 16th-notes, we recognize monumental proportions, long developments, high and low points, intensive and relaxing episodes: a musical "arcus triumphalis."

The Allemande, in contrast, seems almost too overloaded with figuration; the notational picture is irritating because of its multitude of 16th and 32nd-notes. As in earlier works, a diagram of the keys and modulations will facilitate orientation. Bach facilitates such an overview by letting the motion subside when he comes to the supporting and articulating cadences. He then writes longer note values, by virtue of which an agogic accent is, as it were, written out. Double-stops frequently underscore the structural function of such cadences. The harmonic development in one passage, m. 11, puzzles both player and listener at first. The harmony modulates to G major, but in the next measure, without any apparent connection, the dominant of F-sharp minor appears. In terms of music theory, this progression is unproblematic: G major as the Neapolitan sixth of F-sharp minor; but nevertheless, it is difficult to comprehend aurally, since the leading of the upper voices is daring and unusual and the ear cannot supply at once the necessary harmonic background. In Example 155, the situation is clarified by the addition of two harmonic voices, a procedure which is then confirmed in the ensuing m. 13: the implied harmony on the second quarter is a G major sixth chord, and on the 3rd quarter a diminished seventh chord on the seventh scale step, i.e., a dominant function of F-sharp minor.

Example 155.
Suite for Cello solo in D Major, BWV 1012, 2nd movement, Allemande, harmonic sequence, m. 11–12

In contrast to the substantial Allemande, the Courante is immediately accessible. Its skipping principal rhythm ♫♩♫♫, however much it is used, ensures the spontaneity and easy-going joyfulness of the piece.

The Sarabande, with its numerous intervals of a sixth, is arranged almost totally with a view to euphony. It is tempting to characterize it as arcadian in its cheerfulness; it has such a Mediterranean, Apollonian quality, particularly when one recalls the profundity of the Sarabande in the preceding C minor suite. To be sure, the lack of a fifth string is most conspicuous in this movement.

Gavottes I and II maintain the cheerful tone; it is more relaxed by virtue of the livelier tempo, yet it maintains a certain composure and never becomes really high-spirited. Especially charming is the pastoral, Musette character of the second Gavotte, characterized by short, two-measure phrases and the pedal point 'd.'

The Gigue which concludes the work is an authentic "chasse," i.e., hunting music. Bach lets the horns blare; the echoes reverberate in the distance, and the entire range of the instrument is drawn into this joyful music; a merry chase over hill and dale.

Chapter 22

Sonatas for Violin and Clavier

Sonata No. 1 in B Minor, BWV 1014

1. Adagio. A violin melody emerges from the ornate work of the right hand of the clavier. This keyboard part, moving in parallel thirds or sixths, is too rich in substance for an accompanying figure, as will be confirmed later, and seems to come from some "Passion" music. The broadly arched violin cantilena has an expressive,

improvised quality. It seems to go its own way, entirely independent of the clavier; but then it coalesces with the sixths of the keyboard part when the new key of F sharp minor is reached in m. 15–16. What first seemed to be accompanying material now proves to be a basic thematic component. Henceforth, the violin and the right hand of the clavier, now both two-voiced, are inseparable. Together with the bass, which stresses half measures (note the descending thirds), there emerges a five-voiced, rich-sounding structure. It never degenerates into Baroque extravagance, but rather remains clear and transparent, with the eighth-notes in violin and clavier answering each other. The development which began in m. 13 is recapitulated starting with m. 24, this time in the principal key, B minor. In m. 31, a brief, but substantial coda ensues, which culminates in a broad Neapolitan sixth chord in C major. Between this and the preceding F-sharp minor, the pendulum swings between subdominant and dominant; the grandly conceived architecture of the movement is placed between these two poles. One is tempted to view it as the entrance portal to the cycle of the six great violin-clavier sonatas, just as the first "adagio" of the G minor violin solo sonata introduces that series of works.

2. The theme of the first Allegro is concise but still serious. Its seemingly inconsequential m. 4, which plays only a transitional role, a short time later proves to be surprisingly rich in content: first in m. 11 and many times after that, it occurs in inversion; apart from that it serves as an independent continuation motif (violin in m. 31–43, then both right and left hand of the clavier, m. 35–37). A middle section begins in m. 41. It is predominantly in the principal related major keys, and its material derives from the principal theme, although it is differently handled; characteristic development episodes evolve from its first measure (m. 61 ff.). The intensive, interlocking use of the four-note motif taken from the bass line (especially evident in m. 80–81: A-B-C#-d) should also be noted; it occurs in m. 85–87 between the violin and the right hand of the clavier, with the above-mentioned transitional measure serving as bass. In addition there is the charming violin idea (m. 95–101), casually used, as a passing thought. The pianist will have to decide whether to articulate the sustained notes in m. 31–33 and 132–134 with trills. But one need not be overly correct by also adding a trill to the sustained violin note in m. 80–82, for the sound of the violin is sustained anyway. The entrance of the reprise in m. 102 is a literal repetition of m. 1–40.

3. The serenade-like violin melody of the Andante, arioso, is characterized by numerous feminine line-endings of two "trailing off" sixteenths: on the 3rd quarter of m. 2, the 1st and 3rd quarters of m. 3, etc. Bach left very precise indications for phrasing in the violin part; wherever they are missing, it is not difficult to fill them in. In the clavier, the movement begins with a refined accompanying figure—its relationship to the clavier "accompaniment" in the great flute sonata in B minor has often been noted—which is sometimes so similar that it parallels the principal voice, i.e., the violin. This is true, above all, in m. 12–14 and 22–25. I would like to suggest that in these measures, wherever *both* upper parts have a simultaneous eighth rest, the absent bass should be filled in with a b.c. chord. Example 156 gives a model for m. 13. It is not immediately evident that a reprise begins in m. 19, because of the change in the violin part. It reaches its lovely culmination in the interplay of the two melody parts in m. 26–27, in which the e^3 of the violin represents the melodic high point of the movement.

4. After the three rather restrained movements, the concluding Allegro explodes with life. The thematic substance appears in two parts in the form of a

Example 156.
Sonata for Violin and Clavier
in B Minor, BWV 1014, 3rd
movement, Andante, m. 12–
13, with b.c. chord added in
small print

double line: both the violin and the right hand of the clavier could stand alone as a themes. The idea of the fourth measure of the violin, the ♪♪ ♪ rhythm, is introduced very deliberately. Along with its function within the theme we also encounter it as a continuation idea in the first part of the movement (m. 13–15). In the second part it does not appear at all at first, but after two intervening thematic quotations it asserts itself with increasing emphasis from m. 47 on. Thus Bach consciously keeps the idea fresh by shortening the theme, originally four measures long, by one measure: the last measure, containing the above-mentioned motif. This occurs at the beginning of the second part. One only has to imagine the second part, also beginning with the complete, four-measure theme and also featuring the rhythm in question, to acknowledge how much weaker a literal adoption of the theme would have been. It should also be noted that the first part actually ends in the tonic—which is most unusual. The last two measures which modulate to the dominant, are merely appendages.

Sonata No. 2 in A Major, BWV 1015

1. The introductory movement, which Bach provided only with the heading, "dolce," has a pastoral character. This straightforward attitude is reflected in the theme, which is nothing more than a one-measure cadence formula (Example 157a). But in the course of the movement additional material is added to this formula: the continuation idea of m. 8 (Example 157b) and, beginning in m. 17, second half, a new phrase, a measure and a half in length (Example 157c). The first two ideas, 157a and 157b in the example, are combined in a charming manner in about the middle of the movement. The execution of the trill within the movement needs to be looked at closely: the way Bach writes it in m. 1, i.e., with an after-beat, it must be played only as a component of the theme, no matter whether he used the 𝄐 sign or the 〰 sign (m. 18, 22); the latter, of course, also means 'trill.' Apart from that, additional trills are called for, specifically where there is cadencing (m. 7, 17, 26, 32,

Example 157. Sonata for Violin and Clavier in A Major, BWV 1015, 1st movement, Dolce, (a) m. 1, (b) m. 8, (c) m. 17–18

37).[9] Here the trills do not have an after-beat; the anticipatory sixteenth note follows immediately. Since the latter kinds of trills always run parallel in violin and right hand, agreement is necessary.

2. The asymmetrical nature of the principal idea of the Allegro (i.e., its length of five measures) is hardly noticeable the first time it is played or heard, because the construction of the theme is exemplary and the transition from theme to counterpoint in m. 6 takes place effortlessly. The three-part movement has an unusually long middle section in relation to the beginning and concluding sections (m. 30–92). Here we might speak of a new theme; for the continuous sixteenth-note idea—which developed from a broken chord—is treated like a theme for the first time in the right hand starting in m. 30. The accompanying contrapuntal eighth-note voice also consists only of broken triads. It was probably for this reason that Bach felt compelled to refer back to the principal theme very early in this middle section, beginning in m. 40, where it is distributed between the two hands of the clavier. He also extracts another characteristic echo episode (m. 58–69) from the broken triads, which is then followed by a great pedal point exposition (m. 74–92) at the conclusion of this B Section. There is hardly any other chamber work by Bach which features pedal points of this kind; one has the impression of a written out "cadenza" in the tradition of a classical instrumental concerto, which is reinforced by the arpeggios in the violin part. For the latter, which Bach merely noted as chords, we suggest the following solution (Example 158); it avoids overly repetitive arpeggios and can be modified as needed. This pedal point clearly marks the end of the B section. The unison which concludes the A part in m. 29 (likewise a rarity in Bach's chamber music) serves a similar function: clarifying the form of a section of the movement. The reprise of the A section which begins in m. 93 is a literal repetition, and consequently concludes with the same unisono.

Example 158. Sonata for Violin and Clavier in A Major, BWV 1015, 2nd movement, Allegro, m. 74 ff., execution of arpeggios

3. The following tranquil movement is headed Andante un poco, and consists of a canon at the unison of the two melody voices. This is accompanied by a regular sixteenth-note bass which is again derived from broken chords. The various structures of the individual melody lines have already been discussed on pp 150 ff.; they achieve a flexibility of melodic development far removed from the schematization that might have resulted from the constraints of canon. By means of this modification, the canonic line gains vitality, and once again every trace of pedantry is avoided. Then, beginning in m. 26 (in the violin, with an upbeat in m. 25), there is a small coda which ends in the dominant of F-sharp minor, C-sharp major, and moves on at once to the A major of the finale. To connect two movements, Bach apparently liked to use in immediate succession two major keys related by thirds. In this movement the players should also plan the use of trills and turns. Various solutions are possible, but some logic must apply no matter what decisions are made. If one canonic voice features an ornament, the same ornament must also appear in the other canonic voice. To give one example, the original trill of the violin on the 3rd quarter of m. 13 (on b-sharp) must also appear in the corresponding place in the

clavier, although Bach did not write it. Another example: when the pianist on a well-known phonograph recording uses the descending turn in m. 18 and 20, the same mordent must be played in the corresponding measures of the violin (m. 17 and 19), otherwise the idea of the canon is destroyed.

4. It should not be overlooked that the last movement is marked Presto. A lively tempo undoubtedly does the most justice to the dancelike, folk-music quality of its principal theme. The theme itself is a textbook model of linear and rhythmic direction (cf. pp 115, 121). Although it has clear phrases and this regularity is maintained throughout the movement, it is not tiring for player or listener. We have already established the reason for such sustained liveliness: in the first part of the movement the phrase has six measures; in the second, it has four, and, later only three (m. 64 ff.). That being the case, the difference of the motifs at the beginning of the second part carries little weight, especially since the new idea (m. 49–52) is only a counterpoint to the principal theme, as the concluding measures (m. 110–113) demonstrate. The contrapuntal feats involving stretto of the theme, at the unison and at a distance of only a half or quarter measure (m. 92 ff. and 110–111) are a particular source of pleasure.

Sonata No. 3 in E Major, BWV 1016

1. The magnificent introductory Adagio belongs to a type rarely represented in Bach's music: the violin and clavier voices develop entirely independently of each other without thematic overlap. To be sure, one is reluctant to categorize the clavier part as "accompaniment"; it is too interesting for that, even though the rigorous rhythm pattern contrasts strongly with the imaginatively constructed violin line. The balanced proportions of this movement are without equal. For one thing, they are reflected in the tranquility of the bass line, which recalls the pillars of the architectural orders of antiquity. The "salvation" six-four chord in the third to last measure anticipates Romantic music. There are various ways of reading the rhythm of the figure falling on the 3rd quarter of m. 17 and the 4th quarter of m. 27. Since there is no surviving autograph manuscript, the performer will have to decide which interpretation is preferable (Example 159).

Example 159. Sonata for Violin and Clavier in E Major, BWV 1016, 1st movement, Adagio, m. 17: (a) and (b), Eppstein, (c) Schneiderhan and others

2. In comparison with the monumental introductory movement, I find the following Allegro somewhat disappointing. Its principal theme, twice ascending as high as C-sharp, lacks a distinct high point and thus remains weak. Bach also fails to break up the stereotyped eight-measure structure of the phrase in the course of the movement, as he does elsewhere. The middle section, B, begins in m. 63; at first it is defined by a one-measure clavier figure in eighth-notes to which, however, the

violin soon contributes an idea of its own (m. 65–71). This line can be traced back to the violin part of the first movement. Since it does not bear up well when played too rapidly, the overall tempo of the movement should be set at an appropriate "moderato." After m. 75 the principal theme of the movement appears frequently, also in the relative minor. As the movement progresses, tension builds in this middle section: the two upper parts present contrapuntal motifs which are nicely interwoven (m. 102–106), and shortly thereafter the first two measures of the principal theme are imitated five times in succession at two measures' distance (m. 111–120). A return of the A section follows, beginning in the subdominant and significantly shortened (m. 121 ff.).

3. The following Adagio ma non tanto movement is curious. Lyrical and introspective, it evokes the slow movement of the E Major Violin Concerto, BWV 1042, which is also in C-sharp Minor; but as a chamber music piece it is more intimate than the latter: its beauties are not so much out in the open, but must be sought out. In order to interpret this well, we need to get an overall view of its structure. Two melodic lines develop on the foundation of the ostinato-like bass moving in quarter notes: one given to the violin, the other to the right hand of the keyboard part. They are characterized by sixteenth-note triplets (Example 160a) and an additional motif consisting of simple sixteenths phrased in pairs (Example 160b). Along with that,

Example 160. Sonata for Violin and Clavier in E Major, BWV 1016 3rd movement, Adagio ma non tanto, m. 5–6, 9–10

however, both the violin and the right hand must also execute a chordal thoroughbass accompaniment, which is written in eighth-note chords, for example, m. 1–4 in the clavier and m. 13–20 in the violin. A sharp distinction has to be made between these two elements. The keyboard player in particular must separate them acoustically, as if they belonged to two different registers. If the two melody parts now play a duet, as they do for long stretches in the movement, then the thoroughbass harmony is lacking, for there no longer is a voice available for it. This, however, leads to an interruption of the texture. In contrast to other trio movements, in which no b.c. chords are expected because there were no grounds for such an expectation, here the composer has shown how he imagines the b.c.; wherever there was room, he filled it in. In order to avoid this break, I suggest that the b.c. be continued accordingly; it can be suggested by carefully distributing it between the two hands, as shown in Example 161. In this way the movement gains the tonal balance it needs to realize its full beauty. A piano is obviously the preferred instrument for this because variations in touch are possible. On the harpsichord, which cannot accommodate a sustained cantilena, the movement is distorted right from the start.

4. The turmoil of the Allegro finale stands in sharp contrast to the meditative posture of the preceding Adagio. Its infectious vitality had to be countered with some calming element later on, i.e., the triplet idea of the middle section which begins in m. 35. But Bach does not dwell on this idea long; he constantly sprinkles in elements from the sixteenths of the principal theme of the A section. Finally (m. 78) he thrusts the triplets completely aside, although section B is far from over. For a dis-

cussion of the problem of coordinating the eighth triplets and simple eighths notes (*jeu inégal*), see pp. 66 ff. M. 99–102 are proof that long clavier notes can be sustained by the use of trills. This technique would also be appropriate in the 2nd movement of this sonata (m. 88–91), and likewise in many other places in Bach's chamber music, although we shall not point this out in every case. The exact repeat of the opening begins in m. 120, rounding off the A-B-A structure of this movement.

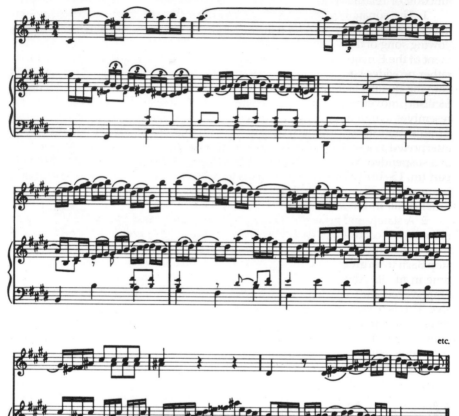

Example 161. Sonata for Violin and Clavier in E Major, BWV 1016 3rd movement, Adagio ma non tanto, m. 24–34 with added thorough-bass.

Sonata No. 4 in C Minor, BWV 1017

In the E major sonata the two slow movements were impressive manifestations of an espressivo style, the rapid movements being rather lightweight in comparison. The situation is reversed in the C minor sonata: here, the two allegros are prototypes of their genre, while the second slow movement in particular serves the function of relaxation.

1. The sonata begins with a subdued, lyrical Siciliano (largo), which, like so many of Bach's movements of this nature, employs ascending, minor sixths.[10] The flowing song of the violin is divided into simple sections. As in the opening movement of the E major sonata, the clavier does not participate in the violin theme, but rather provides background sixteenth-note figures which here have a true accompanying quality. Hence in its distribution of voices the movement resembles the Siciliano movement of the E-flat Major Flute Sonata, BWV 1031, which it also resembles in mood. To point out some specific details: during the second half of m. 22 an extraordinary harmony appears, apparently unintentionally, which can be interpreted as a seventh chord on C; in context, however, it has more the character of a suspended Neapolitan chord. The doubling of the concluding line of the first part (m. 13–16) at the end of the second part (m. 29–32 and 33–36) is of surpassing beauty. In m. 32 the violin evidently has to play an appoggiatura d^2 before the c^2, in order to fill in the leap of a third into the tonic.

2. A stately and powerful theme opens the following Allegro. Its five-measure phrases are captivating, as is the splendid rise of the intervals right in the first measure: fifth-octave-tenth. Its bass also has a straight diatonic line, which does not stop Bach from giving a chromatic counterpoint to the same theme later on; the first time in m. 36. All in all, the polyphonic superiority of the movement should be emphasized: the freedom of voice leading as the theme enters in the bass is impressive. This is reason enough for Bach to repeat this structure two more times (m. 55–59 and 84–88). Other episodes also testify to Bach's contrapuntal artistry, e.g., the combination of the two melody parts in m. 59–62 (Example 162) with criss-crossing imitations (shown by arrows), or the close imitation of an ascending motif developed from the principal theme (m. 42–45, repeated in m. 78–81). This is also a

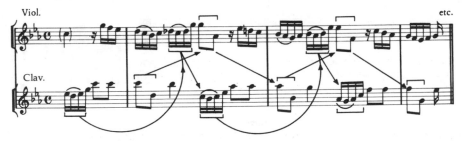

Example 162. Sonata for Violin and Clavier in C Minor, BWV 1017, 2nd movement, Allegro, m. 59–62

three-part movement. The middle part, which enters in m. 34, is marked by a new, brief idea and its chromatic counterpoint; later on, the latter will become independent and lend a new aspect to the principal theme. The 32nd-note figure of the new idea indicates that the overall tempo of the movement should not be too rapid. Still, it has to remain fluid and not become rigid. The reprise of this movement is not easily recognized; it differs noticeably from the exposition, since the idea of the B part has been worked into it. I would place its beginning in m. 84, 3rd quarter—the thematic entrance in G minor. It seems unthinkable to me to read a two-part structure into the movement.

3. The idea behind the straightforward Adagio is to present four-measure melody lines twice in succession, once *forte* and then *piano*. But only the first line is repeated literally; thereafter, Bach varies the echo line and gleans new possibilities from it by means of the inversion of intervals and other variations, ever mindful that the two lines are related. The last line, beginning in m. 41, is doubled in length to eight measures. Its *piano* repetition is then followed by four transitional measures which lead back to the dominant of C minor. The triplet motion of the clavier which had dominated the entire movement is broken off in favor of sixteenth-notes, which reunite the previously separated violin and right hand parts in imitation, thereby clearing the way for the following Allegro movement.

4. The concluding Allegro harkens back to the first Allegro movement, presenting its substance once again, in concentrated form, so to speak. Naturally, the themes are now new and different; on p. 116 we showed how Bach heightens their impact by first introducing only the first four measures of the principal idea, and only later allowing its completion. The movement is binary. The second part seems to open with a new idea, but Eppstein has shown that it is merely a variant of the principal theme.[11] On the other hand, the contrapuntal idea of the principal theme evolves into a new, independent motif. It is interesting to follow its development; the example below illustrates the most important stages (Example 163). The reader

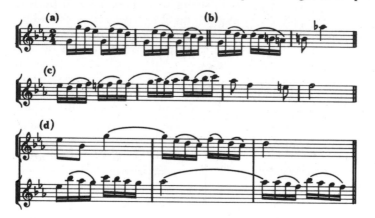

Example 163. Sonata for Violin and Clavier in C Minor, BWV 1017, 4th movement, Allegro, (a) m. 5–6, (b) 55–56, (c) 59–61, (d) 76–78, (e) 80–82

should pay special attention to the inversions and metric displacements (instead of 4 × 4 sixteenth-notes, 5 × 3 sixteenths plus an extra beginning note; see the ties in the example).

In regard to both the quality of its invention and its intellectual penetration of the substance, the C minor sonata is unsurpassed. Taken as a whole or examined in detail, it always offers new insights and is inexhaustibly vital.

Sonata No. 5 in F Minor, BWV 1018

Of the six sonatas for violin and clavier, this work is probably least concerned with effects; one is tempted to state that it is the most introverted of this group. This is not to say that it is of lesser quality; on the contrary, it is better than average. But its beauty unfolds for both player and listener only after a lengthy exposure. A good performance is not achieved without effort, for there are many problems. Right at the beginning we have the great introductory movement:

1. There is no tempo direction, but it should be played in a fluid manner; the correct tempo derives from the dominating clavier figure (Example 164), which

Example 164. Sonata for Violin and Clavier in F Minor, BWV 1018, 1st movement, Largo, m. 1–2

might be called the musical equivalent of a touchingly self-effacing gesture. But the sixteenth figures of the violin, which should not be rushed, also have to be taken into account when choosing the tempo. Many players will find the constant repetition of this figure strenuous, as there is hardly a measure in which it does not occur. Perhaps it will help to think of this figure as "only" a subordinate part—not a mere accompaniment, but a motif of secondary importance which must be correctly articulated, and is damaged by an excess of emotion. For the violin has the lead here: its free, melodic fantasy gives the movement structure and content. It helps to visualize each individual section of the violin part separately, using the following schematic overview:

M. 6–9: prelude; without break.

M. 13–18: *first principal line.*

M. 19–25: its extension with the important third-motif (cf. p. 157).

M. 26–32: *second principal line.*

M. 33–37: its reenforcement with a conclusion in the relative major, A-flat major (m. 32 had concluded with a half cadence.) *End of the first part.*

M. 40–41, 44–45, 48–50: three approaches to the next principal line, each one increasing in intensity.

M. 52–59: *third principal line;* it is longer than the previous ones, starts broadly and reaches a high point when the clavier motif is taken up in m. 55 and 56.

M. 64–68: *fourth principal line,* even more expansive than the preceding one; it consists of three sub-lines: m. 64 ff., m. 74 ff., m. 79 ff. The cadence to the tonic, F minor, in m. 87–88 *concludes the second part,* which is followed by a free reprise.

M. 90–101: *fifth principal line;* at first it appears to be a subordinate part, but becomes the primary focus again by m. 93 at the latest; it then experiences a sharp rise in m. 96–97, from which the descending thirds, having increased in importance during the movement, lead into the concluding section.

M. 102–106, first quarter: reenforcement of the preceding line; the relationships are the same as those at the end of the first part (m. 26–32 and 33–37): the principal line itself concludes with a half cadence, the reenforcement with a full cadence to the tonic, F minor. *End of the third part.*

The remaining three measures form a transition to the next movement.

The interval of the descending third has the value of a "constructive interval" within this movement; it carries, supports and brackets the musical action. This was already thoroughly discussed on p. 157.

A further suggestion might help to master the problems in this movement: Bach reinforces each important increase in tension by means of increased eighth-note motion. M. 20–21, 34–35 and later, m. 94 and 96, are good examples of this. There is a very tight and insistent compression of rhythms in m. 74–82; this is the episode of motion in ascending and descending thirds we mentioned earlier. After this culmination, a modulation to the subdominant, B-flat minor (m. 83), further increases the tension, until finally, in m. 88, this bold melodic curve finds its way back to the tonic and thus concludes. I have devoted considerable space to this movement because I believe that an exact knowledge of its construction is essential if one wants to appreciate the constantly changing light and color that it contains and to understand it in spite of its length.

2. In contrast to most other second movements, the first Allegro of this sonata has a two-part structure, even though there are some signs of a reprise in m. 52 ff. In regard to its thematic material, the movement bears some relationship to the corresponding movement of the C minor sonata, but it is more austere and compact; this can be felt in the severe half notes with which he principal theme begins. These two notes repeatedly enter in diminution, cf. m. 37 or 53, bass voice. Since the principal theme is actually only three and a half measures long (the last seven sixteenth-notes of the violin part in m. 4 are purely transitional), when it enters a third time in the bass (m. 10), there is for the first time a shift of half a measure. Among the numerous contrapuntal ideas, that of syncopation is significant. It appears for the first time in the violin in m. 8–10, and it later combines with the above-mentioned sixteenth runs to form a new motif at the beginning of the second part. Indeed, Bach always begins the second part of a two-part movement with a counterpoint of the principal theme (cf. the last movements of the A major and C minor sonatas). Here it is immediately introduced as a small canon of the melody parts (m. 25–26). But along with these counterpoints, the movement contains a separate idea independent of the theme: the chordal motif of m. 16 ff., which is vaguely reminiscent of the two-part clavier invention in A minor. This idea is also given considerable space in the second part. It is lengthened (m. 32, violin), and is finally condensed in an intensification which leads to two C minor entrances of the principal theme, But we must not forget a further motif: the "sigh" which makes its first appearance in m. 26 as a new counterpoint to the principal theme. None of these ideas is inconsequential; the last 12 measures of the movement (from m. 50 on) contain all the material in question in contrapuntal compression.

3. The next movement is an Adagio, which can be characterized as unique in

Bach's sonatas. It might best be classified as an "intermezzo" type, which we mentioned earlier. A ceaselessly flowing, as it were, whispering series of thirty-second
notes in the clavier is combined with a violin part which consists exclusively of two-
part writing in eighth-notes. The two instrumental parts appear to lack any characteristic contour and move along without any tension. The movement at first seems
enigmatic, but once one is more familiar with the piece, especially by following the
two lines of the violin part, a two-part division of the movement's course becomes
discernable. For purposes of illustration, the violin measures up to the end of the
first part are rendered (in Example 165) in structurally simplified form, showing a
striking similarity to certain Corelli models. Up to this point the movement has 12
measures; the second part beginning with m. 13 is likewise 12 measures long and
concludes on the first eighth of m. 25 in the tonic, C minor. It cannot, however, be
designated a reprise, although it should be noted that the rhythmic compression of
m. 9 and 10 in the first part are paralleled in m. 21 and 22 of the second part; there is
also a melodic similarity. Bach left us two versions of the clavier part of this movement. The earlier of the two consists of simply arpeggiated sixteenth-notes, rather
than thirty-seconds. Without question, the second, richer version, found in all the
modern editions, is superior.

Example 165. Sonata for Violin and Clavier in F Minor, BWV 1018, 3rd movement, Adagio,
m. 1–12, structure of the violin part

4. The last movement was analyzed on p. 140 f. There we pointed out its abundance of ideas and its artistry in the development of motifs, but also its over-
burdened quality, which can produce a feeling of constraint in both musician and
listener. If the direction, "vivace," is interpreted loosely and a relatively leisurely
tempo is selected, one can do justice to all the espressivo passages and the polyphony becomes clear; nonetheless, the movement becomes rather heavy. If the
"vivace" is taken more literally and the movement is played in a buoyant, dancelike
manner, it leaves a strangely superficial impression; the substance seems to lack the
space necessary to unfold. Whatever one tries, a residue of dissatisfaction remains;
like many of the cantata arias, this composition could be called 'manneristic.'

Sonata No. 6 in G Major, BWV 1019

This sonata exists in three versions; their probable sequence and distinctive
qualities were already discussed on p. 34. Here we are following the third version,
the one Bach apparently considered to be final, and which is usually found in the
practical editions. However, it is not only the existence of several versions that
makes this sonata different from the five preceding ones; it also has a fundamentally different sequence of movements. Its five movements correspond to

neither the "sonata da chiesa" scheme nor to that of the "sonata da camera," but with their sequence, fast, slow, moderate (clavier solo), slow, fast, show a symmetrical arrangement not employed anywhere else by Bach. He seems to have had this sequence in mind from the outset, because it can be discerned in all three versions, although it is most convincingly executed in the third version.

1. Allegro. The principal theme of the movement is also very different from the themes of other sonata allegros. It consists almost exclusively of the broken triad of the tonic (in the second entrance it has to be the dominant triad), and seems to belong more to a *Brandenburg Concerto* than to a chamber music piece. This is supported by the fact that the theme does not have a third expositional entrance, and also after this never appears in the bass. But appearances are deceiving: the asymmetrically broken triad of this theme, consisting of groups of three eighth-notes each (a procedure that always leads to irregularities in duple time and reminds one of Bartok's techniques), belongs to the style of Bach's chamber music, not his orchestral music. Another element that is typical for chamber music, and not at all like the "concertino" in a "concerto grosso", is the middle theme (cf. Example 97, p. 131). It carries the principal thought further rather than starting anew, and by virtue of its path of modulation from D major to E minor, produces dynamic tension rather than static continuation. It also appears twice in its complete form (m. 33 ff. and 61 ff.) in the bass. It should also be noted that the entire middle part (B), beginning in m. 22 and ending in m. 69, does indeed apply elements of the principal theme from part A (for example, the continuation episode from m. 17–19 in m. 39–41), but never the opening idea of the broken triad. But such things appeared regularly in the other sonatas. The reprise from m. 70 to the end of the movement is a literal "da capo" of m. 1–22 of the opening A part.

2. The next movement is a relatively short, intermezzo-like Arioso in a tender, slightly melancholy mood. Its tempo indication, Largo, should be modified to a tranquil, flowing Andante, so that the theme, which is only two measures long, will retain that floating quality expressed by the dotted rhythm. In two places (m. 11 ff. and 16 ff.) Bach expands the texture from three voices to four; he first discontinues this when the bass takes over the theme. Some editions have a more interesting trill version (Example 166) in m. 10 of the clavier. If this version is used, the violin in m. 15 will have to be changed accordingly: see the suggestion in Example 166. This gives the final violin trill in m. 20, found in all the editions, a more convincing motivation.

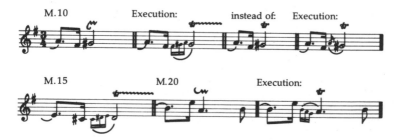

Example 166. Sonata for Violin and Clavier in G Major, BWV 1019, 2nd movement, Largo, various executions of trills in various editions

3. This Allegro for clavier alone is unique in Bach's sonatas. Nor has it occured in any other period that the composer of a duet sonata had one of the partners remain silent throughout an entire movement (with the exception of modern experiments). However, Bach seems to have planned this from the beginning; for one of the other versions also features a clavier solo, albeit a completely different composition. The movement in the third version we are treating here, the one with which Bach was finally satisfied, should not be played too fast. Its delightfully old-fashioned demeanor does not lend itself to virtuosity. For the most part, the clavier movement has two parts which, in a few places, develop into a four part structure. Although the piece is in a two-part form, it still has a true reprise, beginning in m. 45, which is characterized by its transposition to the lower octave. If the two repetitions of the movement are omitted, this three-part structure becomes clearer; and apart from that, the violinist does not have to stand by idly for too long.

4. The second slow movement was not written until the third version. A true Adagio, it must be played very slowly; eighth notes constitute its pulse. Expressive and intense, concentrated into one measure, its thematic line (cf. Example 77, p. 123) is exemplary in proportion, despite its compactness. Whenever the step-wise descending sequential idea makes its appearance (it is vaguely reminiscent of the A minor prelude of *The Well-Tempered Clavier II*), the chromatic structure wins the upper hand, which in two cases (m. 9 and 15) creates interesting cross-relations between the violin and the upper part of the clavier. The degree to which Bach thought contrapuntally can be seen in the upper parts in m. 16, 3rd quarter, and m. 17: at the moment of climax, both melody parts are brought together, moving in simple parallel sixths. This movement actually concludes on the 3rd quarter of m. 19, but Bach provides it, too, with a brief transition from B minor to the dominant of the tonic, G major.

5. In the two earlier versions, Bach intended simply to repeat the first movement of the sonata as a finale. He may have felt that this solution was not entirely satisfying; thanks to this feeling, we now have the 6/8 Allegro as the finale. Its graceful opening theme has the appearance of a bass part for something that is yet to come, but the sixteenth notes which appear in the violin part in m. 5 and provide a counterpoint to the opening theme also lack thematic importance. We wait for the material in the second section (B), which begins in m. 31, and again, it is only a rather ordinary motif! Nevertheless, the movement serves perfectly as a finale. Precisely because of its seemingly insignificant themes, it makes a clean sweep of things. And as it develops further, Bach has some additional surprises in store. He allows us to assume, with the accentuated close in the dominant in m. 71, that the middle section has come to an end, and we are prepared for a reprise of section A. A fermata is called for here, and the violinist should not fail to provide it with an improvised ornament; in Example 167, a suggestion is made in this regard. But in spite of this accentuated fermata, section B is not yet over. Seventeen more measures follow, concluding with a definitive B minor cadence, which establishes a reference to the key of the 4th movement (m. 88). Only then does the literal reprise of the A section begin. Another detail should be pointed out: in m. 31, Bach notes the following rhythm: ♪ ♫ ♩ but in all the later passages featuring the same motif, it is marked ♪ ♫. This could lead one to suspect that m. 31 contained an error in transcription, and since we have no autograph manuscript, this suspicion cannot be disproved. But this difference in notation should never cause both versions to be smoothed into a triplet (♩ ♫), not even at the rapid tempo that is required.[12]

Example 167. Sonata for Violin and Clavier in G Major, BWV 1019, 5th movement, Allegro, m. 71–72

Another note: now and then, one encounters performances of this sonata in which individual movements from different versions are exchanged. Thus, in place of the 4th movement (Adagio) of the third version, the fourth movement of the first version, likewise an Adagio, is played. Karl Klingler always replaced the clavier solo movement of the third version with the third movement of the second version, adapted from the cantata aria. I cannot see the necessity for such exchanges. Apart from the question of whether something is gained by this, one should respect the wishes of Bach, who obviously worked on this sonata for a long time and left us the third version, the one he considered to be the final and best one.

Sonata for Violin and Clavier in F Major, BWV 1022

This sonata does not belong to the preceding cycle of six. It is a transcription of the Trio Sonata for Flute, Violin and b.c. in G Major, BWV 1038. Thus, for a consideration of the individual movements, we refer the reader to p. 220. This work was transposed from G major to F major, and the flute part was given to the right hand of the clavier. For this reason, a "violino discordato" is required here, a violin with all four strings tuned down a whole step. The original flute part is ornamented for the clavier, which is understandable, since the harpsichord's inadequate carrying power had to be reinforced. Nevertheless, one should be somewhat skeptical about the authenticity of these ornaments; they are added rather casually and should not be interpreted literally.

Compared with the trio sonata, Bach makes dramatic changes in the 2nd movement, Allegro e presto. A new theme is introduced and the movement is divided in two. This was also discussed earlier (p. 25; also, see Example 2). The first publisher of the sonata, Ludwig Landshoff, emphasized[13] that this movement, which was perhaps too concise in the trio sonata and the violin-b.c. (BWV 1021) versions, only received its due proportional weight in relation to the other three movements of the work by virtue of this expansion. From the standpoint of style, it is interesting that the introduction of a second theme did not lead to a dynamic sonata movement in the early Classic sense, but rather that the Baroque continuation technique was retained. This is vividly shown by the revised and expanded second use of the new idea in m. 61–75.

The 3rd and 4th movements correspond to those of the trio. In the 4th movement, the 4/2 meter of the trio was transformed into 2/2, Alla breve, which may be attributed to a later copyist. The adroitly handled expansion of the 2nd movement almost leads one to attribute to Bach himself the transcription from trio sonata to sonata for violin and clavier, even though certain indications, like the addition of the ornaments already mentioned, suggest otherwise. Even if the work cannot measure up to the standards of the six great sonatas for violin and clavier, it still commands respect.

Chapter 23

Sonatas for Violin and b.c.

Sonata for Violin and b.c. in G Major, BWV 1021

This sonata is closely related to the Sonata in F Major (BWV 1022), just discussed, and the Trio Sonata in G Major, BWV 1038. (See the discussion of these works, as well as p. 23 f.) But their similarity is only partial, since only the bass of this sonata is the same as that of the two other works. The design of this sonata is obviously simpler than the great violin-clavier sonatas, although it must have been written at the same time or even later. On the other hand, it surpasses the violin sonata with b.c. in E minor in the balance of its proportions. All in all, I would tend to evaluate it as exceedingly "normal," i.e., conventional. It does not approach the high intellectual level of the great chamber music works.

In the introductory Adagio, the violin part is richly ornamented. It is worthwhile comparing this movement with a similarly constructed movement from Bach's late period, the introductory Adagio of the Sonata for Flute and b.c. in E Major, BWV 1035. The embellished melody line in the flute sonata is the product of rich artistic experience and emotional maturity, whereas the violin sonata does not go beyond conventional Baroque patterns. The number and arrangement of its embellishments reveal that Bach was not intensely involved with the composition of this movement. Here, in contrast to the Trio Sonata BWV 1038 and the Violin Sonata BWV 1022, Bach dispenses with writing out the repetitions of the two-part movement and simply uses repeat signs. In the E major flute sonata we mentioned, the two parts are not repeated at all: the signature of the master! The added one and a half measures at the end of the movement, which in the trio prepare the following, lively movement, are also missing in this sonata.

The ensuing Vivace is pleasing by virtue of the boldness of the violin opening; unfortunately, the idea is taken up again only once more, and then only by way of suggestion (m. 32–33). Like the trio, this movement is awfully short.

The third movement is a Largo which seems like a rough draft next to the two other versions of this movement and its related form in the motet, "Jesu meine Freude" written in 1723. This comparison aside, the movement has a character of its own and should not be underestimated. Because the melody part is once again richly ornamented, it should probably be played somewhat slower than the parallel examples we have mentioned.

The concluding Presto is admittedly a disappointing surrogate for someone familiar with the trio sonata. Bach did not write a new upper part, but simply put together a reduced version of the original fugue. But three-part polyphony cannot be transformed into two-part writing without damaging the substance, as Example 168 shows. Thus, the movement seldom rises above a certain superficiality. It is incomprehensible that this has been considered authentic by some, while the Trio Sonata, BWV 1038, has not.

Example 168. Sonata for Violin and b.c. in G Major, BWV 1021 and Trio Sonata for Flute, Violin and b.c. in G Major, BWV 1038: comparison of m. 5–8 of the 4th movement. The b.c. figuration, identical in both cases, was omitted.

Sonata for Violin and b.c. in E Minor, BWV 1023

This little-known sonata deserves attention mainly for its extraordinary introductory movement. The movement consists of two different parts. It begins with a long, toccata-like, improvisational introduction by the violin over a 29-measure long pedal point, 'e,' in the continuo, which should be played "tasto solo," i.e., without any chordal support. Twice during these 29 introductory measures the sixteenth-notes of the violin rise to a high point. The *bariolage* around the open E-string adds to the effect of the pedal point. The second part of the movement, an Adagio ma non tanto, follows without a pause. It is the necessary complement to the one-sidedness of the beginning; as different as they are, both parts form an interdependent whole. The sustaining idea of the Adagio is a broadly unfolding Baroque melody of intense expressiveness. In interpreting this part, one might be tempted to try out playing techniques included in the term "notes inégales" (cf. p. 67); for example, to over-dot the eighths of the figures ♩ ♪ and ♩ ♫, or to adapt the simple b.c. eighths to the triplets of the violin part. But this should be done tastefully and carefully. On the whole, the two parts of the introductory movement recall Bach's clavier toccatas, especially the Toccata in E Minor, BWV 914. There also seem to be some traits found in German violin music of that time, i.e., Pisendel and Biber.[14] For this reason it is reasonable to assume that the sonata was written during the last Weimar years, roughly between 1714 and 1717. We can be certain that the piece came before the great violin works of the Köthen period.

This would also follow from the relatively indecisive posture of the next two movements, an Allemande and a Gigue. If the introductory movement shows the greatest affinity to some free-fantasy models from the violin music between 1690 and 1700 (there is no trace of church sonata influence), the two concluding movements are close to the sonata da camera, i.e., the suite. Here, the figuration of the Allemande exhibits Baroque flamboyance, while the Gigue remains rather conventional and colorless. But it is precisely this unevenness that comprises the charm of the work, the recognition that even a composer like Bach had to go through a learning process before he was capable of writing masterpieces.

Chapter 24

Sonatas for Viola da Gamba and Clavier

Sonata No. 1 in G. Major, BWV 1027

This sonata has also come down to us in a parallel version as a trio sonata for two flutes and b.c. (BWV 1039, compare p. 223).

1. "Adagio." The introductory movement with its pastoral quality has been written so idiomatically for the gamba that a performance on the cello demands great effort, lest the music be distorted by its more voluminous tone. The direction

"adagio" should not lead one to play the movement too slowly: the dotted quarter notes are the beat; otherwise the movement becomes too heavy. The few staccato dots that Bach used, for example in m. 1 and 2 (Example 169), clearly show that the

Example 169. Sonata for Viola da gamba and Clavier in G Major, BWV 1027, 1st movement, Adagio, m. 1–2

composer intended it to have a light, dance-like quality. When playing the principal theme, as in m. 4–6, the pianist must decide whether to play the appoggiaturas exactly as in the gamba part in m. 1–3. Although it is legitimate to proceed logically in such cases, thus, to present a theme absolutely to the letter each time, it can also be very effective to use small variants, i.e., one time with and one time without appoggiaturas. The situation in m. 7 is different, however: the ornaments of the gamba are noted as trills (tr), but those of the right hand as turns (∞). Since the two parts are in canon here, the players have to agree on the same version, the most natural solution being a melodious turn. The same difference in notation can be found in m. 19. If the trio sonata version is consulted to clarify the matter, we find that trills are marked uniformly in both flute parts in the measures in question. The meaning of the trill ⵣ (m. 7, 4th quarter note; m. 8, 4th quarter note) is not clear. Does it mean that the trill should begin on the lower note (Example 170a), or is a turn intended (Example 170b)? I support version (b). The trio sonata has no direction at all for a trill in m. 7, and in m. 8 it has a tr with a wavy line. The variant on the 2nd quarter note of m. 8 is worthy of note. The gamba version surely is the more interesting. Also unclear is the concluding trill in m. 27, which is written differently in the two melody parts. The clavier has the more precise direction: ⵣ must be understood as a turn at the beginning of the trill and an after-beat at the end. Thus, the gamba and the clavier should probably play as follows (Example 171).

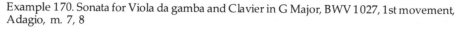

Example 170. Sonata for Viola da gamba and Clavier in G Major, BWV 1027, 1st movement, Adagio, m. 7, 8

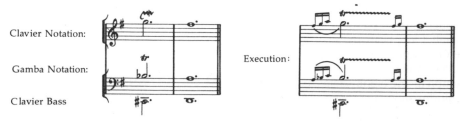

Example 171. Sonata for Viola da gamba and Clavier in G Major, BWV 1027, 1st movement, Adagio, m. 27–28

Although we have spent a great deal of time on the question of the ornaments in this case, this does not nearly cover all the problems of this kind in the movement. In such cases the partners need to reach an agreement concerning the handling of the ornaments before they begin playing.

Musically noteworthy and relatively rare in Bach's music during this period are the brief imitations in m. 9–11 and 21–23. They actually belong to a stylistic period a hundred years before; there are numerous models in Palestrina and Schütz. Comparable treatment also appears in several places in *The Art of Fugue,* although we are certain that Bach had little knowledge of the music of his predecessors.

2. The cheerful, popular aspect of the principal theme of this Allegro ma non tanto temporarily obscures the artistic expertise involved in its composition. The alternation between ascending and descending motion is perfectly balanced: two runs ascending by degrees in m. 1 and 2 are followed in m. 3 by the first stepwise descending progression which, after reaching its culmination-point g^2 in m. 4, is followed by the final stepwise descent. It then is slowed down only once more, from m. 4 to m. 5. The thematic curve begins and ends with d^1; the culmination, marked Kh, lies right at the beginning of the last third of the line, hence in an optimal position. Between the first and second start in m. 2 lies a descending third, which corresponds to an ascending third in m. 3 and 4 (it is appropriately located before the two stepwise descending progressions). It must also be noted that within m. 4, the last of these thirds was moved forward by a quarter note, thus heightening the tension that leads to the culmination-point (Example 172; the thirds are indicated by brackets). Probably to counter the artistic intricacy of this theme, Bach made the

Example 172. Sonata for Viola da gamba and Clavier in G Major, BWV 1027, 2nd movement, Allegro ma non tanto, m. 1–5

divertimenti of this movement very simple. Not wanting to spoil the thematic line by a tonal answer, he keeps the skip of a fourth at the beginning in the *comes* of the gamba as well (m. 5); such a procedure is rare in his music. Once again we have a three-part movement. By inverting the theme's beginning, Bach gains new material for the middle part; moreover, the original theme is transposed in its entirety into minor. The beginning of the reprise is surprising, indeed, misleading, as if Bach were having fun at our expense and making us wonder where the "real" reprise could be (cf. p. 95).

We have already discussed the unusually sustained clavier notes and their embellishment with trills. When the gamba and the melody part of the clavier run parallel, identical ornaments are unavoidable, as in m. 64 ff. Here the mordent in the left hand part, not the trill in the gamba, may be the best solution. It can only be called thoughtless to play the quarter-notes of this movement at exactly the same tempo as the eighth-notes of the preceding 12/8 movement—something that we unfortunately encounter all too often. The two movements have totally different characters, and this should be expressed in the choice of tempos. Measured by metronome, the quarter-notes of the Allegro are slower, to be sure, than the eighth-notes of the Adagio.

3. The very original Andante, which roams freely through a wide range of keys, poses a virtually insoluble problem for the performers: how to produce a homogeneous sound between the gamba and an accompanying keyboard instrument, whether a harpsichord or a pianoforte. The two upper parts are structurally identical and are closely interwoven. It is almost impossible to create this unity with the different timbres of the two instruments. Naturally, this difficulty does not exist in the version for two flutes and b.c. We have no idea why Bach distorted his own idea in such a way when he wrote the gamba version (the trio sonata version had been written earlier); we can only conclude that in Bach's time music was played and listened to with much more intellectual intensity and imagination than it is today, with the result that an actual sound discrepancy did not bother anyone. After m. 13 this problem is no longer a factor: from then on, the gamba goes its own way.

4. This Allegro moderato also appears to be simple and popular, even though this is really not the case. The movement is monothematic and also has no discernable three-part organization. But the theme itself has a surprising construction: it seems asymmetrical, and yet it contains the regular eight measures. The reason for this can be found in the location of the sequence in m. 3–4 and 5–6. It contradicts the normal division of eight-measure phrases into 2×2 measures and demands a division of $2 + 4 + 2$ measures. Notably unpretentious, the divertimenti consist almost completely of broken chords against which Bach writes simple, continuous eighth-note motion, for the first time in m. 26 ff. Occasionally this structure is even further reduced to eighth-note motion, after-beat quarter-notes and a held note (first in m. 34 ff.). As the movement develops, however, the action is intensified again by the canonic motion in the upper parts (m. 49 ff., 59–60 ff.). The constant variants in the basses (already referred to elsewhere) illustrate that Bach never let a movement like this grind away mechanically, but knew how to make it come alive.

Sonata No. 2 in D Major, BWV 1028

This sonata is better suited to the cello than the first gamba sonata. The vibrant tone of the cello is in keeping with the direct, uncomplicated joyfulness of the piece. Anyone mindful of the delicate sound of the gamba will, of course, regret such a change of instrument; but it is easy to understand that cellists also want to be able to play a cello-clavier sonata by Bach.[15]

1. The short introductory Adagio, a simple Arioso type, supplies an introduction to the entire work, as compactly and appropriately as can be imagined. Two melody parts in duet, gamba and right hand, and a calm "walking bass" in eighth-notes determine the structure; the three-part construction is never abandoned. Despite its brevity, the movement contains several problems of ornamentation, since the extant notation is not precise; on the other hand, the appoggiaturas *are*

Example 173. Sonata for Viola da gamba and Clavier in D Major, BWV 1028, 1st movement, Adagio, m. 1–2

important to the music. When the principal theme (Example 173) first enters in the gamba it is notated with an appoggiatura and trill (m. 2). The appoggiatura is written as an eighth but, of course, it has to be played as a sixteenth. This would result in the execution under (b) in Example 173. But as the movement develops, the theme is always noted without appoggiatura, and the trill is marked in only a few cases. The decision has to be made whether to retain the beginning version throughout, or to play only the trill, or to play no ornament at all. Even a version with only an appoggiatura and no trill can be heard. It might seem pedantic to have to adhere to a single version in all cases, but wherever the two parts answer each other directly, one must settle on one version.

2. The fresh, popular quality of the Allegro rests on its clear four-measure groupings. Note how seldom Bach utilizes the characteristic bass of the theme, no matter how ubiquitous this theme may be. The bass appears only at the beginning and end of the two parts, but when it does appear, it influences the theme decisively, even affecting the choice of a correct tempo. This proves that an idea can be important without having been thoroughly worked out. The principal melodic idea, frequently rendered in thirds by the two upper parts, does not appear in its entirety in the bass, but it is employed as a motif (m. 9–12, 65–68), and its syncopated basic idea (compare m. 1 and 2) provides impetus even when it is not actually present. As regards the phrasing of this syncopation: Bach indicated unambiguously what he had in mind; he wanted the first two sixteenths "non legato," the second two, "legato" (♩♩ ♩ ♩). This should be observed everywhere, including the clavier. Bear in mind that "non legato" means a broad, détaché stroke, not short accents.[16] Several times Bach wrote out what amounts to a b.c. realization for the right hand, which suddenly gives rise to a three or even four-part structure (m. 13–14, 59–60, et al.). This can also serve as a model for the treatment of analogous passages in other works.

3. This noble Siciliano melody, marked "andante", resembles many of Bach's important 6/8 or 12/8 arias, which likewise have their roots in the Siciliano tradition. We refer not only to the "Erbarme dich" from the *St. Matthew Passion,* but also to the alto aria "Stirb in mir, Welt," from the cantata, *Gott soll allein mein Herze haben,* No. 169 (which is identical to the middle movement of the Clavier Concerto in E Major, BWV 1053). The thematic development in all movements of this kind is characterized by ascending minor sixths. The melodic phrases become increasingly penetrating in the second half of the movement, the motion becomes more intense and agitated as Bach works with the technique of compressing motifs (cf. p. 160).

4. Allegro. With invigorating directness, the double theme of the finale takes us back to the realm of unproblematic music making. It does not matter whether the sixteenth-note idea of the right hand or the joyful fanfare of the gamba is the principal subject, both ideas require considerable musical temperament, even to the point of brilliance. Bach also frequently lets the theme we have designated as the sixteenth-note idea appear alone (m. 27 ff., 69 ff.). Formally, this movement belongs to the category of three-part A-B-A structures, but the proportions are unusual; the first section (A) has 69 measures, the B section, 28 measures, and the considerably shortened reprise of the A section, 29 measures. Thus, B and the second A together only barely attain the length of the first A. Nevertheless, it would be a mistake to speak of a two-section organization here, i.e., an A-B structure. This is confirmed by looking at the second movement of this sonata, which has two sections and hence only one central thematic group from which the entire movement develops. In the

4th movement, however, the middle section embarks on paths not indicated by the thematic material and the perspective of the first A section. At the beginning of section B (m. 69 ff.), the sixteenth-note line of the principal theme is briefly transposed to the related minor keys, B minor and F-sharp minor, after which a completely new section begins in m. 84, a mere arpeggiation, within which the musical action seems to dissolve almost completely into contourless motion. The clavier is reduced to a whisper, and the gamba plays a vapid bass figure. This has no parallel in any of the three sonatas; Bach never has the gamba merely serve to reinforce the b.c. Then in m. 93 the clavier arpeggios break away from the gamba bass. All in all, the 14 measures, as we have described them, may seem to have little meaning, but just the opposite is the case: they create tension. Their marked contrast to the "healthy" music of the rest of the movement points to a second, background level of the movement's course. Then, in m. 97, the episode ends and the reprise enters powerfully on the dominant. At first, however, the preceding passage seems to continue to make its influence felt: the gamba part is embellished with restless thirty-second notes, and its phrasing (precisely notated by Bach and to be strictly adhered to!) seems to go against the grain. Not until m. 111 are we back on the track again. We also want to call attention to the fact that in one place in the B episode just described, a B^1 is required for the gamba (m. 92), a note that cannot be reached by the six-stringed gamba generally in use. The same is true of the C four measures later.

In conclusion, an observation about the structure of m. 35 (second half) to 38. It seems to consist of simple parallel thirds, but on closer inspection we see that the parallel coupling results in a 3/8 rhythm for the half measures. The following combinations are played together: gamba and left hand, gamba and right hand, both hands, and so on again from the beginning. Written on the basis of 6/8 time, a curious shift occurs, a seemingly asymmetrical sequence. The same structure appears once again in m. 54–58.

A few performance suggestions should be added. In the surviving text, the "fanfare" theme has no turn over the 3rd eighth-note in one place, then in another place it does (m. 5 and 6, clavier). We could proceed in two possible ways: either the theme is played with a turn throughout, or the alternation can be systematized after a fashion, having the clavier always play the turn, the gamba, always omitting it. There are other conceivable ways of making this alternation logical, but since the surviving text has a random character, some agreement has to be reached by the players. In any case, it should not upset us that the turn once is written as a trill (m. 51); the same ornament is meant in all cases. In m. 76–78 there are double stops in the gamba part. They must undoubtedly be broken up into figuration. This way, all three voices in the measures cited play sixteenth-notes, and a heightening of the tension ensues, culminating in the pedal-point which enters in m. 79 on C-sharp and giving the next episode the necessary motivation.

This second gamba sonata is an especially interesting sample of Baroque ornamental technique and for this reason it was treated at length in Part I (p. 76 f.).

Sonata No. 3 in G Minor, BWV 1029

Some scholars are of the opinion that this G minor sonata represents the later version of an original concerto grosso or an instrumental concerto with orchestral accompaniment, or of some other work designed for orchestra. This hypothesis[17] is difficult to support, even if there do seem to be some parallels to thematic material in the *Brandenburg Concertos*. Such parallels can also be found in the Sonata for Violin and Clavier in G Major, but this is no reason to be sniffing about everywhere for an "original version." In any case, the 2nd movement provides absolutely no grounds for such a supposition, and virtually the same can be said of the 3rd movement. We should simply realize that, in contrast to most of his contemporaries, Bach never worked according to a system and that he always sought individual solutions within the general conventions of his epoch. Why shouldn't a sonata have a different look for a change?

1. A primary support for the hypothesis cited is the opening theme of the 1st movement. It is headed Vivace, hence, lively, and therefore outside the "sonata da chiesa" scheme. The theme might indeed suggest a transposition of the opening theme of the 3rd *Brandenburg Concerto* into a minor key, but this is true only of the first two measures. The connection to the above-mentioned G major violin sonata is stronger. The rhythm of m. 7 of the gamba sonata corresponds exactly to that of m. 9 of the violin sonata; structurally, both passages occupy exactly the same places within the themes. Taken as a whole, this movement, more so than other sonata movements, seems to proceed from a concept of terrace dynamics; hence, from two different dynamic levels of, say, a harpsichord. This could be underscored by having the pianist support the *forte* passages with b.c. chords, for example, right at the beginning in m. 1–8. But the player must pay close attention to where Bach writes unisons and not destroy them with b.c. additions. The unisons are a characteristic of the movement. A total unison of all voices accentuates the entrance of the reprise in m. 95–96, and there are further unisons between the gamba and one of the two clavier hands, i.e., m. 9–10 and m. 35. The movement should never be played too fast. A Bach Vivace is not a Beethoven Vivace. The tempo is assuredly slower than that of the often-mentioned G major violin sonata; this is clearly shown by the thirty-second notes of the subsidiary theme (m. 30–31, gamba) which are so important as motifs and should not simply be swept under the table. Also, the polyphony of this movement is so complex that a restrained tempo recommends itself; this, mindful of the fact that liveliness is produced not by a high metronome speed, but by giving the listener the opportunity to hear clearly a contrapuntal structure. Consider m. 60–61: what daring part writing! It would be a misunderstanding of the structural situation, which here as elsewhere is unmistakably that of chamber music, if one were to judge it by orchestral standards. Like most Allegro first movements, this one has a three-part structure. The first section (A) concludes with a cadence to D minor in m. 25. Bach begins the extended middle section (B) in the "normal" relative major key, B-flat major, and introduces it with the "interim" motif already familiar from m. 7 of the theme. Only a few measures later, a new idea appears. It seems unimportant at first, but in fact, it increases in importance as the movement proceeds. Then in m. 95, section A has its reprise, with the striking unison entrance that has already been mentioned. It is a variant, rather than a literal repetition of the first A. However, as in the first A section, there is an interesting detail: the quasi-canonic leading of the two upper voices on the second and third appearances of the above-mentioned secondary motif from m. 9 in m. 17–18 and m. 107–108.

2. The leading of the three voices in the Adagio movement is highly unconventional. On the one hand, the structure is based on an expansive 3/2 meter, as clearly documented in the bass line; on the other hand, we have two melody parts richly

colored with small note values and ornaments. It cannot definitely be ascertained which one is the principal voice and which the secondary, but the gamba will probably always attract most attention. There are hardly any cross-references between the motifs of these three voices. Not until the second section is there any common material: the beginning motif of the right hand of the clavier in m. 17 appears again one measure later in the gamba, and in m. 20–22 the bass motif is imitated, in succession, by the two upper voices. Within the movement as a whole, however, the two cases are of little importance. Its uniqueness rests precisely in the fact that the individuality of the three voices is carried to the extreme. For the 4th eighth-note of the penultimate measure (m. 29) in the gamba part, the *BGA* offers the alternative of a g^1 instead of the B-flat^1 printed in the edition. This would bring about a very noticeable cross relation with the immediately preceding G-flat^1 in the right hand—not impossible for Bach, especially in a movement in which the voices are so independent.

3. The Allegro, like the first Vivace, should not be rushed either. This is already indicated by the sixteenth-note triplets of m. 5, which are repeated later. The imitation by the gamba of the principal theme which first appears in the upper clavier part provides a classic example of a tonal thematic answer. In contrast to this rather uncharacteristic idea, the new middle theme is more interesting. It is a true melodic "second theme" in the sense of the Classic sonata. As it unfolds, the clavier drops into an accompanying role; its sixteenth-note arpeggiations could have been written in the second half of the 18th century. Starting in m. 24, the two upper voices are interchanged, and now the gamba takes over the accompaniment. There follows a duet episode between the two melody parts up to m. 37, after which the "theme-and-accompaniment" structure continues. The entire complex is surprising, but this should not cause any doubt as to the authenticity of the movement, or even of the entire sonata, as has been the case. Bach was capable of more than he is credited with by pedantic authorities on style. Apart from this, the attentive player and listener very soon will realize that what appeared to be an "accompanying figure" acquires importance as a motif in the course of the movement. One can hardly speak of a reprise in this movement; neither the two entrances of the principal theme in C minor and G minor in m. 79 and 81 nor the G minor entrance of the gamba theme in m. 93 justify this designation. Bach finds another way to round off the movement convincingly: by means of the contrapuntal virtuosity of m. 98–104, within which the interlocked, advancing cadence formulas press on to a conclusion.

A footnote: on the first eighth-note of m. 58 August Wenzinger plays the lower 'c' instead of the printed 'g'; he is correct.

Chapter 25

Partita for Flute Solo in A Minor, BWV 1013

Whether or not this work, the only work Bach composed for flute solo, was indeed originally written for the flute is uncertain.[18] There may have been earlier versions for a keyboard instrument; this is supported above all by the observation that the first two movements, Allemande and Courante, cannot be played adequately on the flute because Bach did not provide any rests for breathing. But the same problem exists in other flute works by Bach, e.g. in the concluding movement of the E-flat Major Sonata, BWV 1031, which we know was intended for the flute. We do not know whether Baroque flutists had scruples about either inserting pauses or omitting notes; the former possibility is conceivable in unaccompanied solo pieces. Today the problem should be treated in an unorthodox manner: since the partita is not particularly appropriate for public performance, interrupting the metric flow is no sacrilege; the player will be able to mentally fill in the musical gaps.

Precisely because of the previously mentioned sixteenth-note motion, the introductory Allemande seems more like a prelude than a dance movement, even a highly stylized one. There are no authenticated dynamic marks, but it is clear that echo effects are expected between m. 2 and m. 3, for example, perhaps even between half measures. But this effect should not be achieved at any cost. The line contains enough vitality in itself to hold our attention, and it gains in interest the more intensely one follows its development. Thus, for example, the passage ascending to the climax (m. 35 to m. 41) and the ensuing descent to the 3rd quarter-note in m. 43 is an evolving process that must not be disturbed by echo effects.

The following Corrente begins with an idea which is rhythmically profiled, but it is soon abandoned in favor of a continuous run of sixteenth-notes. The extent to which the latter is to be rendered more fluid and playable by the additional articulation of legato and staccato is a matter of controversy among flutists. It could probably be justified stylistically to add short slurs, giving a more interesting articulation to passages like the one in m. 31–34, which has no phrasing at all in the original. Bach himself (i.e., the surviving manuscript) indicates a legato tie only once, namely in m. 16, where the first and second groups of four sixteenths are each tied together with legato slurs. In any case, the phrasing situation of this movement is fundamentally different from that of the first movement, which is not compatible at all with legato.

The melodic line of the following Sarabande is wide-ranging, especially the second part, which is no less than 30 measures long and composed of heterogeneous elements. The player has the difficult task of molding it into a unit. One will have to select a tempo that is not too slow, and one must not get too carried away in "espressivo."

The concluding Bourrée-Anglaise (there is no Gigue in this partita) draws its vitality from a jovial inspiration at the beginning, whose characteristic broad, concluding quarter-note at the end of the line (m. 2 and 6) has a truly dancelike feeling. Bach indulged in a popular idiom here—something he enjoyed doing—and thus the otherwise rather dry suite comes to a sprightly conclusion.

Chapter 26

Sonatas for Flute and Clavier

Sonata in B Minor, BWV 1030

This greatest of Bach's flute works (the Overture in B Minor, BWV 1067, is no exception) has been the subject of a great deal of literature. Spitta's famous interpretation in his great biography of Bach is obviously inspired by direct experience; he completely forgets historical research and allows himself to be carried away to almost poetic formulations, especially in regard to the 1st movement (quoted on p. 119). Of the Gigue section in the last movement, he writes, ". . . an Italian Gigue in 12/16 time, . . . entirely new and yet familiar, since it is developed most beautifully from the fugue theme in the manner of Buxtehude."[19] We have already devoted a detailed analysis to the first, and surely most important, movement on pp. 116 ff. and 114 ff. One might also mention that the work was written over a period of more than a decade, beginning with a G minor version which originated in Köthen in about 1720. The autograph of the final version belongs to the Leipzig period, 1736–37.

Not only the B minor sonata but also the two other sonatas for flute and clavier differ in two respects from the sonatas for violin (and gamba) and clavier. First, they have three movements in the sequence fast, slow, fast (which corresponds to the arrangement of movements in several of the *Brandenburg Concertos* and all the instrumental concertos), and hence belong neither to the "sonata da chiesa" nor the "sonata da camera" type. Secondly, the bass hardly ever carries the theme. The "presto" fugue is the only exception to this; in a fugue, all the voices are, naturally, of equal importance. But otherwise, in comparison with the string sonatas, there is a shift of emphasis in the musical action toward the two melody parts. The bass is usually only a b.c. This, however, does not impoverish the music; on the contrary, the two upper voices gain a sharper profile. This is especially clear in the great introductory movement of the B minor sonata.

1. One should observe that the tempo indication for this movement is Andante; it should not be played too rapidly. Even if it does take the place of an opening allegro, its tempo shows a kinship with opening movements in many Bruckner symphonies, which also occupy the place of an allegro, but are, in reality, measured and often in a solemn moderato. In the case of our flute sonata Andante, only a restrained tempo will give its numerous themes that characteristic coloration that is indispensable for clarifying its complicated structure. For here Bach wrote virtually no continuous developments, transitions, divertimenti, or whatever one may call these structural elements; rather, the movement's course always consists of themes. It is necessary to recognize the various functions of these themes, i.e., to know what place they occupy in this course. Thus, for example, the principal idea (see Example 65) has a supporting function and is crucial in determining the development, whereas the following idea in m. 21–22 (see Example 117) merely serves to continue the composition. Throughout the entire movement, the structural members

are condensed into themes. But it would be a mistake to allow the beauty of these themes to lull us into playing (or listening to) each of them with the same expressive intensity. A careful, nuanced distribution of values is called for, lest uniformity or even fatigue occur.

There is much polyphonic intertwining of the two melody parts. The contrapuntal texture changes constantly, and it is remarkable how deliberately Bach handles the gradations of contrapuntal density. Voices may be heard, at first one after another, then in simple sequence, then they combine, overlap, and are finally bound together in canon. Then the texture unravels again, with voices completely separated, and finally they once more are enmeshed. Let us take a look at the beginning figure in the right hand. The sixteenth-notes which consist of broken two-part chords at first play the role of an accompanying figure. But as the movement develops, they increase in importance until, finally, they become constructive material, on equal terms with the other themes. The first step in this direction can be seen as early as m. 3–4, when the flute pauses. When it starts again in m. 5, this time with the full theme, the clavier figures immediately recede into the background. They swing back and forth like this between independent motif and dependent accompaniment throughout the entire movement. As early as m. 12 there is another important thrust in the direction of emancipation: a new figure, typical of Bach, has come into being (Example 174). We shall encounter it again many times, even in the bass (see m. 37, 48 ff. et al.).

Example 174. Sonata for Flute and Clavier in B Minor, BWV 1030, 1st movement, Andante, m. 12–13, clavier

The form of the movement's principal themes has its origins in the polarity between the diatonic and the chromatic. Bach often took this route, for example, in *The Art of Fugue*.[20] The sonata is an exception in that Bach's B minor works are often either totally chromatic in the origins of their themes (see the *B Minor Mass*, 1st Kyrie; *The Well-Tempered Clavier I*, B minor fugue) and remain chromatic, or else they restrict themselves to pure diatonicism (see the Overture in B Minor, BWV 1067). An antithetical posture as in the 1st movement of the flute sonata is an exception. The beginning of the opening theme is clearly diatonic; but in m. 9, an added measure (cf. p. 119), it takes its first steps toward chromaticism. By use of inversion a new chromatic idea emerges out of this four measures later, in m. 13. In order to see just how important it is we must trace m. 48–52; even the bass of these measures is dominated by chromaticism. Earlier, in m. 36–37, there is another chromatic motif. Later, certainly after m. 59, when the flute enters with sixteenth triplets, we have again returned to the realm of pure diatonicism and remain there until shortly before the reprise in m. 80. (The fermata in the flute in m. 79 should be ornamented.) But immediately afterward there is another venture into chromaticism. The entire movement is arranged in this manner: a constant ambivalence between chromatic and diatonic is manifest in the mutual relationship of its ideas. It is no exaggeration to view this tension as one of the basic elements of Western music.

2. Bach counters the high intellectual level of the 1st movement with the necessary relaxation in the following Largo e dolce. The movement is a Siciliano, heavily

interspersed with figurations and, hence, should be played broadly. The melodic lead redounds to the flute alone, while the clavier has a kind of artfully worked out b.c. accompaniment. Only here and there, at the ends of the flute lines, does it emerge into alternating figures. Formally, the movement is arranged like a simple song: 8 + 8 measures.

3. Bach divided the final movement into two sections: it consists of a Presto fugue in alla breve, followed by a Gigue in 12/16 time. There is no parallel for this kind of division in his chamber music, which leads to the supposition that Bach wanted to conclude this sonata, which had begun so ambitiously, in an equally special way. We would probably be on the wrong track if we interpreted this two-section movement as being two movements bound together by a simple *attacca*, with the Presto representing the scherzo and the Gigue the finale. Analogies of this kind would relate the sonata to later, Classic conventions which are most certainly alien to it. No, the two sections of the movement have grown from one root, as Spitta already perceived. A very lively movement after the extended Andante and Largo is necessary for contrast. The Presto satisfied this need. Yet it is more difficult to reconstruct the reason for following it with another movement in which the straightforward presto motion is dropped in favor of an interlocking syncopation of the theme. The 12/16 movement has no tempo indication; therefore, it could be assumed that the presto of the preceding fugue applies to it as well. But even if it is played very briskly (which is not necessarily desirable), it has a more measured effect than the fugue. Did Bach want the calmer Gigue to establish a link to the 1st movement, thus rounding off the sonata? It is just as easy to imagine the other solution, that of concluding the sonata with the fugue, which would then have to be lengthened. Its material could have easily supported this; the way it is now, it is broken off rather abruptly. Such a combination of movements would not have been unusual; the 4th *Brandenburg Concerto* serves as a prototype.

As enticing as such speculations are, we have to proceed from what Bach actually provided: the division of the finale into two sections. The Gigue itself is again divided into two sections and hence is a complete movement, whereas the fugue appears incomplete. Thematically, m. 5–6 form a free inversion of m. 2–3. A downward-upward motion thus results, providing a forward thrust. In contrast to this, the Gigue theme is constructed according to an upward-downward curve and can thus be seen as an inversion of the idea of the fugue theme. Accordingly, it has a soothing effect (cf. Example 80a,b). The fugue theme is provided with a bass at its first entrance. This bass line does not have a contrapuntal function, but should be viewed as the "simplest version" of the later contrapuntal bass line (m. 9–16). All in all, the polyphony of the fugue is distinguished by its clarity. Careful analysis shows how economically the contrapuntal material is handled here, whence arises the compelling radiance of the movement.

In contrast to such clarity and verve, the Gigue at first seems rather unexciting. Perhaps it would make a better impression in a different setting; here it stands in the shadow of the fugue, even though it is a complete movement in its own right. It is interesting that Bach chooses not to overdo the syncopation idea of the beginning, despite the dominance of syncopation in the movement. He always balances this with episodes in even rhythm. We can see from this the importance of correctly measuring out a thematic idea. Instead of the prescribed trill in the clavier in m. 47–48 (counting from the beginning of the Gigue), simple mordents would probably be better; the same goes for a few parallel passages.

Sonata in E-flat Major, BWV 1031

Compared to the B minor sonata, which is exacting in its intellectual demands, and often quite convoluted, the E-flat major sonata is relaxed, cheerful, immediately appealing. This may have moved some specialists in recent times to doubt its authenticity, as if it were not worthy of Bach. On p. 26, we gave our reasons for not sharing this view. From the standpoint of the art of composition, the work is anything but mediocre; a great deal of artistic expertise went into its creation, and, in any case, nobody would speak of a lack of inspiration. Bach has many facets; why should this sonata not be credited to him?

1. The Allegro moderato opens with an eight-measure clavier solo. It is more than a ritornello, even if it is used as such several times later in the movement. But motifs from it are also used as supporting material in the interaction between flute and clavier (m. 5–6, 22), and in general the arrangement of the eight introductory measures points the way for the course of the entire movement. To be sure, when the flute enters in m. 9 with its principal theme, it shows a determination to go its own thematic way; this theme never appears in the clavier. The optimistically ascending major sixth at its beginning finds its answer later (flute, m. 40) in another descending major sixth. Now the clavier is allowed to take part (m. 42), which results in an intimate connection between the two upper melody parts in these measures. The movement is remarkably short, only 71 measures, and therefore easy to grasp. An expositional section concluding with a cadence to the dominant (m. 25–26) is followed by a middle section which employs essentially the same ideas and ends with a cadence to the relative minor. Several transitional measures lead back to the tonic key. However, a reprise is only implied; the material that begins in m. 53 constitutes a significant abbreviation of what was utilized in the exposition and the middle section, so that the principal theme of the flute, for example, does not appear at all in this concluding section. Even more than normally, the pianist will need to work with b.c. reinforcements which are apparently expected wherever the right hand pauses. One must, however, be circumspect in filling in the chords; two voices (parts) suffice, and at times only one. Example 175

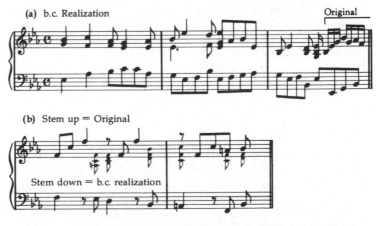

Example 175. Sonata for Flute and Clavier in E-flat Major, BWV 1031, 1st movement, Allegro moderato, m. 9–11, 18–19

offers a suggestion in this regard. Naturally, the b.c. realizations must be clearly set off from the thematic sections in the right hand.

2. The delicate Siciliano has been especially well written for the flute. It is related to the introductory movement of the C minor violin sonata; in both cases, the melody part and the accompanying clavier are always separate. But Bach concedes to the clavier at least a few motifs from the flute part, which yields Rococo-like echo effects in a couple of places (m. 17–18 and m. 27–28).

3. If in the first two movements the themes of the upper parts were only occasionally linked together, they are almost constantly connected in the lively Allegro finale. There is no flute motif that is not imitated by the clavier, and vice versa. The brevity of the individual motifs demands this procedure. Although the movement has a certain breathless quality, since the sixteenths hardly pause at all, it should not be hurried. 3/8 measures weigh more heavily than 12/8 measures, and the flutist will be grateful for a moment to catch his or her breath. Some practical editions have trills marked over the long held notes (flute, m. 33–35, 121–123; clavier, m. 39–41, 115–117); the BGA does not have these trills, and the NBA does not contain the sonata. Stylistically, trills would be more than appropriate here and there are precedents in other works. However, one might still consider whether it isn't enough to give the trill only to the clavier, thus introducing more variety into the course of the movement.

Sonata in A Major, BWV 1032

1. The first movement, Vivace, has come down to us as a torso: its last third is missing (see Figure 2 and p. 29). Capable editors and experts in Bach diction have made successful attempts to fill in the gaps; it is not necessary to invent much in the way of new material, only to rearrange and transpose what is there. On this basis, Bruno Todt's edition, published by Breitkopf and Härtel, presents an acceptable solution for those who are not necessarily concerned with musical philology, but would like to save the work for playing purposes.

Like the E-flat major sonata, this sonata also begins with a clavier solo, an eight-measure introduction which is taken up later in abbreviated form. And here, too, the flute follows with its own theme, but soon is so intimately linked with the upper clavier part that one cannot speak of separate themes for the two instruments. On the contrary, m. 49–51 show an intimate intertwining of all parts. In the extant autograph, the movement breaks off in m. 62; there is a gap, and then only the last two measures are preserved. For this reason, it is impossible to give reliable information concerning its structure, and only the length of the missing material can be estimated.

2. The slow movement has the heading Largo e dolce, just like the middle movement of the B minor sonata, which is also in 6/8 time. But here we do not have a Siciliano; the movement belongs, rather, in the company of the slow movements of the C Major Concerto for Two Claviers, BWV 1061 or the A Minor Triple Concerto, BWV 1044, even though it does not reach their level of quality. Fortunately, its relative brevity conceals this inadequacy. It is interesting that it also exists in a version for violin, cello and b.c.;[21] this is the only time Bach wrote for this instrumentation.

3. The spirited, concluding Allegro is the most inspired movement of the sonata. Here again there is an introductory clavier solo, but then the flute follows in m. 9 with the same theme. Instead of a third entrance by the bass in the tonic, which we would expect, the right hand has the theme in the tonic for the second time in m. 31 ff. As the movement develops, there are numerous secondary themes, so that it is tempting to call it a rondo. The most important of these themes can be found in m. 53–54, 89–93, 118–122 and 128–129. Of these, the sixteenth-note passages also appear in the bass, which otherwise plays no part in the movement's thematic work.

Sonata for Flute (Violin) and Clavier in G Minor, BWV 1020

It is not immediately evident from the sources whether this work was written for flute or violin. But in practice, judgment has fallen on the side of the flute. Not only does the melody part sound more convincing on the flute, but the range of the part also supports the flute: it never falls below d^1, the lowest note a transverse flute was capable of reaching at the time. There is no other violin work by Bach in which the low register of the g-string is omitted.[22]

The parallels between this sonata and the Flute-Clavier Sonata in E-flat Major, BWV 1031, were already evident to its first publisher, Wilhelm Rust, and to Philipp Spitta. The two works are indeed very similar in arrangement: three movements, one of which is a sustained quasi-Siciliano middle movement; different themes in the flute and the clavier, etc. It is unlikely that this sonata could have been composed before the Köthen period; it was probably written around the time of the E-flat major sonata.

The 1st movement has no tempo indication, but is the normal Allegro. After the twelve-measure clavier introduction characterized by passage work, the flute enters with the expressive principal theme. Its ascending sixth acts like a clarion that always calls the substance of the movement together. The presence of the theme is so powerful that we are hardly aware of how infrequently it is used. For the rest, the movement consists of richly figured passages which, however, should not be played casually, in a busy, empty manner; they contain structural and dynamic differentiation which demands time and space to develop.

A delicately lyrical Adagio follows, in 9/8 time. Its close relationship to the slow movement of the double concerto for two violins and orchestra has often been pointed out. However, this sonata movement has a charmingly intimate quality; it is definitely not a "public" composition, as the largo of the double concerto, being an instrumental concerto and orchestral work, necessarily has to be. An admirable quality of this poetic E-flat major movement is the balance of the proportions and lines, and likewise the balance between the extended principal theme and the short secondary themes.

In the concluding Allegro the verve of the concise principal idea is captivating; its syncopation in m. 2 animates all the passage work with its energy. Here, too, we have the short clavier soli which are typical for the flute sonatas, further supporting the assumption that it was written as such. The movement has two sections. The striking two- and one-measure character of its many auxiliary motifs—in m. 12, 15–16, 32–33, for example—gives it the air of a true finale, i.e., last dance, or *Kehraus* quality.

Chapter 27

Sonatas for Flute and b.c.

Sonata for Flute and b.c. in E Minor, BWV 1034

Parts of this four-movement sonata seem like an early work. Certain parts, especially of the 2nd and 3rd movements, have a conventional flavor and stand in the shadow of Corelli or Telemann. Since we know that Bach did not use the transverse flute before the Köthen period, we will have to accept Schmieder's date, "Köthen, c. 1720." The expressive Adagio ma non tanto that opens the work makes real demands on the flutist who wants to reproduce effectively passages like m. 21 and 22 (which move through all the registers and allow little time for breathing) with the necessary fullness of tone. It is also difficult to portion out the requisite espressivo correctly throughout the lengthy movement and to keep the numerous sixteenth-notes from sounding too mechanical.

The 2nd movement, Allegro, is dominated by brisk motion which carries the rather schematic sequences of the theme effortlessly. In two places, m. 16–24 and 40–47, the running passages are reduced to mere broken chords. A suggestion for the b.c. realization in these passages: the right hand should not be played the way it is realized in the Urtext edition of Peters[23] (Woehl), *on* the stressed beat, but rather, *afterwards,* along with the bass, and as eighth notes. This not only vitalizes the structure but also offers the flutist a better solution for the problem of breathing.

The basis of the following movement, Andante, is almost a "basso ostinato." Its manner of construction demonstrates Bach's proximity to the Italians.

The concluding movement, on the other hand, bears the personal stamp of Bach. It is composed with verve and should be played accordingly. The compression of motifs in this Allegro has already been pointed out on p. 142 ff. But it never for a moment gives the impression of calculated construction. On the contrary, the movement captivates by its infectious enthusiasm. One should not be misled into playing the important second motif, alternating between flute and bass (m. 13–16), with a crescendo on the five repeated eighth-notes. That would be putting an *espressivo* in the wrong place, which would only diminish the freshness of the movement. Five equal, evenly stressed eighth-notes are necessary.

Sonata for Flute and b.c. in E Major, BWV 1035

This work has also been discussed repeatedly. It is a late work, composed in the last decade of Bach's life along with the *Musical Offering,* with which it has superficial similarities. Bach wrote this sonata in either 1741 or 1747 for Fredersdorf, Frederick II's chamberlain. Like his master, Fredersdorf played the flute and apparently requested that Bach write a flute piece for him. In accordance with his wishes, Bach followed exactly the conventions for a sonata accompanied by b.c. He probably was aware of the type of music the chamberlain was accustomed to playing, since the latter was schooled by Quantz, and provided what was expected. But Bach fills in this narrowly circumscribed frame with the wisdom of an old master. It is difficult to think of a chamber music work that gives us as concentrated an example of his compositional art. The sonata is not merely concentrated, it is inspired. The themes of the 2nd and 3rd movements display a particularly vigorous immediacy.

1st movement: Adagio ma non tanto. The movement seems to be an homage to the age of sensibility (*Empfindsamkeit*), with its richly ornate figure work in the flute part. Yet we cannot help but note how Bach wields a moderating hand: the line is never overloaded, it always flows, and keeps things in balance. M. 18–20 should be singled out for their expressiveness. The movement actually seems to be over, when a short minor epilogue over a chromatic bass is added, which sets it off from the bright preceding material.

The following Allegro is completely unburdened and joyful. Its principal theme is so lively that Bach manages to make do entirely without divertimenti and allows the movement to develop in a completely songlike manner.

The Siciliano in C-sharp minor has its own great beauty that must, however, be sought out. Through most of the movement the bass imitates the melody, at times canonically, and after m. 21 even in inversion. The harmony of the b.c.'s beginning is extraordinary for that time. The upbeat on the dominant is followed not by the tonic, but the subdominant six-four chord (m. 1–2 and 13–14). Today we can scarcely imagine how bold this was in the mid-18th century.

Another observation regarding the b.c.: some of the old editions have the right hand play along from the beginning while the bass remains silent. This is incorrect; as long as the bass does not play, there is no chordal support in the upper voice. The same applies to the beginning of the second section.

4th movement: Allegro assai. The opening theme of this extremely virtuosic finale provides constant surprises by virtue of the ending of its first and second lines (m. 1 and 2), which is, so to speak, "suspended in air."

Chapter 28

Trio Sonatas

Considering the central importance of the trio sonata for two melody instruments in the first half of the 18th century, an importance we can gather from the great number of trio sonatas written by Bach's contemporaries, it is strange that Bach himself wrote only a few. To be sure, one would arrive at a considerably larger number if one subscribed to the hypothesis of Hans Eppstein, who surmises that nearly all the sonatas for melody instrument and clavier originally were trio sonatas. In one case, the Gamba Sonata in G Major, BWV 1027, a preceding trio sonata version does exist: the Sonata for Two Flutes with b.c., BWV 1039. If Eppstein's assumptions concerning the other sonatas turned out to be correct, this would still not result in the discovery of any *new* trio sonatas by Bach; and, in any case, the versions for melody instrument and clavier would still have to be regarded as the definitive ones.

Currently only two trio sonatas are considered authentic by Bach experts: the Trio Sonata for Two Flutes and b.c. in G Major, BWV 1039 just mentioned, and the Trio Sonata for Flute, Violin and b.c. in C Minor, from the *Musical Offering,* BWV 1079. As I indicated on pp. 23 ff., I cannot subscribe to this view, for which reason the other two surviving trio sonatas—the one for flute, violin and b.c. in G Major, BWV 1038, and the one for two violins and b.c. in C Major, BWV 1037—will be included in our study.

Sonata for Flute, Violin and b.c. in G Major, BWV 1038

According to current opinion, only the bass of this trio sonata was written by Bach. It is identical to that of the Sonata for Violin and b.c. in G Major, BWV 1021. Bach supposedly gave one of his students in Leipzig the assignment of writing two new voices over this bass, something which would be eminently conceivable as part of instruction in composition. But in this case there are some arguments to the contrary. The violin sonata is the weaker piece; its concluding movement is a poor reduction of the corresponding movement of the trio sonata (see p. 202). Also, the decided similarity between the 3rd movement of the trio sonata and a movement from the motet *Jesu meine Freude,* not only in the two melody parts, but also in the bass, supports the conjecture that Bach himself is the author of the trio. And if hypotheses are in order, I would argue that the violin sonata was a student assignment.

The sequence of movements in the work again corresponds to that of the church sonata. It is striking that the most contrapuntal movement, the fugue, here is the finale; in church sonatas such movements traditionally stand in second place.

In the opening movement, a Largo in two sections, Bach does something that he does virtually nowhere else: he writes out the repeats of both sections as a charming variation. The flute and the violin alternate in dotted rhythms and present new melodic lines, while the bass, which remains the same and had been ornamental in the first transition, now appears in a simple manner. Equally noteworthy is that both sections have exactly the same length, 2×16 measures. Bach usually preferred longer second sections.

The jolly Vivace which follows has only one theme and as a result is unusually short.

The next movement is an Adagio of the arioso type. We have already referred to its relationship to the motet *Jesu meine Freude* (i.e., its 9th movement, "Gute Nacht, o Wesen"), which was composed in Leipzig in 1723. Here, however, Bach continues the melody parts differently; only their beginning (m. 1–3) and the reprise (m. 13–15) are the same as those of the motet (cf. Example 1, p. 24). Apart from that, the melody parts consist of richly ornamented lines in which the effortlessness of the imitative polyphony of m. 5–11 is especially delightful (Example 176).

Like the first Allegro of the trio sonata the concluding fugue, Presto, is brief. Its theme appears immediately in stretto (Example 177). In the subsequent development its descending fourth is not only changed to a fifth, according to the *comes* tradition, but also to an octave or unison; (m. 11, 13, 17) and to a second (m. 24, 25). If the bass was independent of the melody parts in the three preceding movements, it now participates fully in the thematic substance; in a fugue it cannot be otherwise. For this reason it is tempting to play the movement as a pure, three-part

Flute

Violin

b.c.

Example 176. Trio Sonata in G Major, BWV 1038, 3rd movement, Adagio, m. 5–11

Example 177. Trio Sonata in G Major, BWV 1038, 4th movement, Presto, m. 1–4

fugue without b.c. realization, although an original bass figuration is extant.

All in all, the trio appeals by virtue of its conciseness and vitality. One could almost speak of its youthful charm, which is unhindered by its formal and contrapuntal mastery.

Here, too, Bach calls for violin scordatura: the a^1 and e^2 strings must be tuned down to g^1 and d^2. This is important, since it strongly affects resonance and partials. (Cf. also the discussion of the sonatas BWV 1021 and 1022, p. 200 f.).

Sonata for Two Violins and b.c. in C Major, BWV 1037

Bach's only surviving original work in the instrumentation so richly represented by Handel, Corelli, Telemann and others, leaves all these works far behind. Even within Bach's own chamber music this trio sonata holds a special position. This alone would suffice to refute the claim of some scholars that this is not an authentic Bach composition. (Regarding this question see p. 22).

Here, too, we have a "sonata da chiesa" arrangement. Also, the movement that is most polyphonic, a fugue, appropriately stands in second place. The opening Adagio seems conventional for the first two measures. But by m. 3, when the 2nd violin enters, the 1st violin plays a counterpoint with the unmistakable style of Bach (Example 178). This syncopated motif subsequently becomes the most important material in the movement; once it even moves down to the bass which otherwise moves in regularly-paced eighth-notes (m. 18–19).

A note about the resolution of the melodic suspension in the 1st violin on the 2nd quarter of m. 2: it has to be played as a full eighth note; otherwise poor voice leading results. The same is true for the corresponding passage in m. 4 (see Example 178). But in m. 17, the syncopated solution ♫ ♩ is preferable, so that parallel seconds with the bass are avoided.

Example 178. Trio Sonata in C Major, BWV 1037, 1st movement, Adagio, m. 3–4

In the 2nd movement, Alla breve, we have a veritable triple fugue. Both violins immediately and simultaneously present the first and second themes. Then, after the dominant cadence in about the middle of the movement, the bass enters with the third theme in m. 57, last quarter. At first it looks like a variant of the second theme, but then as the movement develops it shows its independence, especially when all three themes are combined starting in m. 91. The second statement of this triple combination occurs in m. 101 ff.; the third, in m. 113 ff.; the fourth, in m. 131 ff. Thus, of the six possibilities of triple counterpoint, three are offered. The first and the second statements have the same arrangement: each of the three themes has one turn as the upper, middle and lower voice. The triple fugue "problem" has been solved with ease. In the process, Bach built in a special artistic *tour de force:* the first and second themes are in double counterpoint at the octave; the first and third and the second and third themes, however, are in double counterpoint at the twelfth. The movement is notable for its structural density. There is hardly a secondary theme that goes unexploited. Nevertheless, Bach's technique is not at all academic. He constantly sees new combinations; the more familiar one becomes with this fugue, the more surprising, indeed, ingenious elements come to light. The same conventional Baroque formulas that Bach's contemporaries often merely mechanically strung together, the same "Cantor's counterpoint," is imbued with vitality as if the material were being used for the first time. Thus, for example, in m. 82–87, each voice maintains its individuality, yet in an almost chummy together-ness they fashion a durable organic structure. The same is true of his use of pedal point (m. 121–130), which is so overworked by other technicians of the fugue.

This effervescent, vivacious piece of music is followed by the Largo in A minor, a solemn canon of the two melody parts. The line seems to express pain; we hear it in the "exclamatio"[24] of the ascending sixth in m. 5 (7), 15 (17), and later again in m. 22 (24). Melodic caesuras are important technical devices in the composition of canons and Bach uses them to organize the melodic line into phrases. Nowhere is he shackled by the formal demands of canon.

The concluding Gigue, in two sections with the hint of a reprise, is overflowing with high spirits. One is hardly aware that Bach is breaking with the tradition of the church sonata by introducing a dance suite movement. He is vindicated by its success: one could not wish for a livelier finale to this splendid work. It is a stroke of genius to have the theme begin each time with an empty first count, which lends it a spirited, bouncy quality.

Along with the qualities already mentioned, this trio sonata is distinguished by two general characteristics. The first is its unflagging inspiration, to which the work owes its freshness and its tight formal construction, extraordinary even for Bach. Secondly: it is supremely suited to the two violins. It is difficult to understand why our violinists so rarely play this masterpiece, so that this trio sonata is relatively unknown.

Sonata for Two Flutes and b.c. in G Major, BWV 1039

This sonata is identical to the Sonata for Gamba and Clavier in G Major, BWV 1027. A few changes occur in the bass line. The trio sonata is probably the earlier version. We do not know whether Bach was dissatisfied with it and for that reason rewrote it as a gamba sonata or whether he considered it especially suited for the gamba because of its "gentleness." It is difficult to reconstruct what Bach's motivations might have been; the unique 3rd movement, Adagio e piano, requires two absolutely homogeneous upper voices and hence can hardly be effectively realized in the gamba version. Flutists always like to play this work.

For details, we refer the reader to our discussion of the gamba sonata (p. 203 ff.).

Sonata for Flute, Violin and b.c. in C Minor from the Musical Offering, *BWV 1079*

The work bears the original title, *Sonata Sopr'il Sogetto Reale à Traversa, Violino e Continuo.* We made earlier reference to its special status both as a part of a cyclic work and as a product of Bach's last creative period. We likewise assume familiarity with the occasion of its origin, Bach's visit to Frederick the Great in Potsdam and Berlin in 1747.[25] As a matter of fact, in its structure and personal style, the trio sonata differs substantially from the Köthen works, even though, like those works, it outwardly follows Baroque chamber music tradition: a four-movement church sonata with the movement sequence slow, fast, slow, fast.

1. In its opening theme, the introductory Largo employs the descending diminished fourth that had been in use since Monteverdi and could be called a *topos* which spans many stylistic periods. Bach himself employed this progression many other times; and apart from that, we find it not only in the 2nd Symphony of Robert Schumann, which is mentioned most often in this connection, but also in Schubert (Piano Trio in E-flat Major, Opus 100), Mendelssohn (Violin Concerto), Brahms (Piano Quartet in G Minor, Opus 25) and elsewhere. It is a two-section movement. At the beginning of the second section, the motif we have mentioned appears as an inversion, although the fourth has now become a third. The ratio between the lengths of the two sections is striking, 16 : 32 measures, or 1 : 2. The extended second section demands a reprise, which enters punctually at the beginning of the last third of m. 33 in the subdominant.

2. Without a doubt the most substantial movement of the work is the following Allegro, really an Allegro moderato. Its length alone is extraordinary: 249 measures. Bach apparently intended to present the "royal theme," which had not been quoted in the first movement, in its due breadth (Example 179, lower line). It appears no less than six times, completely stated, as a cantus firmus. It is paired each time with the theme of Bach's invention (henceforth we shall call this the "principal theme"— Example 179, upper line), with which it is treated in double counterpoint. All three voices play the royal theme: first, the bass in G minor (m. 47 ff.) and in C minor (m. 68 ff.); then the violin in C minor (m. 118 ff.); after that, the flute in C minor (m. 161

Example 179. Trio Sonata in C Minor, BWV 1079, 2nd movement, Allegro, m. 67–75. Principal theme, royal theme

ff.), and finally, because of the reprise of the first section, twice more in the bass (m. 208 ff., m. 229 ff.). These cantus firmus entrances have a somewhat asymmetrical relationship to the three-section arrangement of the movement. The entrance of the flute in m. 161 overlaps the beginning of the reprise. Bach could already have presented this cantus firmus in the exposition, but he refrained from doing so, probably because he wanted people to give their full attention to his own theme first. Perhaps he also wanted to save the extremely bold three-part texture at the start of the reprise (m. 159–169) until this significant moment. Such an assumption could be supported by the fact that at this point Bach's principal theme receives a new bass which is more complex than the one at the start of the movement.

The most important material of the movement derives from the principal theme. Not only does it undergo many transformations, but is itself constructed with considerable artistic expertise. The variant of the opening motif of m. 1 in the sequence in m. 3 (one would have expected the same rhythm here as in m. 1) has two functions: it prepares the way for the later sixteenth passages and it prevents the motif in m. 1 from wearing thin too soon. For this motif is used again in m. 9 in inversion, and later on is also thoroughly explored. Hence the original form of the motif and its inversion, in immediate succession, comprise the material of the middle (B) section, beginning in m. 89. Thus section B uses the same material as section A, although with a different interval for the upbeat. Also, it is clearly set off from section A and its reprise by beginning in E-flat major (relative major) and cadencing with a half-cadence to the tonic, C minor, in m. 158–159, Adagio. The opening motif is dramatically concentrated in this middle section in m. 126–132, which is reminiscent of Bruckner's development techniques (Example 180).

Example 180. Trio Sonata in C Minor, BWV 1079, 2nd movement, Allegro, m. 126–135

Back to the principal theme: its second, no less important motif appears in m. 5 (indicated by brackets in Example 179). Its later employment can be so easily distinguished by the listener that further references are not needed. On the other hand, another divertimento-like motif enters for the first time in m. 34. It does not belong directly to the principal theme, but it derives from it and must not be overlooked (or "overheard"). Far from being a spur-of-the-moment formula, it obviously was carefully planned. The first half of its first measure carries m. 5 further by also embellishing the interval of a sixth. After this, the four sixteenth-notes form the counterpoint to the second half of the measure, which now stems directly from the opening measure of the principal theme. Within the overall development, this divertimento motif usually precedes the cantus firmus, preparing the listener for it.

Coming back once again to the second motif from the principal theme (bracketed in Example 179): in the B section (m. 97–103), it causes Bach suddenly to drop all polyphony. He presents it in simple, homophonic sequences of thirds, quite in the style of the northern German early classicism of his son, Carl Philipp Emanuel (cf. for example, m. 97–100). As in another passage in the 3rd movement (see that section), we may see this as a gesture of homage to the "age of Sensibility" and the person to whom the *Musical Offering* was dedicated.

In contrast to the works of the Köthen period, the strongly individualized bass is conspicuous in this movement, at times showing Baroque extravagance. It too is repeatedly involved in the principal theme. In general, the movement is extremely contrapuntal; thus the homophonic insertions we have mentioned have, in contrast, a relaxing effect. They do not arise by chance but are prepared well in advance, as shown by m. 32. In summary, we hardly notice the extreme length of this movement due to many details of its composition, the continual cross-referencing of its material and its perfectly balanced proportions.

3. In the following movement, Andante, the syncopation of the theme accounts for its different, *espressivo* quality. The adoption of the theme by the bass (m. 3–4, 20–21) should be noted, for it does not seem to be inherently suitable as a bass line. Bach's solution is masterful and surprising. We have already referred to the use of the "sigh patterns" from the *galant* age; they constitute an homage to the musical fashions of the King of Prussia to whom the *Musical Offering* was dedicated. We also want to point out that Bach provided careful dynamic indications for this movement and that there are several bold harmonic progressions (see m. 15–17).

4. The concluding Allegro has the only theme in the entire trio sonata to derive directly from the "royal theme" (Example 181). The original idea of the *Musical Offering* is thus fully integrated into the work rather than being a mere cantus firmus quotation, as in the 2nd movement. Now the theme even allows a transposition into major (m. 45 ff., E-flat major, m. 54 ff., B-flat major). Within the movement, which is mostly diatonically oriented, the descending chromaticism lends a special color to

Example 181.
Trio Sonata in C
Minor, BWV 1079,
4th movement,
Allegro, m. 1–8

the accompanying voices. We should note that several times, e.g. m. 39–44, the 6/8 time suddenly changes to 9/8 time, although this change, in accordance with practices of the time, is not notated. Like the first Allegro, this movement also has three sections, albeit with somewhat blurred contours. The beginning of the B section would be in m. 62; that of the reprise, in m. 90.

What style features, then, characterize this as a late work? It was written, after all, very close to the time of *The Art of Fugue*.[26] Comparing it with the earlier chamber music we would like to emphasize two things: (1) the characteristic shapes of the individual lines, which do not shy away from occasional contrapuntal abruptness; and (2) an indifference, perhaps stemming from old age, as to whether the work might be too rambling, too tiring. Similar symptoms are thought to be evident in late Beethoven works. Bach had reached a stage of maturity at which he no longer concerned himself much with questions of interpretation and reception. At this point he followed only the demands of his creative imagination. Precisely for this reason we repeat the suggestion we made earlier concerning this work: to try playing it without continuo realization, i.e., with only flute, violin and cello. It is easy to dispense with the harmonic substance of the continuo as the three voices contain all that is necessary. But in such an experiment the linear structure emerges with captivating clarity, so that the traditional method of interpretation can be disregarded with a clear conscience.

Finally there are two other short, individual movements in trio sonata instrumentation that should be mentioned. On the last page of the *Hunt* cantata, *Was mir behagt, ist nur die muntre Jagd,* BWV 208 (Weimar, 1716), Bach wrote a movement of 27 measures for oboe, violin and b.c. in F major. Schmieder gave it the BWV number 1040. The thematic material of the movement is a rocking eighth-note figure (Example 182), which had been used in the cantata itself (in the aria, "Weil die wollenreichen Herden"), and which is also familiar from other Bach works, e.g., the Pentecost cantata, *Also hat Gott die Welt geliebt,* BWV 68. The little movement is a masterpiece, making us regret that Bach did not enlist the oboe elsewhere in his chamber music. The movement is much too short to be performed by itself in a concert program. Nevertheless, it has become customary to play it during performances of the *Hunt* cantata as a kind of instrumental ritornello after the aria. It works extraordinarily well here and is thus kept in the repertoire.

Example 182.
Trio Movement in
F Major,
BWV 1040, m. 1–2

The other movement is an inversion canon for flute, violin and b.c., which belongs to the *Musical Offering,* BWV 1079. Bach seems to have added it to the trio sonata as a kind of "encore", because it is written in the same instrumentation, and because the *Musical Offering* has no other indications of instrumentation. It is a so-called "canone perpetuo," that is, a perpetual (endless) canon of the two melody parts over a free bass. In quality, however, it does not measure up to the other canons of the work.

Works for Lute

We have already seen that Bach's lute compositions are only partly original works, the rest being transcriptions of solo string works (see Part I, Chapter 2). There are still some particulars to add concerning Bach's lute notation. Bach always wrote for the lute on two staves, which was unusual not only in his own time, but also before and after. During the 16th and 17th centuries, the great epoch of the lute, compositions were always written in tablature, i.e., in finger notation, a system which differed from country to country. Later, in the 19th century, the one-line, treble clef notation, which is played an octave lower than written, predominated. It had its origins in guitar practice and is still used today. Bach wrote at the actual pitch. He used (and his copyists imitated him) the soprano clef for the upper line and the bass clef for the lower line, which corresponded to the keyboard notation customary at the time. Two of his lute works, however, are written differently. The upper line of BWV 995 is written in the tenor clef, probably because of the low register of the work. And in BWV 997, the most reliable copies (there is no surviving autograph) use the treble clef for the upper line, an octave higher than it is played. The only discrepancies are in the last movement of this Partita, the Double (see pp. 231, 233). Bach uses tablature only once: at the end of BWV 998. He did this for reasons of space, because he had run out of staff lines. However, he used German organ tablature, not lute tablature.

Suite in G Minor, BWV 995

The work is a transcription of the fifth suite for Cello solo in C Minor, BWV 1011. On the title page of the autograph of the lute version is the dedication, in Bach's own hand, "Pièces pour la Luth à Monsieur Schouster par J. S. Bach," from which we can gather that Bach adapted it for a specific occasion, perhaps as a paid commission by the otherwise unknown Schuster. The date of origin is assumed to be during the Leipzig period, between 1727 and 1731. The transposition to G minor must be termed successful because it preserves the characteristic dark tonal quality of the C minor cello original. Since the low note G_1 appears repeatedly, the work calls for the little-used 14-course lute with 26 strings.

The musical text follows the cello version quite closely,[27] diverging primarily on basic chords, which obviously were capable of more fullness on the 14-course lute than on the 4-string cello. But in some places there are also changes in rhythm, as well as added "Manieren" (ornaments). Example 183 gives an idea of the latter. Two additional variants of the adaptation are noteworthy. First, in the "très-viste" section of the Prelude, a fugue in the tradition of the French overture, Bach uses real two-part texture at the second entrance of the theme in m. 36–43, while here the cello original remains monophonic. Thus he follows the dictates of a fugal exposition more precisely than was possible with an unaccompanied string instrument. Second, in the Sarabande, Bach resists every temptation to provide chordal filling, although this would have been technically easy to do. He had a justifiable fear of

Example 183.
M. 22–23 of the
Allemande in
(a) the cello version
(BWV 1011) and
(b) the lute version
(BWV 995)

watering down the concentration of the monophonic cello version by filling in harmonies, thereby diminishing the impact of this great movement. Only in two places, m. 15 and 19, is a bass line indicated.

Regarding the individual movements we refer to the discussion of the Solo Suite for Cello in C Minor, BWV 1011 (p. 182). All in all, this piece is the most successful of Bach's lute transcriptions. It was written wholly in the idiom of the lute, without, however, violating the original cello work.

Suite in E Minor, BWV 996

This suite is an original composition for the lute. Though considered doubtful by Schmieder in the BWV, its authenticity is not questioned by Kohlhase. It is assumed to date from the decade *before* Köthen, i.e., between 1707 and 1717. This would mean that here we have one of Bach's few early chamber music compositions. One might find this confirmed by several conventional characteristics, for example, by the theme of the fugal Presto of the 1st movement (Praeludio), which consists of only one motif with simple stretto and sequential treatment. The suite is nevertheless charming, largely because of its simplicity and compactness, which distinguishes it from the expansive suite, BWV 995. Its first movement, the Praeludio, is divided into Passaggio and Presto and is almost like a study for the corresponding movement in BWV 995.

Comparing the substance of the Allemande, Courante and Sarabande with similar later works we can see that later Bach was able to provide these traditional forms with content in a much more personal manner. But in this case he scarcely rises above mediocrity. The Bourrée, on the other hand, is a real gem; its splendid principal idea (Example 184) has justifiably made it the most famous of Bach's lute

Example 184. Suite in E Minor, BWV 996, Bourrée, m. 1–4

pieces. I would rate the following Gigue almost as highly. A smooth performance of this virtuosic movement, unhindered by distortions of tempo and unintended accents, is a difficult, but nonetheless rewarding task for any lutanist.

Partita in C Minor, BWV 997

In contrast to the suite in E minor, this partita is obviously a mature work. The history of its transmission is complicated. No autograph exists, and Thomas Kohlhase, the editor of the lute works for the NBA, had to take into consideration no fewer than 16 different copies from the 18th and 19th centuries.[28] He sets its date of origin "not much earlier than 1740," and considering the quality of the piece, we would be inclined to agree.

The partita has five movements. After the introductory Prelude there is an extended da capo fugue instead of the expected Allemande and Courante; this is followed by the Sarabande and the concluding Gigue, which is provided with a Double.

The expansive scope of the Prelude recalls the great introductory movements of the suites for cello solo, with which it also shares its well-reasoned organization. It is in three sections. From m. 36 to the end there is a free reprise of certain elements of the exposition, which is brought to a close with a cadence to the dominant in m. 16–17. It is worth following the way Bach transforms these elements in their details and reinserts them in the course of the movement. The continuation of the beginning idea also merits interest, above all, in m. 33–34. There is a fermata in both m. 53 and 54; each demands an improvised ornament. A broad arpeggio might suffice.

The Fugue is worked out with extraordinary density and concentration. Earlier (pp. 32 and 127), we called attention to its bizarre theme, whose rhythmic imbalance (m. 1, eighth note; m. 2 and 3, dotted quarters) and abrupt downward leap of a major seventh has no parallel in any of Bach's numerous fugue themes. Bach provides it with a counterpoint starting right in m. 2, so that the second entrance of the theme (m. 7 ff.) already leads to a three-part texture. In the further development, even in the divertimenti, m. 1, the eighth-note scale is employed almost incessantly, "rectus" and "inversus," (Example 185a), both in its entirety and in fragments. The fugue has a clear three-part structure, its first section, which concludes in the tonic in m. 49, being repeated in its entirety after the middle section, so that we have a da capo fugue. The first and second sections are approximately the same length. In the latter, the eighths are dissolved into sixteenths, which are seldom interrupted. More importantly, however, the theme of the fugue now appears as an inversion in the middle section, thereby further accenting its unwieldy character. But the original theme is also used again, occasionally in a modified form suited to the lute (Example 185a, b).

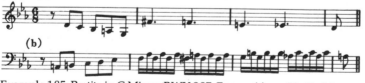

(a) (inversus)

(b)

Example 185. Partita in C Minor, BWV 997, Fugue, (a), m. 59–61, (b), m. 105–107

In the Sarabande one can recognize an echo of the concluding chorus of the *St. Matthew Passion,* "Wir setzen uns mit Tränen nieder."

The ensuing Gigue also shows the hand of the master: one rarely finds such well thought out developments of principal ideas in the numerous gigues of Bach's contemporaries. The ensuing Double movement is a headache for the lutanist. Musically, it is an exact variation of the preceding Gigue, but as notated in the sources it is unplayable on the lute. In order to play it, certain parts of both the upper and the lower lines have to be transposed down an octave. We already know that the most important transcriptions of this partita employ the G-clef throughout in the upper part, which is written an octave higher than it is played, corresponding to later guitar notation. In the Double, however, this no longer seems to be the case. For this reason Kohlhase, who has investigated the problem thoroughly, considers the Double to be one of the few original compositions for the lute-harpsichord (see p. 57) But since the movement clearly forms a unit with the preceding four movements, and particularly with the Gigue, we should not hesitate to make the necessary changes, so that the work as a whole can be performed on the lute.[29]

Prelude, Fugue and Allegro in E-Flat Major, BWV 998

This three-movement work has sometimes been considered a torso, since combinations of movements like this do not occur elsewhere. On the evidence of the autograph, however, Kohlhase has established that the surviving version is complete. Bach did not give the work a title; over the first line of the music he wrote simply, "Prélude pour la Luth ò Cembalo." The date of origin is assumed to be 1740–1745.

The Prelude, with its even eighth-note triplets, should not be played too rapidly; as it unfolds it shows less contour and elaboration than the Praeludio of the C Minor Partita, BWV 997. The continuation of the Neapolitan sixth chord, F-flat major, to the dominant of the dominant of E-flat major (m. 35–40) is a striking episode. This has moved some specialists to doubt the authenticity of the work. But these doubts have since been competently refuted. The harmonic progression is indeed daring, but correct in regard to form.

The theme of the following Fugue goes against everything we know about fugues since it has too little profile (Example 186). Yet the variety of the material developed from it is surprising. All in all, however, the fugue seems to be somewhat loosely constructed. What is interesting and certainly of significance for establishing the time of composition, is the relationship of the motif from m. 17–20 to the 3rd movement of the trio sonata and to the three-voice Ricercare from the *Musical Offering.* Like the fugue from BWV 997, this is also a da capo fugue. Its middle section, from m. 29 to 75, seems to belong more to a prelude than to a fugue; the already rather low contrapuntal standards of the piece are completely thrust aside in favor of concertante sixteenths, and what few thematic quotes there are are lost in this motion.

Example 186. Prelude, Fugue and Allegro, BWV 998, Fugue, m. 1–2

A sprightly Allegro follows, which with its constant running passages faintly recalls the concluding movement of the E-flat Major Sonata for Flute and Clavier, BWV 1031. A comparison of the sixteenth-note structures of this movement with those of the two preceding movements reveals that they are more integrated. Bach may not attain the level of concentration of the Presto from the Sonata for Violin Solo in G Minor, BWV 1001, but he never lapses into empty motion.

It should also be pointed out that, in contrast to other lute compositions by Bach, this work has long passages with a two-part texture.

Preludium in C Minor, BWV 999

This small prelude, developed from a single broken chord idea, has also become widely known as a keyboard work. As such it is very easy to play and probably has introduced Bach to many a youthful beginner. Nevertheless, it sounds better on the lute, as Bach intended it. It is impossible not to hear echoes from *The Well-Tempered Clavier;* in fact, the piece was written in Köthen at about the same time, which makes it the sole lute composition of the Köthen period. The conclusion on the dominant is striking. Was further material to have followed, perhaps a fugue? Did it remain a plan or has the continuation been lost in this case?

Fugue in G Minor, BWV 1000

This fugue is a transcription for the lute of the 2nd movement of the G Minor Sonata for Violin solo, BWV 1001. It exists only in French lute tablature, which Bach himself never used. The tablature manuscript probably was done by Johann Christian Weyrauch, a lutanist from Bach's Leipzig circle, which does not rule out the possibility that Bach himself made the transcription. To be sure, the lute adaptation does contain some significant variants from the original. The exposition is lengthened by two measures, that is, by an additional entrance of the theme, and the sequence of seventh chords in m. 47–48 (m. 45–46 of the violin version) receives additional basses. Neither of these effects could have been produced by a mere technician; hence it is probable that Bach at least had a hand in the transcription.

Suite in E Major, BWV 1006a

This work is also a transcription. Its original is the last in the series of solo Partitas for violin, in E major, BWV 1006. The adaptation probably also originated in Leipzig between 1735 and 1740. Whether Bach himself was responsible for the adaptation has not been definitely confirmed, not even by the fact that an autograph manuscript survives. For the transcription was made rather carelessly; Kohlhase calls it "scantier and more like an assignment" than the other transcriptions. On the other hand, Bach wrote two other versions of the Prelude which he used for cantatas no. 29 and 120a.

Also misleading is the title, "Suite pour le Clavecin composé Jean Sebast. Bach. Original," affixed to the autograph by an unknown hand. For this reason Philipp Spitta (1889) surmised it was for pedal harpsichord; Hans-Dagobert Bruger (1921) claimed it was a lute work, and Hans Joachim Zingel (1964) thinks that it was written for the harp. These claims are not convincing; the transcription's range is too low for either the harpsichord or the harp. But even on the lute, there is an unmistakable loss of quality. Unlike the transcription of the C minor cello suite, which was an interesting new version of the already magnificent original, here the original is far superior to the adaptation. The E major partita is unique as a violin composition, a high point in the entire field of violin literature; here any adaptation constitutes a devaluation, even if Bach himself were to have undertaken it. For a discussion of the individual movements we refer the reader to the original (pp. 177 f.).

Appendix

Abbreviations

BGA: Bach-Gesamtausgabe: *Johann Sebastian Bachs Werke,* ed. by the Bach-Gesellschaft in Leipzig, 46 volumes, Leipzig, 1851–99

BJB: *Bach-Jahrbuch,* published by the Neue Bach-Gesellschaft, Leipzig, 1904– , Berlin, 1952– .

BWV: Bach-Werke-Verzeichnis: Wolfgang Schmieder, *Thematisch-systematisches Verzeichnis der musikalischen Werke von Johann Sebastian Bach,* Leipzig, 1950, Wiesbaden, ⁵1973.

MGG: *Die Musik in Geschichte und Gegenwart,* Comprehensive (General) Encyclopedia of Music, ed. by Friedrich Blume, 16 volumes, Kassel (etc.), 1949–79.

NBA: Neu Bach-Ausgabe: Johann Sebastian Bach, *Neue Ausgabe sämtlicher Werke,* published by the Johann-Sebastian-Bach-Institut, Göttingen, and the Bach-Archiv, Leipzig, Volume 1– , Leipzig/Kassel (etc.), 1954– .

b.c. basso continuo, thorough bass, figured bass

K,Kh,Kt culmination point; high-point, low point

M.,m. Measure

T,S,D Tonic, subdominant, dominant

Tp,Sp,Dp Tonic parallel (relative major or minor), subdominant parallel, dominant parallel

Var. Variation

Notes

PREFACE

1. Hans Eppstein, *Studien über J. S. Bach's Sonaten für ein Melodieinstrument und obligates Cembalo,* Uppsala, 1966 (Acta Universitatis Upsaliensis—Studia musicologica Upsaliensia, N.S., vol. 2).
2. Bach bibliographies can be found in the following places: until 1905, in BJB 1905 (Max Schneider), until 1910 in *BJB,* 1910 (Max Schneider); until 1951 in *MGG* (Friedrich Blume); until 1972, in *Riemann Musiklexikon,* supplementary vol. 1, Carl Dahlhaus, ed., Mainz, 1972. There is also a convenient summary in Luc-André Marcel, *Johann Sebastian Bach in Selbstzeugnissen und Bilddokumenten,* Reinbeck bei Hamburg, 1963– , (rowohlt monographs, 83). For further bibliography the reader may wish to consult the detailed lists in *The New Grove Dictionary of Music and Musicians,* S. Sadie, ed., London, 1980, vol. 1, pp. 836ff.

PART I

1. [Johann Mattheson], *Der Vollkommene Capellmeister, Das ist . . . zum Versuch entworffen von Mattheson,* Hamburg, 1739, facsimile edition, ed. by Margarete Reimann, Kassel (etc.) ²1969 (Documenta Musicologica, Series 1 (R. 1). vol. 5), § 8.
2. Mattheson, *Der Vollkommene Capellmeister* § 106. A Revised Translation with Critical Commentary by Ernest C. Harris, UMI Research Press, Studies in Musicology, Ann Arbor, 1981.
3. Wolfgang Schmieder, *Thematisch-systematisches Verzeichnis der musikalischen Werke von Johann Sebastian Bach (Bach-Werke-Verzeichnis, BWV),* Leipzig 1950, Wiesbaden ⁵1973.
4. Hans-Peter Schmitz considers it unequivocally a flute sonata: compare H.-P. Sch., *Querflöte und Querflötenspiel in Deutschland während des Barockzeitalters,* Kassel/Basel, 1952, p. 74; there is also a reference to the Foreword to the new edition of the Sonata in G Minor, BWV 1020 (for flute) by Leo Balet in "Nagels Musikarchiv."
5. Bach designated as "Opus I" only the edition of the 6 clavier partitas—*Clavir-Übung*—which appeared in 1731 published by Bach himself.
6. Charles Sanford Terry, *Johann Sebastian Bach,* Leipzig, 1929, Berlin³ 1950, p. 65. The author of the text of the opera was probably the Arnstadt rector, Treiber. See also Percy M. Young, *The Bachs, 1500–1850,* New York, 1970. *Die Bachs.*
7. *Other important works written in Köthen* include the clavier works "Chromatic Fantasy and Fugue," *The Well-Tempered Clavier, Part 1,* two and three part Inventions ("Sinfonien"), as well as the *Brandenburg Concertos,* the violin concertos in A minor and E major, the double concerto for 2 violins in D minor, the orchestral suites (overtures) in C major and B minor, and the Fantasia and Fugue for Organ in G minor, BWV 542.

239

8. The following works by Bach were published during his lifetime, mostly by Bach himself:

   1. The cantata, "Gott ist mein König" (No. 71), Mühlhausen, 1708 (written for a town council election);
   2. Clavierübung, part 1, 6 partitas for clavier, in individual editions starting in 1726, collected in 1731 as *Clavir-Übung, Op.1;*
   3. Clavierübung, part 2: *Italian Concerto* and *Suite in B Minor,* 1735;
   4. Clavierübung, part 3: Prelude and triple fugue in E-flat major and chorales for organ, 1739;
   5. Clavierübung, part 4: *Goldberg Variations* for clavier, 1742(?);
   6. 6 organ chorales (so-called Schübler chorales), between 1746 and 1750;
   7. Canonic variations on the Christmas song *Vom Himmel hoch,* not before 1746;
   8. *Musical Offering,* 1747.

9. Cf. Georg von Dadelsen, *Bemerkungen zur Handschrift Joh. Seb. Bachs, seiner Familie und seines Kreises,* Trossingen, 1957 (Tübinger Bach-Studien, Book 1). Also important to the theme of this entire chapter is Georg von Dadelsen, *Beiträge zur Chronologie der Werke Johann Sebastian Bachs,* Trossingen, 1958, (Tübinger Bach-Studien, Books 4–5).

10. The most important chamber music volumes of the *BGA* are vol. 9, 27 and 42, which appeared in 1860, 1879 and 1894.

11. Edited by Wilhelm Rust and Alfred Dörffel.

12. A selection of contemporary documents about Johann Sebastian Bach was brought out by Hans-Joachim Schulze: *Johann Sebastian Bach. Leben und Werk in Dokumenten,* compiled by H.-J. Sch., Leipzig/Kassel (etc.)/ Munich, 1975; it is based on vol. 1–3 of the critical edition, *Bach-Dokumente,* which appeared in 1963, 1969 and 1972 as supplements to the NBA.

13. cf. Paul Kast, *Die Bach-Handschriften der Berliner Staatsbibliothek,* Trossingen, 1958 (Tübinger Bach-Studien, Books 2–3), and Karl-Heinz Köhler, "Die Bach-Sammlung der Deutschen Staatsbibliothek. Überlieferung und Bedeutung," in *Bach-Studien,* vol. 5, edited by Rudolf Eller and Hans-Joachim Schulze, Leipzig, 1975.

14. Wolfgang Schmieder, "Foreword" to Phillip Spitta, *Johann Sebastian Bach,* abridged edition with notes and addenda by W. Sch., Wiesbaden, [3]1949, p. IV.

15. Alfred Dürr, "Zur Echtheitsfrage bei Johann Sebastian Bach," in *Musica 7,* (1953), p. 292.

16. Vienna, June 12, 1890. The correspondence between Brahms and Mandyszewski was published in *Zeitschrift für Musikwissenschaft* 15, (1933), pp. 337 ff.

17. Ischl, June 14, 1890.

18. Vienna, June 15, 1890.

19. Vienna, July 2, 1890.

20. Related to me by my teacher, Prof. Dr. Georg Schumann, who was Director of the Berlin Singakademie from 1900 to 1950. See also Friedrich Welter, "Die Musikbibliothek der Singakademie zu Berlin," in *Singakademie zu Berlin. Festschrift zum 175 jährigen Bestehen.* ed. by Werner Bollert, Berlin, 1966.

21. An additional source was: NBA VI, 1 (works for violin), critical commentary by Rudolf Gerber and Günther Hausswald, pp. 25 ff. In the Foreword to *BGA* XXVII, which contains the solo works for violin and cello, the editor, Alfred Dörffel, cites as his primary sources two manuscripts of the violin solo works,

one of which allegedly was purchased by Georg Pölchau in 1814 from a St. Petersburg pianist named Palschau. The other, which had a French title, is supposed to have been inscribed "écrite par Madame Bachen. Son Épouse." These two manuscripts also do not appear to have been in the possession of Philipp Emanuel.

22. In a letter to the author dated June 8, 1978.
23. Here I am thinking particularly of the interpretation of the *B Minor Mass* as not planned as a single, coordinated work as Friedrich Smend maintained in connection with the edition of Vol. II, 1 of the NBA which contains the Mass.
24. In an undated letter to the first Bach biographer, Johann Nikolaus Forkel, Carl Philipp Emanuel Bach wrote, "Apart from his sons, I can think of the following pupils: organists Schubert and Vogler, Goldberg at the court of Count Brühl, organist Altnikol, my late brother-in-law; organists Krebs, Agricola, Kirnberger, Müthel in Riga and Voigt in Anspach." Carl Philipp Emanuel's memory was not completely accurate; he forgot Bach's pupils Gottfried August Homilius and Johann Christian Kittel. Forkel included this information in his biography, *Über Johann Sebastian Bachs Leben, Kunst und Kunstwerke*, Leipzig, 1802, modern edition, Augsburg, 1925, p. 63. Concerning Goldberg he added, "He was a very strong keyboard player, but had but little talent as a composer." Carl Philipp Emanuel's letters to Forkel were published by Max Schneider in *Bach-Urkunden*, Leipzig, (1917) (publications of the Neue Bach-Gesellschaft, vol. 17 no. 3.)
25. cf. Ernst Dadder, "Johann Gottlieb Goldberg," in *BJB* 1923, pp. 57 ff.
26. Werner Danckert, *Beiträge zur Bach-Kritik*, vol. 1, Kassel, 1934 (Jenaer Studien zur Musikwissenschaft, vol. 1) pp. 35f. The quotation refers to m. 9–11 of the first movement of the E-Flat Major Flute Sonata. In this essay, Danckert draws a comparison between the E-Flat Major Flute Sonata, BWV 1031, and the Sonata for Violin (Flute) and Clavier in G Minor, BWV 1020. Using his own system of typological theory (Ibid p. 9), he considers the latter, unlike the former, to be not authentic. He characterized the G minor sonata as follows: ". . . the construction of the motifs is de facto basically forward moving, up-beat; both the harpsichord opening [example from the music follows] and the initial motif of the flute [example from the music follows] were conceived in this spirit." Danckert contrasts this description of an "unauthentic" Bach work to the "authentic" E-Flat Major sonata.
27. See Friedrich Blume, "Eine unbekannte Violinsonate von Johann Sebastian Bach," in BJB, 1928, pp. 96 ff.
28. Hans Eppstein, *Studien über J. S. Bachs Sonaten für ein Melodieinstrument und obligates Cembalo*, Uppsala 1966 (Acta Universitatis Upsaliensis—Studia musicologica Upsaliensia, N.S., vol. 2)
29. NBA., VI, 1. Critical commentary by Rudolf Gerber and Günter Hausswald, pp. 118 ff., 121 ff.
30. On the question of the correspondences between and the authenticity of the three works, BWV 1021, 1022, and 1038, see also Ulrich Siegele, *Kompositionsweise und Bearbeitungstechnik in der Instrumentalmusik Johann Sebastian Bachs*, Neuhausen bei Stuttgart, 1975, pp. 23 ff.
31. Compare Friedrich Smend, *Bach in Köthen*, Berlin, 1952.
32. In his story, *Fälschungen*, Frankfurt a.M. 1953, Hermann Kasack uses this problem as his central theme. Although he is only talking about woodcarving,

the same applies to all the arts.

33. According to NBA VI, 3. Critical commentary by Hans Peter Schmitz, pp. 48 ff.
34. Bach made two trips to Berlin and Potsdam, the first one in 1741, to visit his son, Carl Philipp Emanuel. On this trip he did not meet King Frederick II who was probably involved in the First Silesian War at the time. However, he probably did meet with the King's "privy counsellor," the chamberlain Fredersdorf who likewise played the flute, and to whom he gave the E Major Sonata. In the BWV, Schmieder mentions a copy of the sonata from the 19th century, on which was written: "Following the autograph of the author, which was written by him for the chamberlain Fredersdorf in the year 17– , when he was in Potsdam." Hans Peter Schmitz, in the "Critical Commentary" to *NBA* VI, 3, p.24, footnote 6, mentions another note in an old music catalog: "Sonata per il Traverso e Continuo. Written for the Privy Counsellor, Fredersdorf, when he was in Potsdam. von Radowitz." Schmitz doubts this origin (p. 24), but I do not find his stylistic arguments convincing. Bach's second trip led to his famous meeting with Frederick the Great and to the composition of the *Musical Offering*. See also Hans Eppstein, "Über J. S. Bachs Flötensonaten mit Generalbass," in BJB 1972, pp. 12 ff. Concerning a third trip by Bach to Berlin, compare Note 58.
35. Eppstein, *Studien über J. S. Bachs Sonaten für ein Melodieinstrument und obligates Cembalo.* p. 161.
36. Hans Eppstein, "Chronologieprobleme in J. S. Bachs Suiten für Soloinstrumente," in BJB 1976, pp. 35 ff.
37. Thomas Kohlhase, *Johann Sebastian Bachs Kompositionen für Lauteninstrumente. Kritische Edition mit Untersuchungen zur Überlieferung, Besetzung und Spieltechnik,"* Typewritten diss. Tübingen, 1972. The work will appear as the "Critical Commentary" to NBA V, 10, which contains the lute works edited by Kohlhase. The author and the publisher have graciously made the manuscript, i.e., the galley proofs available to me (hence the lack of page references in the following).
38. Kohlhase, *Johann Sebastian Bachs Komposionen für Lauteninstrumente.*
39. Hans Eppstein, "Johann Sebastian Bachs Sonate für Violine und Klavier in G Dur, BWV 1019," in *Archiv für Musikwissenschaft 21* (1964), p. 221.
40. The history of this sonata has been frequently dealt with in the literature. The chief sources of perplexity are 1), that the two cantatas cited, No. 120 and No. 120a, were not written until 1728 or possibly even later, in Leipzig, whereas the sonata was in all probability written in Köthen; and 2), that the *cantabile* movement (B 3) can only have been derived from the cantata aria, not the other way around. For this reason, it was speculated that the B version was written at a later date, after the move to Leipzig (which meant that C could only have been written in Leipzig too, sometime in the 1730's). But Friedrich Smend's hypothesis is the most likely one, namely, that the movement "must have been taken from a lost vocal work from the Köthen period" (Smend, *Bach in Köthen,* pp. 61 ff.). Hans Eppstein agrees with Smend's hypothesis (compare Note 39.).
41. The first version appears in both the BGA IX, p. 250 and the NBA VI, 1, p. 195. Hans Eppstein's new edition of the 6 violin-clavier sonatas by Henle-Verlag, Munich/Duisburg, 1971, which is superior to the NBA in many respects, does not contain the first version.
42. Leipzig, 1930 (Veröffentlichungen der Neuen Bach-Gesellschaft, Vol. 1, No. 1.)
43. The following section was based primarily (along with various individual essays

and lexicographic articles) on: Eberhard Preussner, *Die bürgerliche Musikkultur,* Kassel/Basel ²1950: Bernhard Paumgartner, *Das instrumentale Ensemble,* Zurich, 1966: François Lesure, *Musik und Gesellschaft im Bild,* transl. by Anna Martina Gottschick, Kassel (etc.). 1966; Kurt Gudewill, "Collegium musicum," in MGG II, col. 1554–62. In addition, the standard biographies by Philipp Spitta, Albert Schweitzer and Charles Sanford Terry have been consulted here as elsewhere.

44. The work has been published in a new edition by Guido Adler in *Denkmäler der Tonkunst in Österreich,* Vol. 10, Vienna, 1903. According to the latest research, Orazio Benevoli's authorship of the mass is contested; it is thought that Heinrich Ignaz Franz Biber could have been the composer, but this would mean that the mass was not written for the dedication of the Salzburg cathedral in 1628, because Biber did not arrive in Salzburg until 1673.

45. Preussner, *Die bürgerliche Musikkultur,* pp. 19 ff. Johann Friedrich von Uffenbach (1687–1769), alderman and councillor in Frankfurt-on-the-Main, was a passionate lover of music. He traveled through Alsace, Switzerland, Italy, France, and Brabant and recorded his impressions (unpublished).

46. Reproduction of the Chodowiecki engraving in Preussner, *Die bürgerliche Musikkultur,* facing p. 43; reproduction of the Thun illustration in MGG II, col. 1557 f.

47. Preussner, *Die bürgerliche Musikkultur,* p. 38, footnote.

48. The word "academy," denoting a concert, is still used today in the "Akademie-Konzerte" of the National Theater Orchestra in Mannheim, founded in 1779, and in the Bavarian State Orchestra in Munich, founded in 1811. The Concert Society in Winterthur still calls itself "Musikkollegium," continuing its tradition since it was founded in 1629 as "collegium musicum."

49. Occasionally concerts were publicly announced, usually on special occasions: ". . . tomorrow, Wednesday, the 17th of June, in the Zimmerman Garden in Grimm Lane we shall begin with a fine concert, including a new harpsichord, the like of which has not been heard in this area, and all lovers of music, as well as musicians themselves, are cordially invited to attend" (bulletin announcing the end of national mourning, in *Nachricht auch Frag—und Anzeiger Leipzig,* June 16, 1733). Or: "On the celebrated name-day of his Royal Majesty in Poland and Electoral Highness (Friedrich August II) of Saxony, the Bach "Collegium Musicum" will humbly present an evening concert of solemn music with illumination in the Zimmerman Garden by the Grimm Gate" (*Leipziger Zeitungen,* August 3, 1735). See also Schulze, *Johann Sebastian Bach. Leben und Werk in Dokumenten,* pp. 65 f.

50. On the title of *The Well-Tempered Clavier,* Part I, Bach writes, "I have written this for the use and edification of young people interested in understanding music, as well as for those already proficient in this field . . ."

51. Paumgartner, *Das instrumentale Ensemble* p. 114. The presentation corresponds to a model by the Celle organist Wolfgang Wessnitzer, who characterized it as a desirable standard for what "makes up a good *Capell,* and what persons would contribute to it." In fact, there was probably always a dearth of musicians, as was the case with Bach in Leipzig.

52. Princes who played music were no rarity in the 18th century. Emperor Leopold I conducted and composed, the accomplishments of Frederick the Great in the area of composition and flute playing are well known; Joseph II was a cellist; Prince Louis Ferdinand of Prussia was a brilliant pianist and composer.

53. Apart from the works cited in note 43, I used the following sources for this section: Rudolf Bunge, "Johann Sebastian Bachs Kapelle zu Cöthen und deren nachgelassene Instrumente," in BJB 1905, pp. 14 ff.; Smend, *Bach in Köthen;* Walther Vetter, *Der Kapellmeister Bach,* Potsdam 1950.

54. Another group of musicians released from service at the Berlin Court was probably hired by Margrave Christian Ludwig von Brandenburg, to whom the *Brandenburg Concertos* were dedicated; see Heinrich Besseler, critical commentary to NBA VII, 2, p. 17.

55. Father of the well-known gamba virtuoso, Carl Friedrich Abel, who among others, frequented the home of Goethe's parents.

56. Interestingly, in his memorandum on the church music of Leipzig, written in 1730, *Kurtzer, iedoch höchstnötiger Entwurff einer wohlbestallten Kirchen Musik; nebst einigen unvorgreiflichen Bedencken von dem Verfall derselben.* ("A brief, but highly necessary plan for a well-organized program of church music, along with some speculative thoughts about the decline of such music.") Bach also listed a total of 18 instrumentalists, although in different combinations: 4 (6) violins, 4 violas, 2 cellos, 1 contrabass, 2 (3) oboes, 1 (2) bassoon(s), 3 trumpets, 1 player of kettledrums. Transverse flutes are noted separately. The numbers in parentheses are ideal (optimal) instrumentations. But, in fact, Bach had a core of only 8 musicians in Leipzig "whose quality and musical expertise, modesty forbids me to describe truthfully" (Schulze, *Johann Sebastian Bach, Leben und Werk in Dokumenten,* p. 103).

57. This was nothing unusual. Dittersdorf reports that nine servants, in livery, a valet and a pastry cook also played in the Bishop of Grosswardein's orchestra and a cook sang the buffo parts in "Singspiele." See *Karl von Dittersdorfs Lebensbeschreibung . . . ,* Leipzig, 1801, new edition, Leipzig, 1940, pp. 125 and 133.

58. On the basis of these account books, Smend and Besseler conclude that Bach made a third trip to Berlin in 1718, where he supposedly discussed the construction of the harpsichord with its builder, Michael Mietke and commissioned the instrument (compare Note 91).

59. Terry, *Johann Sebastian Bach,* p. 120.

60. Carl Philipp Emanuel Bach, in *Bach-Urkunden,* (cf. Note 24).

61. I do not share Vetter's view that Bach was thwarted from achieving his real goals all his life due to his church service (Vetter, *Der Kapellmeister Bach*); however, I can imagine that he occasionally groaned under the pressure of constantly having to write cantatas during his first decade in Leipzig.

62. Records show that in Köthen, Bach experimented not only with the lute harpsichord, also called a "Lautenwerck" (a harpsichord with double gut strings that had a resonating board similar to a lute, and hence sounded somewhat like a lute)—but also with early forms of the *viola pomposa,* the *viola da spalla* and the *violoncello piccolo,* which he ordered to be built in Leipzig. It is certain that he only employed the transverse flute since the Köthen period. Regarding the lute-harpsichord, see Kohlhase, *Johann Sebastian Bachs Kompositionen für Lauteninstrumente* and André Burguéte, "Die Lautenkompositionen Johann Sebastian Bachs," in BJB 1977, pp. 26 ff. Regarding the transverse flute, see Schmitz, *Querflöte und Querflötenspiel in Deutschland während des Barockzeitalters* and Bunge, "Johann Sebastian Bachs Kapelle zu Cöthen und deren nachgelassene Instrumente," p. 29. More important than his experiments with new instruments, however, were Bach's sallies into new composi-

tional terrain, i.e., the sonatas for melody instruments and obbligato clavier, *The Well-Tempered Clavier*, Part I, and the *Brandenburg Concertos*.

63. Beginning in 1718, he received an annual compensation of 12 Thaler for this.

64. In the church records for the parish of Köthen, Anna Magdalena's maiden name appears in the wedding entry as "Wülckeln." Other spellings encountered elsewhere are 'Wülken,' 'Wilke' and 'Wilcke.' The spelling 'Wülckelns' resulted from misunderstanding the genitive 's' in the marriage document: ". . . Und mit ihm Jungfer Anna Magdalena, Hn Johann Caspar Wülckens Hochfürstl. Sächssl. Weissenfelsischen Musikalischen Hof—und Feld Trompeters ehel. jüngste Tochter . . ."

65. In a letter to a friend from his student days, George Erdmann in Danzig, October, 1730: ". . . it is beginning to look as if the musical interest of the Prince is waning, especially since the new Princess does not seem to be interested in music . . ." (Schulze, *Johann Sebastian Bach. Leben und Werk in Dokumenten*, p. 12).

66. See the letter to Erdmann cited in note 65: "Although at the outset it did not at all seem appropriate for me to become a cantor after having been a 'Kapellmeister . . . (Schulze, *ibid.*)

67. Bach performed the same duties at the court at Weissenfels.

68. This probably also explains why Bach's second wedding was performed at home. As court Kapellmeister, he belonged to the parish of the castle, but, as mentioned, he did not recognize the reformed rite. Hence the solution: "on the Prince's orders, married at home."

69. Apart from the works already cited, I also used the following sources concerning the situation in Köthen: Wilhelm Bethge/Walter Götze. *Johann Sebastian Bach und sein Wirken in Cöthen*, Köthen, 1925; Wolfgang Frohberg, *Johann Sebastian Bach in Köthen 1717–1723*, Köthen 1977, as well as information related personally by the present cantor of St. Jakob's Church in Köthen, Michael Christfried Winkler.

70. From the abundant literature available on the topics covered in Chapters 4, 5 and 6, I list only a small selection. For bibliographic material, please refer to the sources mentioned in Note 2 to the Preface of this book. Regarding the literature on performance practices in the early 18th century, a distinction must be made between publications of that time and contemporary publications. Of the former, we shall cite here only those which have appeared in new editions and are currently available.

Georg Muffat, *Suavioris harmoniae instrumentalis hyporchematicae florilegium*, Part 1, Augsburg 1695, Part 2, Passau, 1698; new edition by H. Rietsch, in *Denkmäler der Tonkunst in Österreich*, vol. 1 and 4 (according to the old numbering system, Vol. I, 2, and II, 2), Vienna 1894. The work is a collection of compositions by Muffat; its 'Prologue' deals in part with the playing practices of the time.

[Johann Mattheson], *Der Vollkommene Capellmeister . . .*, Hamburg, 1739; facsimile-reprint, ed. by Margarete Reimann, Kassel (etc.). ²1969 (Documenta Musicologica, Ser. 1, Vol. 5)

Francesco Geminiani, *The Art of Playing the Violin*, London, 1751 (1740?), German, Vienna (1785–1805) facsimile-reprint of the original Engl. edition, ed. by David D. Boyden, New York, Toronto, 1952.

Johann Joachim Quantz, *Versuch einer Anweisung, die flûte traversière zu spielen . . .*, Berlin, 1752; facsimile-reprint of the 3rd edition, Berlin, 1789, ed. by Hans Peter Schmitz, Kassel/Basel, 1953 (Documenta Musicologica, Ser. 1, vol. 2). Engl.

transl. by E. Reilly, London. 1966.

Carl Philipp Emanuel Bach, *Versuch über die wahre Art, das Clavier zu spielen* . . ., 2 parts, Berlin, 1753–62; facs. new impr., ed. by Lothar Hoffman-Erbrecht, Leipzig, 1969. Engl. transl. by W. Mitchell, New York, 1949.

Leopold Mozart, *Versuch einer gründlichen Violinschule* . . ., Augsburg, 1756; fcs.-reprint, Frankfurt a.M., 1956, Engl. transl. by E. Knocker, Oxford, 1948.

Jacob Adlung, *Musica mechanica organoedi* . . . (published after Adlung's death by Johann Lorenz Albrecht), 2 vols., Berlin, 1768; facs. reprint, ed. by Christhard Mahrenholz, Kassel, 1961.

Selection of 20th century publications

A. Books

Anthony Baynes (ed.), *Musical Instruments Through the Ages*, Harmondsworth, 1961, New York, 1966 (page references here follow the latter).

David D. Boyden, *The History of Violin Playing from its Origins to 1761—and its Relationship to the Violin and Violin Music*, Oxford, 1965.

Friedrich Ernst, *Der Flügel Johann Sebastian Bachs*, Frankfurt-on-the-Main London/New York, 1955.

Thomas Kohlhase, *Johann Sebastian Bachs Kompositionen für Lauteninstrumente. Kritische Edition mit Untersuchungen zur Überlieferung, Besetzung und Spieltechnik,* diss., Tübingen, 1972; expanded as "Critical Commentary" to NBA V, 10 (in preparation).

Klaus Marx, *Die Entwicklung des Violoncells und seiner Spieltechnik bis J. L. Duport (1520–1820)*, Regensburg, 1963 (Forschungsbeiträge zur Musikwissenschaft, vol. 13).

Hanns Neupert, *Das Cembalo*, Kassel/Basel, ²1951.

Raymond Russell, *The Harpsichord and Clavichord,* London, 1959.

Gustav Scheck, *Die Flöte und ihre Musik*, Mainz, 1975.

Arnold Schering, *Aufführungspraxis alter Musik*, Leipzig, 1931.

Hans Peter Schmitz, *Prinzipien der Aufführungspraxis alter Musik. Kritischer Versuch über die spätbarocke Spielpraxis*, Berlin, 1950.

Hans Peter Schmitz, *Über die Wiedergabe der Musik Johann Sebastian Bachs*, Berlin 1951.

Hans Peter Schmitz, *Querflöte und Querflötenspiel in Deutschland während des Barockzeitalters*, Kassel/Basel, 1952.

Hans Peter Schmitz, *Die Kunst der Verzierung im 18. Jahrhundert. Instrumentale und vokale Musizierpraxis in Beispielen*, Kassel/Basel, 1955.

Charles Sanford Terry, *Bach's Orchestra*, Oxford, ²1958.

B. Articles

Rudolf Bunge, "Bachs Kapelle zu Cöthen und deren nachgelassene Instrumente," in BJB, 1905, pp 14 ff.

Willibald Gurlitt, "Das historische Klangbild im Werk Johann Sebastian Bachs," in BJB, 1951/52, p. 80.

Max Rostal, "Zur Interpretation der Violinsonaten Johann Sebastian Bachs," in BJB, 1973, pp. 72 ff.

Alte Musik in unserer Zeit, Papers and discussions from the Kassel conference, 1967 (with contributions by Karl Grebe, Ludwig Finscher, August Wenzinger, Rudolf Ewerhart, Kurt Blaukopf, Wolfgang Gönnenwein, et al.), Kassel, etc., 1968 (Musikalische Zeitfragen, vol. 13).

Further references will be given in the notes in each case.

71. "Organ movement" was the name given to the revival of Baroque organ-building techniques. It began in Freiburg i. Br. when Willibald Gurlitt, the Freiburg musicologist, and the Ludwigsburg organ-builder, Oscar Walcker, made an organ precisely following the plans of Michael Praetorius (1619, in his *Organographia,* cf. Note 79). Besides Gurlitt, the most important members of this movement were Karl Straube (Leipzig), Christhard Mahrenholz (Hannover) and the writer Hans Henny Jahnn (Hamburg). Even before 1921, Albert Schweitzer had called attention to the need for changing the way organs were built. The organ in Freiburg was destroyed during the war (1944) and rebuilt in 1954–55.

72. The B Minor Sonata for Flute and Clavier, BWV 1030, in the early G minor version, is sometimes also played on the oboe. There is no information available on this, but it is musically defensible. The only (extant) chamber music work by Bach for the oboe is the short Trio Movement for Oboe, Violin and b.c. in F Major, BWV 1040. In contrast, almost all of Bach's contemporaries wrote chamber music for the oboe.

73. g^3 can be found in m. 86 of the Chaconne from the D minor Partita for Violin solo, BWV 1004, and in the Finale (allegro assai) of the C Major Sonata for Violin solo, BWV 1005, m. 89 ff.

74. David D. Boyden, *The History of Violin Playing from its Origins to 1761,* Oxford, 1965, p. 271f.

75. Boyden, *op. cit.,* pp. 324ff; see also Plates 40 a/b

76. Albert Schweitzer, *Johann Sebastian Bach,* Leipzig, [6]1928. pp. 192 f. and 361 ff.

77. Characteristically, Johann Christoph Weigel's collection of illustrations, *Musicalisches Theatrum* (1720), consisting of 36 full-page engravings of musical instruments of the time, does not show a cello, although the gamba and the "Violon" (contrabass) are both included. This could be accidental, however, since the work was originally published as separate sheets and was not compiled in one volume until our own time: *Musicalisches Theatrum, auf welchem alle zu dieser edlen Kunst gehörige Instrumenta in anmuthigen Posituren lebhafft gezeiget und allen Music Liebhabern zu gefälliger belustigung vorgestellet werden. Nürnberg zu finden bey Jo. Christoph Weigel,* facs.-repr., ed. by Alfred Berner, Kassel (etc.,) [2]1964 (Documenta musicologica, Series 1, vol. 22).

78. Wolfgang Boettcher in the Program Notes for the 44th German Bach Festival, Heidelberg, 1969: "Chamber music II—Bach: Three solo suites for the cello."

79. Michael Praetorius, *Syntagma musicum,* Part 2: *De Organographia,* Wolfenbüttel, 1618, facs.-repr., ed. by Willibald Gurlitt, Kassel (etc.) [2]1964 (Documenta Musicologica, Series 1, vol. 14); coll. of plates: XXI, no. 5 and 6.

80. Robert Hausmann, cellist of the Joachim Quartet for many years, played without an end pin into the 20th century (he died in 1909). Hausmann published Bach's solo suites in a reliable edition at the turn of the century (Steingräber-Verlag, now out of print).

81. Hubert Le Blanc, *Défense de la basse viole contre les entreprises du violon et les préten-sions du violoncel,* Amsterdam, 1740.

82. Leopold Mozart, *A Treatise on the Fundamental Principles of Violin Playing*, Oxford, 1948, pp. 10f.

83. Sylvestro Ganassi, *Regola Rubertina. German: Lehrbuch des Spiels auf der Viola da gamba und der Laute*, two Parts, Venice, 1542–43, translated and edited by Hildemarie Peter and Emilia Dahnk-Baroffio, Berlin-Lichterfelde 1972, p. 12.

84. The bowing position of the angel playing the gamba in Matthias Grünewald's Isenheim Altar painting is an absurd misrepresentation.

85. Marx, *Die Entwicklung des Violoncells und seiner Spieltechnik bis J. L. Duport (1520–1820)*, p. 39; compare also Ganassi, *Regola Rubertina*, p. 10.

86. Johann Sebastian Bach, *Sechs Suiten für Violoncello solo*, ed. by August Wenzinger, Kassel, 1950 (Bärenreiter-Ausgabe, No. 320).

87. Cf. Note 78.

88. Museum of Musical Instruments of the National Institute for Musical Research, Preussischer Kulturbesitz, located in what used to be the Joachimsthal Gymnasium, Bundesallee 1–12, 1000 Berlin 30.

89. Illustrated in Scheck, *Die Flöte und ihre Musik*, p. 29.

90. Ernst, *Der Flügel Johann Sebastian Bachs*, pp 22 f., 30. f.

91. Thus, Heinrich Besseler in his Critical Commentary to NBA VII, 2 (*Brandenburg Concertos*), pp. 17f. Besseler proposes that Bach was in Berlin in 1718 to order the instrument and discuss its construction.

92. Quantz, *Versuch*, translated by E. R. Reilly as *On Playing the Flute*, London, 1966, p. 259

93. Le Blanc, *Verteidigung der Viola da gamba*, pp. 85 ff.

94. Kohlhase, *Johann Sebastian Bachs Kompositionen für Lauteninstrumente*, names, among others, Johann Christian Weyrauch and Johann Kropffgans from Leipzig, a "Monsieur Schouster," about whom no more is known, and Silvius Leopold Weiss from Dresden. Weiss belonged to the Court Chapel of Dresden from 1718 to 1750 and probably was introduced to Johann Sebastian by Wilhelm Friedemann. He was an extremely prolific composer for the lute (a complete edition of his works is in preparation), and is considered today as the last important lute player of that period.

95. See Alexander Buchner, *Musikinstrumente im Wandel der Zeiten*, Prague, ²1957, Ill. 186–189.

96. Konrad Ragossnig, *Handbuch der Gitarre und Laute*, Mainz, 1978, p. 14.

97. Kohlhase, *Johann Sebastian Bachs Kompositionen für Lauteninstrumente*.

98. Franz Julius Giesbert, "Bach und die Laute," in *Die Musikforschung* 25 (1972), pp. 485 ff.

99. Details of the particular tunings used by Yepes are in the supplement "Die Instrumente" (by Jürgen Eppelsheimer) to L. P. Cassette No. 7 (Chamber music II) of the complete works of Bach in the *Archiv-Produktion* of the Deutsche Grammophon-Gesellschaft, No. 2722013, Hamburg, 1975. See also Kohlhase, *Johann Sebastian Bachs Kompositionen für Lauteninstrumente*.

100. Kohlhase, *Johann Sebastian Bachs Kompositionen für Lauteninstrumente*.

101. Bunge, "Bachs Kapelle zu Cöthen und deren nachgelassene Instrumente," p. 29.

102. Young, *Die Bachs 1500–1850*, pp. 127 ff.

103. Compare Adlung, *Musica mechanica organoedi*, p. 139.

104. Regarding the question of the lute-clavier, see also Kohlhase, *Johann Sebastian Bachs Kompositionen für Lauteninstrumente* and Howard Ferguson, "Bachs

'Lauten-Werck'," in *Music and Letters* 48 (1967), pp. 259 ff.

105. Neupert, *Das Cembalo*, p. 66.

106. Strangely enough, Pablo Casals did not arpeggiate these measures, but played them instead exactly as written.

107. Matters of interest concerning these questions from an editorial point of view in Georg von Dadelsen, "Die Crux der Nebensache. Editorische und praktische Bemerkungen zu Bachs Artikulation," in BJB, 1978, pp. 95 ff. There is also a detailed discussion of the suites for cello solo, which have not yet been included in the NBA.

108. Compare Rolf van Leydens Preface to his edition of the sonatas for gamba and clavier, Frankfurt a.M./New York/London, 1935 (Edition Peters, No. 4268).

109. Various editions number the measures of the 1st and 2nd movements of this sonata continuously, and likewise the 3rd and 4th movements, so that the 2nd movement begins with m. 29 and the 4th with m. 19. Since, however, these are both entirely new movements which are only connected to the preceding movements by an *attacca*, this seems to make little sense. In each case, we begin the numbering of these movements with m. 1.

110. Francesco Maria Veracini (1690–1768), *Sonata accademica*, No. 10 (F Major) and No. 11 (E Major), ed. by Walter Kolneder, Frankfurt a.M./New York/London, 1971 (Edition Peters, No. 12561–62), here in Veracini's original (translated) Preface.

111. Scheck, *Die Flöte und ihre Musik*, p. 137.

112. Johann Friedrich Agricola, quoted in *Johann Sebastian Bach. Leben und Werk in Dokumenten*, p. 74.

113. See Hans Eppstein's Preface to his edition of the Violin-clavier sonatas (compare Note 41.).

114. There is also extensive literature concerning the "notes inégales," including Christel Pfeiffer, "Die 'notes inégales,' ihre Bedeutung und Anwendung aus der Sicht deutscher musikgeschichtlicher Quellen des 18. Jahrhunderts," in *Melos* 6 (1978), pp. 512 ff., and Newman W. Powell, *Rhythmic Freedom in the Performance of French Music from 1650–1735*, diss., Stanford University, 1959 (University Microfilms Inc., Ann Arbor, Mich.).

115. Quantz, *op cit.*, p. 123.

116. There would be no objection to a "swing" version of Bach, the like of which has been fairly common recently, if it did not also relate to the practice of "notes inégales", thus advertising itself as "historically correct." This may well be a short-lived fashion, as was the case with "Play Bach" or the "Swingle Singers" who, however, never claimed to be historically correct, but honestly characterized their works as new interpretations.

117. Compare Note 40.

118. Obituary of Johann Sebastian Bach, written by Johann Friedrich Agricola and C. P. E. Bach in Lorenz Christoph Mizler's periodical, *Neu eröffnete Musikalische Bibliothek, oder gründliche Nachricht nebst unpartheyischem Urtheil von musikalischen Schriften und Büchern*, vol. 4, Part 1, Leipzig, 1754; reprint in BJB, 1920, pp. 12 ff., here, p. 24.

119. Two letters written to Johann Nikolaus Forkel by Carl Philipp Emanuel Bach, probably within a short span of time; the first is not dated, the second, on January 13, 1775. The letters give a very vivid description of Bach's manner of playing since they derive from first-hand experience. They were an important

source for Forkel's Bach monograph, the first of its kind, which appeared in 1802. Compare Note 24, also in regard to the first publication of the letters.

120. Compare Note 70 regarding publications of C. P. E. Bach and, later, Leopold Mozart and Johann Mattheson.

121. In his book *Die Flöte und ihre Musik*, Gustav Scheck gives interesting examples of ornamentation as used by Bach contemporaries like Chambonnières, Anglebert, Couperin le Grand, Hotteterre le Romain, Rameau, Tartini, et al. (pp 112 ff.). Edward Dannreuther's article, "Die Verzierungen in den Werken von Johann Sebastian Bach" (BJB, 1906, pp. 41 ff.) is still worth reading.

122. NBA VII, 7 (lost solo concertos in reconstructed form) contains a facsimile of the autograph of the first page of the score of this concerto, in which Bach did not indicate any ornaments. Perhaps the signs were taken from old parts; otherwise, the source of BGA XVII is unclear.

123. The turn sign is frequently written incorrectly, though probably not deliberately; namely: ∞ . However, this would signify a turn from below which was first used by Richard Wagner in *Rienzi*. Wagner, however, noted it with a ✠ ,—a sign otherwise not used. See the following, which contains both Richard Wagners turn notation (from Richard Wagner, *Sämtliche Werke*, vol. 3, 1: *Rienzi*, Mainz, 1974, ouverture, m. 19, 130 and other corresponding passages) and its execution, as found in more recent *Rienzi* editions.

Wagner:

Execution:

Richard Wagner, Overture to *Rienzi* m. 19–20

124. New edition by Friedrich Hermann, Frankfurt a.M./New York/London, 1967 (Edition Peters, #237a). Unfortunately the original figuration is missing in this edition.

125. Bach's pupil, Johann Philipp Kirnberger (1721–83), set down this method of instruction in outline form (albeit extremely drily) in his work *Grundsätze des General Basses als erste Linien zur Komposition*, Berlin, 1781.

126. From the edition cited in Note 41.

127. From the edition cited in Note 108.

128. Quoted from Baynes (ed.) *Musical Instruments Through the Ages*, pp. 126 ff. On the same topic, see also Frank Hubbard, *Three Centuries of Harpsichord Making*, Cambridge, Mass, ³1970.

129. The fortepiano, i.e., the *Hammerklavier* without a rigid connection between key and hammer, was invented by Bartolomeo Cristofori in Florence in 1709.

130. Ernst, *Der Flügel Johann Sebastian Bachs*, p. 23.

131. Compare Note 70. To quote from the text: "Herr Gottfr. Silbermann had originally constructed two of these instruments. One of these was seen and played by the late Kapellmeister, Herr Joh. Sebastian Bach. He (had) admired and praised its beautiful sound; however, he complained that it was too weak in the high register and was very difficult to play. Herr Silbermann, who could not tolerate any criticism of his productions, took extreme umbrage at this and remained angry with Bach for a long time; nevertheless, his conscience told him that Bach was not in the wrong. Hence, and this should be said to his great

credit, he considered it best not to distribute these instruments any further. Rather, he occupied himself all the more assiduously with correcting the flaws noted by Herr J. S. Bach, on which he worked for many years. That this is the true cause of the hiatus I have no doubt, especially since Herr Silbermann himself candidly admitted this to me. Finally, when Herr Silbermann had in fact effected many improvements, particularly in regard to the action, he again sold one of them . . . Herr Silbermann also had the estimable ambition to show one of these products of his recent work to Kapellmeister Bach and submit it for his perusal. This time he received total approbation." (Adlung, *Musica mechanica organoedi*, pp. 116f.)

132. See Forkel, *Über Johann Sebastian Bachs Leben, Kunst und Kunstwerke*, pp. 34 ff. Also, Theodor W. Adorno, "Bach gegen seine Liebhaber verteidigt," in Th. W. A., *Prismen*, Frankfurt a.M., 1955, pp. 162 ff., esp. p. 175.

133. Le Blanc, *Verteidigung der Viola da gamba*, p. 101.

134. Compare also Alfred Brendel, *Nachdenken über Musik*, Munich/Zurich, 1977.

135. Schweitzer, *Johann Sebastian Bach*, pp. 370 ff.

136. From a letter of Siegfried Behrend to the author. Thomas Kohlhase defends a similar point of view in a letter to the author.

137. In his book *The Great Conductors*, New York, 1967, Harold Schonberg, the music critic for *The New York Times*, gives a vivid picture of the inadequacies of rehearsal and ensemble practices in the 18th and early 19th centuries (Chap. 5).

138. Being tied to one's own epoch in regard to the art of earlier times is the case even when it is not intended. Thus forgeries of "old masters" in the 19th century are exposed not so much by the materials used—pigments, canvas, etc.— but rather by the fact that the forger had a completely different way of seeing which is not like that of a camera (observation by Prof. Dr. Gert von der Osten, Cologne).

139. Valuable contributions to this topic have been made by Reinhold Hammerstein in "Musik als Komposition und Interpretation," *Deutsche Vierteljahrsschrift für Literaturwissenschaft und Geistesgeschichte* 40, 1966, no. 1; esp. chap. 4, pp. 14 ff.

PART II

1. See also August Halm, *Von zwei Kulturen der Musik*, Munich, 1913. He discusses monothematics on pp. 7 ff., and classical sonata form on pp. 35 ff.

2. In his *Entwurf einer neuen Ästhetik der Tonkunst*, Leipzig, 1916, Feruccio Busoni pointed out that in the music of Wagner, the dynamic composer "par excellence," there is a constant crescendo directed toward climaxes. Once a climax has been reached, it immediately subsides only to begin intensifying again (p. 29).

3. See Werner Danckert, *Ursymbole melodischer Gestaltung*, Kassel, 1932, and *Personale Typen des Melodiestils*, Kassel, 1933.

4. Hermann Abert, "Wort und Ton in der Musik des 18. Jahrhunderts," in *Archiv für Musikwissenschaft* 5, 1923, pp. 31. ff.

5. Bartók's 4th and 5th string quartets and his Concerto for Orchestra are particularly significant.

6. See Igor Stravinsky, "Answers to 35 Questions," Question VIII, in I. Str., *Leben und*

Werk . . ., Zurich/Mainz, 1957, p. 252.

7. Along with the various studies by Eppstein, also refer to Siegele. *Kompositionsweise und Bearbeitungstechnik in der Instrumentalmusik Johann Sebastian Bachs;* see his discussion of the Sonata for Viola da gamba and Clavier in G Minor, BWV 1029, pp. 97 ff.

8. The tempo of the Baroque minuet should not be confused with that of the minuet of Viennese Classicim, the tempo of which is actually closer to a "Scherzo." When Mozart or Beethoven wrote an "authentic" minuet—in *Don Giovanni*, for example, or the 8th Symphony—they both used a slow, leisurely tempo.

9. For example, in the "Confiteor" of the "Credo" of the *B Minor Mass*, the first setting of the "et expecto resurrectionem mortuorum," which is completely different, m. 121–146.

10. Cf. Part I, Notes 119 and 132.

11. Ernst Kurth, *Grundlagen des linearen Kontrapunktes*, Bern, [4]1946.

12. For works in the minor mode, this is always the *minor* key of the 5th degree, since, strictly speaking, a minor dominant is a major triad.

13. Philipp Spitta, *Johann Sebastian Bach*, 2 vols., Leipzig, [4]1930, vol. 1, p. 730.

14. The second theme of the 1st movement of Brahms' String Sextet in G Major, Op. 36 is noteworthy in this regard. In a "normal" course there would have to be a quarter-note in m. 5, or at the very latest, m. 6; however Brahms, makes the idea, which begins somewhat conventionally, specially attractive by sticking with the ♩. values.

Johannes Brahms, String Sextet in G Major, Op 36, 1st movement, m. 135–142.

15. For this, too, there is a unique example: the subsidiary theme of the 1st movement of Mozart's Piano Concerto in C Major, KV 503. It contains four completely symmetrical phrases with four masculine endings!

Wolfgang Amadeus Mozart, Piano Concerto in C Major, KV 503, 1st movement, m. 51–57.

16. Anton Bruckner, *Vorlesungen über Harmonielehre und Kontrapunkt an der Universität Wien*, ed. by Ernst Schwanzara, Vienna, 1950.

17. There are some differences in the counting of measures in the Chaconne. The NBA counts the first, incomplete measure, which begins on the 2nd quarter in three-four time, as m. 1. Other editions, for example the Peters edition of Carl Flesch, only count the first complete measure as m. 1 and disregard the two preceding quarters. We have always followed the latter method. Hence, when

comparing measures with the NBA one must add one to each measure number cited here.

18. For a key to the abbreviations, see p. 237.

19. Strangely enough, the final movement of the Clavier Concerto in F Minor, BWV 1056, gives the same intertwined impression. Not only is it in the same key, but also in 3/8 time.

20. Some readers may not agree with the division of this phrase into 4 lines. Other groupings are, of course, possible. Thus the 4th line could be sub-divided, which would result in a 5-line phrase. Then, the first half of the 4th line (up to the eighth-note pause) would be considered an "extra" line. The 3rd line could also be divided in half. But whatever division is preferred, the two primary characteristics—the heterogeneity of all the lines and the lengthening of the 3rd line in the reprise—remain the same.

21. There are also numerous monographs on this topic, most of which are scattered in periodicals. Eppstein (*Studien über J. S. Bachs Sonaten für ein Melodieinstrument und obligates Cembalo*, pp. 48–67) calls it the "principle of integration." For him, however, this is not the central theme. Among the more interesting new publications is Amy Dommel-Diénys, *Étude pour la première sonate pour clavecin et flûte de J. S. Bach en si mineur*, Paris, 1977. A basic explanation of the problem (not confined to Bach) is found in Rudolph Reti's *The Thematic Process in Music*, London, 1961.

22. On this important question, compare Carl Dahlhaus, "Motivbeziehungen—real oder fiktiv?" in *Melos* 6, 1968, p. 476.

23. The exposition of Beethoven's Piano Sonata in D Major, Op. 28, 1st movement, can serve as an example of this technique.

24. The English lyric poet Gerald Manley Hopkins (1844–89), in his poem, "Henry Purcell": "It is the forged feature finds me."

25. George Frideric Handel, Sonata in D Major, Op. 1, No. 13 for Violin and b.c.; Hallische Handel-Ausgabe, vol. IV, 4, pp. 34 f.

26. Letter to Felix Braun, March 14, 1913, in Hans Carossa, *Briefe*, ed. by Eva Kampmann-Carossa, vol. 1, Frankfurt a.M., 1978, p. 80.

27 Thus Paul Hindemith, in "Johann Sebastian Bach, ein verpflichtendes Erbe," lecture given at the Bach Festival in Hamburg on September 12, 1950, Wiesbaden, 1953, pp. 11 ff. (Publ. in Engl. as *J. S. Bach, Heritage and Obligation*, New Haven, 1952.)

28. The popular "Theory of Affections", as represented by Athanasius Kircher, Johann Kuhnaw, Johann Mattheson in Bach's time, apparently did not interest him. He showed equally little interest in the rational enlightenment aesthetic of Diderot and Rousseau.

29. Felix Mendelssohn-Bartholdy: "What communicates itself to me in music I love is not ideas that are too ill-defined to put into words, but rather, those that are too well-defined." Quoted from Josepf Rufer (ed.) *Bekenntnisse und Erkenntnisse—Komponisten über ihre Werke*, Berlin, 1979, p. 44.

30. "The findings of sociology, psychology and behavioral science probably do not apply when it comes to what is probably most imponderable: creativity." Horst Bienek, in *Werkstattgespräche mit Schriftstellern*, Munich, ²1969, p. 10.

31. In this regard, see Carl Dahlhaus, *Die Idee der absoluten Musik*, Kassel (etc.)/Munich, 1978.

PART III

1. Apart from Schumann, Felix Mendelssohn-Barthody and several other composers wrote keyboard accompaniments to some of these works. See NBA VI, 1 (Works for violin), critical commentary by Rudolph Gerber and Günter Hausswald.

2. Regarding the numbering of the measures, see Part II, Note 17.

3. Brahms arranged the Chaconne as a piano work for the left hand (Studies, #5).

4. This movement has been arranged for piano, transposed into G Major; it is listed in *BWV* as #968, but its authenticity is in doubt.

5. Kurth, *Grundlagen des linearen Kontrapunktes.*

6. A great musician's lifelong struggle for the correct interpretation of this fugue is narrated in Yehudi Menuhin's autobiography, *Unvollendete Reise,* Munich, 1976, (originally published as *Unfinished Journey,* New York, 1977) p. 118.

7. Practical suggestions for studying the solo works for violin can be found in Richard R. Efrati, *Die Interpretation der Sonaten und Partiten für Violine solo und der Suiten für Violoncello solo,* Zurich/Freiburg i. Br., 1979. There are, however, misgivings about the author's treatment of the solo works for violoncello, all of which he consigns to the viola.

8. Since the suites for cello have not yet appeared in the NBA, we are using August Wenzinger's edition for our phrasing (See Part II, Note 86), unless otherwise noted

9. Hans Eppstein adds these trills in brackets in m. 7 and 38 (see Part II, Note 41), but not elsewhere. In my opinion they should be played in all the places cited.

10. Arnold Schmitz characterizes this ascending sixth as the musical equivalent of a rhetorical 'exclamatio': *Die Bildlichkeit der wortgebundenen Musik Johann Sebastian Bachs,* Mainz, 1950, pp. 37 ff., 59 ff.). The regularity with which the interval appears in Bach's minor *Siciliani* is striking. See also the discussion of the Sonata for Gamba and Clavier in D Major, BWV 1028, 3rd movement.

11. Eppstein, *Studien über J. S. Bachs Sonaten für ein Melodieinstrument und obligates Cembalo,* p. 63.

12. Compare Eppstein's Foreword to his edition of the sonatas, vol. 2 (see Part II, Note 41).

13. In the Foreword to his edition, Frankfurt a.M./New York/London, 1936, (Edition Peters, No. 4460).

14. See NBA, VI, 1, Critical Commentary by Rudolph Gerber and Günther Hausswald, pp. 131 ff.

15. In 1958, the 82-year-old Pablo Casals played this arrangement of the D Major Sonata—cello and piano—at the U.N. General Assembly with Mieczyslaw Horszewski.

16. Cf. Part I, Notes 78 and 86.

17. Siegele, *Kompositionsweise und Bearbeitungstechnik in der Instrumentalmusik Johann Sebastian Bachs,* pp. 97 ff. See also Eppstein, *Studien über J. S. Bachs Sonaten für ein Melodieinstrument und obligates Cembalo,* pp. 103 ff.

18. See the Preface by Hans Peter Schmitz to his edition of the Partita, Kassel (etc.), 1963 (Bärenreiter-Ausgabe No. 4401), and NBA VI, 3 (works for flute), Critical Commentary by Hans Peter Schmitz, pp. 7 ff.

19. Spitta, *Johann Sebastian Bach,* vol. 1, p. 730.

20. We should note here that in many of his works, Béla Bartók went in the opposite

direction, from chromatic to diatonic, for example, in his *Music for String Instruments, Percussion and Celesta.*

21. Reproduced in NBA VI, 3, Critical Commentary by Hans Peter Schmitz, pp. 55 ff.
22. See the Preface by Leo Balet to his edition of the sonatas, Kassel, n.d. (Nagels Musikarchiv, No. 77).
23. Edition Peters, No. 4461b.
24. Compare Note 10.
25. The details are very vividly described by Forkel, *Über Johann Sebastian Bachs Leben, Kunst und Kunstwerke,* pp. 26f., 74.
26. The term "Late style" has been bandied about a great deal; there is no real definition of what it means. See Gottfried Benn, "Altern als Problem für Künstler," in his *Gesammelte Werke,* ed. by Dieter Wellershoff, vol. 1, Wiesbaden, [3]1965, pp. 552 ff.
27. In the Critical Commentary of his much-cited edition of the suites for cello solo (see Part II, Note 86), August Wenzinger offers some interesting speculations about the putative priority of the lute or the cello version. He also enumerates all the differences between the two versions (pp. 66 ff.).
28. See Kohlhase, *Johann Sebastian Bachs Kompositionen für Lauteninstrumente,* especially the specific discussion of the work in chap. 1. Later in the chapter there is an interesting note that Robert Franz published this suite in 1881 for piano "with appropriate chordal complement."
29. In the recording of the work by Narciso Yepes cited in Part I, Note 99, the problem is convincingly solved.

Illustrations

1. Johann Sebastian Bach in his Youth. Portrait by Johann Ernst Rentsch, the elder (?). Städtisches Museum (Anger-Museum), Erfurt. By permission of the museums of the city of Erfurt.
2. Autograph of the Sonata for Flute and Clavier in A Major, BWV 1032 (below) and the Concerto for 2 Claviers and Strings in C Minor, BWV 1062. Deutsche Staatsbibliothek, Berlin, DDR (Sign. : Mus. ms. Bach P 612).
3. *The Rémy Family in Coblenz,* painting by Januarius Zick (1776). Germanisches Museum, Nürnberg.
4. Development of the violin bow from Mersenne (1620) to Viotti (1790). From David D. Boyden, *The History of Violin Playing from its Origins to 1761 and its Relationship to the Violin and Violin Music.* London, Oxford University Press, 1965. Plate 35.
5. Lutenist from the *Musikalisches Theatrum* by Johann Christoph Weigel. Copperplate engraving, c. 1720. From Johann Christoph Weigel, *Musikalisches Theatrum.* Facs. reprint publ. by Alfred Berner. Kassel (etc.), Bärenreiter, 1961. ²1964. Plate 16.
6. Continuo part of the Trio Sonata in C Minor, BWV 1079, from the original edition of the *Musical Offering,* Leipzig, 1747. From Johann Sebastian Bach, *Musical Offering.* BWV 1079. Photographic reprint of the original edition, Leipzig, 1747. Edited with commentary by Christoph Wolff. Leipzig, Edition Peters, 1977, p. 1.
7. Autograph of the Sonata for Violin Solo in G Minor, BWV 1001, p. 1. From Johann Sebastian Bach, *Sonatas and Partitas for Violin Solo.* Reproduction of the autograph. With an epilogue, ed. by Günther Hausswald. Leipzig, Insel-Verlag, 1958, no page numbers.
8. Suite for Cello Solo in C Minor, BWV 1011, in the hand of Anna Magdalena Bach, p. 1. From J. S. Bach, *6 Suites for Cello Solo.* Reduced facs. edition. Munich/Basel, Edition Reinhardt, undated, no page numbers.

Index of Works

Page number in italics refer to the main discussion of a work.

Index of Names

DATE	ISSUED TO
NOV 0 3	
NOV 2	
NOV 2 4 1997	*Yasuko Kirihaa*
	Renew